INDIA'S FOREIGN POLICY AND ITS NEIGHBOURS

INDIA'S FOREIGN POLICY AND ITS NEIGHBOURS

J.N. Dixit

GYAN PUBLISHING HOUSE
New Delhi - 110002

INDIA'S FOREIGN POLICY AND ITS NEIGHBOURS

ISBN : 978-81-212-1091-1

Published in 2015 in India by
Gyan Publishing House
5, Ansari Road, Daryaganj,
New Delhi - 110002
e-mail : books@gyanbooks.com
gyanbook@vsnl.com
website : gyanbooks.com

CONTENTS

PREFACE

Let me begin by stating that this book is not a preplanned or prestructured exercise on more recent events and trends affecting India's foreign policy, and India's relations with its neighbours. This book is a collection of articles that I have written over the last seven years in various Indian and foreign newspapers and magazines. The book is essentially based on a suggestion put forward by the publishers Gyan Publishing House and more specifically its Director, Publications, Shri Amit Garg. He met me about eight months ago and said he would like to bring out a book containing a collection of my articles, as they would collectively constitute an analysis and commentary on events over the last seven years related to foreign policy with a contemporaneous flavour. I agreed, subject to the precondition that the selection of the articles, their structured arrangement in the book and the required editorial work will be entirely the publisher's responsibility. Mr. Garg agreed to take on this responsibility. The result is this book.

I retired from the Government of India on the 1st of February, 1994 and have tried to reincarnate myself as a political columnist. That the Editors of the newspapers in which I have been writing and the general public continue to give me encouragement to write is a matter of great satisfaction. The articles in modified form which are published in this book are published due to the courtesy of *The Indian Express, The Hindustan Times, The Telegraph, The Hindu,* and the Indian language newspapers *Sakaal, Dainik*

Hindustan and *Amar Ujala*. While acknowledging that these articles reached the public through these newspapers, I thank the editorial managements of these newspapers for enabling me to print the articles (with amendments and modifications) in book form.

I thank the publishers Gyan Publishing House for the initiative that they took in publishing this book. I also place on record my appreciation to my two Secretaries Mr. R.N. Sharma and Mr. N. Ram Narayan, without whose painstaking and attentive efforts these articles would not have been written.

The contents of this book express my personal assessments and views. I do not expect everybody to agree with the views and assessments on issues which they cover, these are entirely my responsibility, but if producing this book provokes an interest and a debate on foreign policy issues and on the nature of inter-State relations in our region, the book would have served its purpose.

July, 2001 **J.N. Dixit**

INTRODUCTION

This kind of a book which is a collection of articles written over a period of the last five to seven years prompts the relevant questions: The contents of the book have already been in public domain. Why publish them in consolidated form? What is the relevance of comments and assessments of the past events, particularly, when they are not transformed into in-depth studies underpinned by academic research?

Answers to the two questions are that general patterns of human memory being short, the articles if re-produced in book form would recall events and developments and their underlying impulses, to the public mind. The answer to the second question is that media articles and comments have the virtue of contemporaneous assessments and analyses of trends and factors in terms of what in modern jargon is called "Real Time Response and Analyses". These assessments and analyses are not burdened by deductive over-analysis, though they lack the virtue of being based on post facto information which becomes available with the passage of time.

The contents of this book cover roughly the period from 1995 till to date. The decade of the 90s of the last and first two years of this century have seen dramatic changes in global power equations, economic developments and the forward march of technology. India itself has gone through a period of political upheavals. The Soviet Union disintegrated, the cold war ended, ideological confrontations which characterised world politics after the Second

World War for nearly 44 years disappeared. India lost leverages which it had in international politics and strategic options with the disappearance of the former Soviet Union. She had to forge new equations, diversify her economic, technological and political relations, seeking out contacts with the emerging new power centres of the world. The transformation of former Soviet Central Asia into independent Central Asian Republics, the emergence of the democratic regime in South Africa ending Apartheid, dealing with increasing clout of new regional groupings like ASEAN, were challenges to India's foreign policy. The non-aligned movement became progressively ineffective losing its unity as well as commonality of objectives. The SAARC remains in the doldrums. Relations with Pakistan went through a roller coaster ride with Vajpayee's visit to Lahore followed by the Kargil war and then a military coup in Pakistan, bringing General Parvez Musharraf to power. India and Pakistan conducted nuclear tests in 1998, changing the entire strategic and security environment in South Asia. These ups and downs are moving towards some possibilities of normalisation of relations with the recent Vajpayee—Musharraf summit though it has not achieved any dramatic breakthrough.

India's relations with the US have improved qualitatively since President Clinton's visit to Delhi in March 2000 and Prime Minister Atal Behari Vajpayee's trip to Washington in September 2000. Parallely India's relations with the Russian Federation stand revived with the advent of President Putin to power in Moscow. India has overcome the highly critical reactions on her nuclear weapons tests from important powers and has managed to stabilise its relations with all of them, particularly with Japan, China and the countries of the Western Europe. Despite difficulties and political limitations India's economic reforms and re-structuring though slow in implementation have remained on track. These events and trends evolved and occured in the context of an over-arching political limitation, namely the national consensus which underpinned our foreign and security policies for nearly five decades after its independence does not exist any more. The Government of India had to cope with this new challenge in fashioning its foreign and security policies.

This exercise had to be undertaken in the context of another complicating factor, namely, all of India's neighbours being subject to political tensions and uncertainties off and on during the last ten years. Pakistan has had a military coup, and before that successive changes of government due to the dismissal of elected Prime Ministers. Sri Lanka remains enmeshed in the ethnic crisis compounded by a civil war situation. The entire Royal family of Nepal was assassinated on the first of June 2001. Assassinations took place in the context of incremental violence perpetrated by the Communist Party (Maoist) in that country. The Koirala Government is on the defensive. There have been eight changes of government since the restoration of democracy there in 1990. The presence of refugees of Nepalese origin from Bhutan and the Inter-Services Intelligence Agency of Pakistan and other dissident groups from India in the country adds to our difficulties.

Bangladesh is going in for elections hopefully in October, 2001. But the period leading to elections has already witnessed incremental violence and disruption of law and order. Bhutan remains challenged by dissidence amongst its Nepalese subjects and the presence of separatist movements from North-Eastern India on its territory.

Structuring of practical and stable relations with its neighbours is the complex challenge which India has faced over the last several years. Specially because with each one of its neighbours, India has a number of issues which remain unresolved, whether it is the question of Kashmir, problem of illegal migration and enclaves in adverse possession with Bangladesh and so on. Domestically a succession of coalition governments have succeeded the Narasimha Rao government which lasted till 1996. Indian domestic politics has undergone profound changes with the emergence of coalition governments, the incremental empowerment of new segments of Indian civil society, higher levels of political consciousness and consequent rise in political expectations. These developments have had an impact on the dynamics and objectives of Indian foreign and security policies.

India is going through a period of domestic and international transitions. India's policies therefore have been an exercise in successfully coping with the challenges inherent in this predicament.

The articles presented in this book in collated form contain assessments and analyses as the events took shape and developments occurred. The objective is to jog public memory about these important events in their contemporaneous context. The book will also serve the purpose of judging the correctness of value-judgements and assessments when analysts and scholars look upon these developments and events with the facility of historical perspective later. In some ways the book may serve the purpose of comprehending what India has gone through and how India managed external relations and security concerns during the last decade of the 20th century and beginning two years of the current one.

I would like to thank publishers Gyan Publishing House for coming up with the proposal to publish my articles in book form. Profound thanks are also due to the newspapers and magazines in which these articles originally appeared over the last decade.

J.N. Dixit

PART—I
INDIA'S FOREIGN POLICY

1

INDIA'S FOREIGN POLICY—AN OVERVIEW

As we move into 21st century, it is time to indulge in some critical introspection as to how we have been dealing with the world around us, what has been the nature of our behaviour as an Independent and sovereign member of the international community, after a gap of about 300 years since the disintegration of India's politico-diplomatic identity as the Mughal Empire.

Whatever interpretative differences may be about the politico-territorial identity of India in pre-British times, there can be no fundamental difference on the point that it is the first time in recorded history that the people of the sub-continental India have welded themselves into a nation-state in 1946-47. We are in the process of consolidating this new national identity amidst our tense diversities and tensions, of centrifugal aspirations of characteristic different segments of our society. Fifty odd years may not be a sufficiently long period in the life of a country for arriving at a holistic or historical evaluation of the perspectives and policies which characterised different activities related to the governance of the concerned society of State. Nevertheless, half a century is a time long enough to undertake an interim evaluation about the perspectives and policies which I have mentioned.

In the current perspective, India seems to have moved from an organic to the critical period in its existence from the ordained vision which dealt with a world of certainties (to the extent that such certainties can be abiding) into an era of ferment which is compounded by uncertainties and doubts about our own reaction to the world around us. The validity of our orientations and perspectives, of necessity, stands questioned in the context of the end of the cold war and the ideological confrontation which affected the international community for nearly seven decades since the end of the First World War.

A recapturing of the origins of our foreign policy in terms of our ethos and our motivations would be pertinent. These origins precede India's achieving dominion status in 1946 and independence in 1947. They had their roots in the thought process of the leaders of our renaissance in the late 19th century and of the national freedom movement during the first four decades of 20th century. That if India was to find an appropriate place in the comity of nations, it would have to redefine its geo-political identity and cultural individuality was felt by leaders of the Indian renaissance from the late 18th century onwards. The intellectual and cultural interface between the British and Indian intellectuals in areas in India where the British had acquired direct control perhaps led to this broad consciousness. The initial processes of cross-cultural and cross-linguistic connections between colonial powers in India at that point of time like the British, the French, the Portugese and to some extent Danish and the Dutch made the Indian elite aware of the world beyond its traditional political and diplomatic cogitations of the international community which was limited perhaps to Turkey at the one end, and South-East Asia at the other. Raja Rammohun Roy was the earliest and most impressive articulator of the terms of reference required for India to be the part of the world a large which was coming closer due to the expanding facilities and increasing speed of communications between different parts of the world. The intellectual side effects of Indian entrepreneurs like the earlier Tagores of the Jorasanko family who came to know about the industrial revolution and the new economic trends permeating Europe led to a realisation that India could not remain isolated from the macro-level political and economic forces at work in different parts of the world. The consequence was the urge to learn english, the desire to emulate British political institutions, to eliminate the negative and pernicious orthodoxies of religions practised in India and to visualise an India which would be similar to the nation states of Europe. Raja Rammohun Roy, Dwijendranath and Dwarkanath Tagore, the earlier leaders of the Brahmo Samaj Movement, advocated India's modernisation and establishing relations with other societies with the above objectives. It could be said that this was the first phase of India's developing an international consciousness and acquiring aspirations to become a part of the modern world. This phase was characterised by curiosity about the western world, being impressed by the military, technological and economic power of the European countries being in awe of the resulting political influence and the reach of their power in different parts of the world, all this leading to a desire to metamorphose Indian society and the Indian policy in a manner where India, in subordinate partnership with England, would merge into the international community.

The second phase in the evolution of India's international consciousness dates back to the aftermath of the Indian mutiny of 1857. Several parts of India had become familiar with Europeans generally and British particularly over a period of nearly one hundred years by then. This familiarity and the resulting knowledge about the motivations of the colonial power, led to the general discontentment resulting in the mutiny. There was a fundamental change in the attitudes of the British towards their Indian subjects after the mutiny, not just in terms of political postures and administrative practices, but also in terms of cultural, intellectual and psychological attitudes. A pernicious sense of racial superiority and intellectual arrogance permeated not only the British Government, but the migrant British population in India as well. The previous comparatively harmonious social relationship between the foreigners and Indians were replaced by above attitudes. Expansion of Christian missionary activities backed by the political authority of the colonial regimes in India (not only in British India but in the residual pockets of Portuguese and French colonies in the sub-continental India) accentuated the process of looking down upon the natives, questioning the very existence of their culture, the value of their literature and the relevance of their social mores. An Indian impulse to affirm its identity, its religio-cultural integrity and to define a sense of nationhood in western terms, but rooted in Indian history, the Indian value system and the Indian religio-cultural ethos, was, therefore natural. The political and intellectual renaissance which characterised the sub-continent had two broad strands in terms of attitudes and reactions towards foreign countries and societies. One strand was in linear continuity of the attitudes and movements initiated by Indian leaders from the late 18th century onwards. The strand of emulating the West, trying to adopt and adapt themselves to western value system, western institutions, to the Indian milieu. This strand found expression in the ideologies, movements and attitudes of the newly emerging middle classes in urban British India. The second strand was an assertive reaction to the arrogance of the western rulers. There was an emphasis on not just the relevance, but the importance of Indian values. There was critical questioning of the western analyses and assessments regarding India's history, its intellectual heritage, its cultural and religious identity. Bankim Chandra, Swami Vivekananda, Maharishi Dayanand, Maulana Altaf Hussain Hali and Justice Akbar Allahabadi personified this strand, this reaction.

Increasing familiarity of the Indian intelligentsia with British political writings added another dimension to India's awareness of the wider world. The gradually increasing number of Indians going to England for study or for economic purposes contributed to this awareness. The sense of self and the desire to make it known to the rest of the world received a fillip by the work of Western scholars, especially British and German scholars on Indian history and the Indian scriptural texts, and the translation of the works of classical Indian literature into English and western languages. The works of Max Mueller, Professor William Jones and Sir William Wilson Hunter, are illustrative of the inputs which the collective psyche of Indians received, making them rediscover their identity in contemporary perspectives at that point of time. While individuals like Sir Syed Ahmed, Surendra Nath Bannerjee and Dadabhai Naoroji personified the first strand described earlier, the second strand found expression not only through the individuals whom I have mentioned, but also in the rise of cultural and religious movements and nationalistic Indian literature in different parts of the British India. The synergy of these impulses ultimately led to the founding of the Indian National Congress in 1885. India had the beginnings of an organised political party capable of articulating Indian aspirations and expectations not only regarding domestic affairs but also regarding India's attitude towards the rest of the world.

Gandhiji's experience during the Boar War and his assuming a leadership role in the Indian National Congress immediately after the end of the First World War made him conscious about the possibilities of utilising India's contributions to the British Empire for demanding an appropriate role for India in the British scheme of things. A British Indian delegation being given separate representation in the post-First World War international conferences and deliberations, and India's being allowed a role of a founding member of the League of Nations intensified India's international consciousness and initiated Indian experience in foreign relations. These developments germinated ideas which between the first and second World Wars, crystalised into Indian foreign policy orientations.

This embryonic and emerging Indian world view could be summed up as follows: India being the most important constituent element of the British Empire deserved Dominion status and a recognised identity in the British imperial system. Secondly, India had to be self-governing under the umbrella of the British empire, if it were to achieve this status, and if it was expected to contribute to the stability and strength of the British empire. Third, India wished to evolve into a modern nation state with modern democratic political institutions. And fourth, India expected to be treated as an equal by other dominions in the British empire and by extension by other countries which had dealings with other British dominions. This constituted the moderate initial framework of India's foreign policy till about 1920.

The period between 1920 and 1946, should be considered the time when the fundamental terms of reference for Independent India's foreign policy were formulated. Mahatma Gandhi's influence was the predominent factor in this process. While Gandhiji defined the framework for India's foreign policy, Nehru fashioned its orientations and details. It would be pertinent to recall their conceptual contributions to India's foreign policy.

A commitment to freedom based on truth, a commitment to democracy predicated on safeguarding diversity and individual freedom and commitment to encourage reason and impulses of peace in international relations were the terms of reference which Mahatma Gandhi provided for India's foreign relations before India became free. Certain statements of his are worth quoting to remind ourselves of the abiding norms which the Father of the Nation gave us to navigate through the complexities of international relations. He said: "I would rather that India perished than that she won freedom at the sacrifice of truth." He went on to say: "Democracy is not a state in which people act like sheep. Under democracy individual liberty of opinion and action is zealously guarded." And finally his assertive desire that India remains committed to the imperatives of peace. He said: "I am not pleading for India to practise non-violence because she is weak. I want her to practise non-violence being conscious of her strength and power. No training in or collection of arms is required for the realisation of her strength."

Two major influences on Jawaharlal Nehru, the first Minister for External Affairs in free India in the sphere of foreign relations were his participation in India's freedom struggle within the ideological framework of Gandhian thought. The second influence was the Socialist ideology of early 20th Century Europe emphasising the imperatives of social equality and economic justice, and opposition to all forms of oppression and exploitation. Looking back to the last fifty years of our participation in international relations, the first notable trend in our foreign policy was the impact of these two influences in our attitudes and stances on problems characterising the world situation in the immediate aftermath of the Second World War.

Our foreign policy views were only at the conceptual level before we became free. It became operational only after the profound transition that India underwent from being a colony to an independent and sovereign state. Our notions of how the international community should be structured and organised were deeply influenced by our freedom struggle and a certain perception about our historical identity as a people and civilization. Self-perception of India's historical identity was selective and normative. We perceived ourselves as inheritors of a great moral and rational tradition in dealing with inter-state and inter-societal relations. The concepts of concretising this tradition were those of tolerance, non-aggression, a commitment to reason in resolving controversies, conflicts and an acknowledgement of the supreme virtue of nurturing peace through a non-expansionist, non-acquisitive approach, not just in inter-state relations but towards life itself. This was not an objective or multi-dimensional perception of our past in its totality. It was a selective, self-adulating perception. This was based on what we as a people collectively thought was good for our survival and socio-economic well-being in a complex, competitive world. It was, therefore, motivated perception. The nature of our freedom struggle as it evolved under the Indian National Congress, particularly during the phase when Mahatma Gandhi guided it, consolidated the conceptual terms of reference based on selective historical perception which I have detailed.

India was also firmly opposed to the competitive and aggressive politico-military policies of different world powers enmeshed in the Cold War. India sought the achievement of these aims not through acquisition of military might or exploitative economic power. Unrealistic it might have been, but India desired to influence international relations through its commitment to reason and through whatever moral influence it could project. India succeeded unexpectedly and remarkably in this.

exercise in the 1950s and early 1960s. India was not just the most prominent but the first voice to be heard at the United Nations and in the Chancelleries of the world, emphasising the danger and irrelevance of the phenomenon of colonialism, imperialism and all forms of discrimination. India achieving independence through a non-violent freedom struggle and its vigorous advocacy for freedom and liberation of peoples under subjugation in different parts of the world, was an important influence leading to the dismemberment of imperial and colonial regimes and the emergence of practically all the countries of Africa and Asia into independence. India's role in the liberation of Indonesia and other South Asian countries and its firm advocacy for the liberation of the African countries are a matter of historical record. India's support for resurgent and revolutionary People's Republic of China, for the people of South Africa and the Palestinians generated impulses which came to positive fruition decades later from the 1970s to the 1990s.

India and China jointly defining the five Principles of Peaceful Co-existence, the *Panchsheel,* provided ideological foundations for the establishment of Non-aligned movement in 1961. This was a structured and rational response to the abrassive competition of the Cold War with its militaristic ramifications. More importantly, the rationale and the objectives of the movement subserved the fundamental interests of the vast majority of countries in the international community which had emerged from colonial and imperial domination into freedom and liberty. Foreign policy orientations of India and her cooperation with other like-minded countries were a stabilising factor in the international situation.

A brief survey of the changing concerns in Indian foreign policy and Indian interests since our achieving independence would be relevant. It would provide linear perspective to this analysis. The evolution of India's foreign policy went through four chronological phases. The first phase was from 1946 to 1954, the second phase from 1954 to 1962 and the third phase from 1962 till mid-80s and the fourth phase from mid-80s todate.

During the first phase (1946-1954) India's foreign policy concerns were— first to territorially consolidate the Indian polity which was subject to the possibility of some large and important princely states opting to remain independent, which would have fragmented the geographical cohesion of the Indian Republic, still recovering from the trauma of partition and creation of Pakistan. The deliberatively ambiguous role of the departing colonial government in relation to the princely states of Hyderabad, Travancore, Bhopal and Kashmir, imparted this concern to the Government of India. Pakistan's intrusion into Kashmir in 1947-48, compounded Indian worries about its territorial consolidation.

Secondly, India had to cope with the problem of defining its political and strategic world view in the conflict between Western allies led by the USA and the Socialist and Communist group of nations led by the USSR. Thirdly, India had to structure relations with two of its most important neighbours, Pakistan and China, one of whom was manifestly hostile (Pakistan) and the other was an uncertain commodity (China with its new communist government, which could create an unstable regional environment). Fourthly, while India, correctly anticipating the disappearance of colonialism and the emergence of a large number of independent states in Asia and Africa, was also concerned about former colonial powers working at retaining their political clout in these countries for their (the ex-colonial powers') own strategic and economic interests.

Indian foreign policy responded to these concerns with (i) the adoption of a non-aligned stance on cold war confrontation; (ii) assuming a decisive politico-military posture in consolidating the territorial integrity of India *vis-a-vis* Pakistan and the princely states of India; (iii) attempting a measured friendly equation with China (India's compromise on Tibet, and supporting China's admission to the UN and the Security Council), and (iv) a move to unite newly independent countries on matters of common concern, so as to ensure that they retain their freedom of option to take decisions on domestic, foreign and defence policies without being influenced by external powers, or extraneous pressure to the extent possible.

The next phase of India's foreign and defence policies was from 1954 to 1962. India went through a period of vulnerability culminating in India's military defeat by China in October/November, 1962. This was so despite the intriguing conundrum in international politics of India and Jawaharlal Nehru being at the peak of his leadership role in multilateral political developments during this very period, from being the Chairman of the Neutral Nations Repatriation Commission on Korea, to being the catalyst for the Geneva Conference on Indo-China after the French defeat at Dien Bien Phu, to founding the non-aligned movement and playing a major role in the UN peacekeeping operations in the Middle East and Congo.

What caused the vulnerabilities? Answer to this question will provide the explanation for shifts in India's policies, as well as for the Osmoses and failures from which they suffered. India's apprehension regarding Pakistan increased by a quantum dimension when Pakistan signed a defence and military cooperation agreement with the USA in the mid 1950s. Pakistan's joining the SEATO and CENTO accentuated Indian threat perceptions especially in the context of Pakistani interpretation of the implications of its becoming a member of the western military alliance systems. Pakistan claimed that its bilateral defence arrangements with the USA, and its membership of the CENTO and SEATO, obliged the West to support Pakistan politically and militarily in any confrontation with India. This was the *quid pro quo* which Pakistan claimed for becoming party to the anti-communist alliance. Add to this Indian experience of the western countries' reluctance to be of technological and defence assistance to India and India's worries took concrete shape. Simultaneously, Sino-Indian relations were coming under strain. From 1954-55, China's increasingly assertive presence in Tibet, eroding the authority of the Dalai Lama, its commencing road construction in Aksai-Chin, which was part of Ladakh in Jammu and Kashmir, her publishing maps of the Indian sub-continent showing parts of India as Chinese territory and her open questioning of Jawaharlal Nehru's leadership role in Asia (at Bandung) contributed to the evolving estrangement between the two countries.

Other critical developments were: Pakistan continuing its cogitations about Kashmir, both at the UN and in Kashmir itself on the one hand, and Chinese involvement with secessionist insurgencies in the North Eastern States of India. There were also domestic challenges to the country's security and stability. While food assistance and inputs for the softer sectors of Indian economy were coming from the Western countries, they continued to resist giving investment and technological inputs to the core sectors of Indian economy. The most glaring example of this attitude was UK, US and Germany initially refusing to cooperate with India in setting up steel plants. UK and Germany only came in after the Russians gave a positive response to Indian requirements in the field. India's efforts at diversifying and modernising its economy to move out of its essentially agricultural groove suffered from this limitation.

Ethno-linguistic centrifugal tendencies were emerging in the domestic political situation, as manifested in the demand for linguistic States. New strategic and security compulsions were impinging on Indian politics requiring new orientations, new responses.

With Khruschev replacing Stalin as the leader of the Eastern Bloc, old Soviet ideological and political prejudices against India disappeared. The creation of CENTO and SEATO, Pakistan and South-East Asian countries joining these anti-Soviet system of alliances created Soviet strategic interests in South and South-East Asia. Mao Tse-tung's disagreements with Khruschev and the evolving distances between China and the Soviet Union provided additional impetus to Russian interest in India. India's involvement with the non-aligned movement, her support to Nasser during the Suez crisis, her silence on the Soviet intervention in Hungary, her firm resistance to western pressure exerted bilaterally and through the UN to compromise on Kashmir, and her support to Palestinians and Arabs after the creation of Israel, had widened the gulf of mutual suspicions and contradictions in political and security interests between her and the Western democracies. India was therefore, in search of equations and cooperative relations with other countries which would meet her political and economic interests and her security concerns. A convergence of interests emerged between the Soviet Bloc countries and India. India seized this opportunity, Jawaharlal Nehru's visit to the Soviet Union in the mid-fifties and Khruschev and Bulganin's joint state visit to India in 1955, laid the foundation of Indo-Soviet equations which served the vital interests of both countries—and equation which continued uninterrupted for thirty-five years, till November/ December, 1991.

The cooperation which developed between India, the Soviet Union and the Soviet Union's allies had a clearly defined ideological and political framework. India was not transforming itself into a communist country. The Soviet Union was agreeable to a relationship based on the concepts of peaceful co-existence and non-alignment. India's motivations were to strengthen its economic and defence capacities with the assistance of the Soviet Union to use the leverages of Indo-Soviet friendship and Soviet Union's super power status to counter politico-strategic challenges to India's territorial integrity and national consolidation processes. There was also the unarticulated objective of balancing off Pakistan's growing proximity to the USA and China. Sino-Pakistani equations grew in tandem with Sino-Indian estrangements from 1956—1959 onwards. The point to be kept in mind is that India turned to the Soviet Union only after Western countries failed to respond to her expectations and requirements.

India managed to tackle various problems related to its foreign policy during this period except in one case, viz. Chinese challenge to India's territorial integrity. Chinese maps incorporating Indian areas into China, and Chou En-lai's exchanges with Nehru had signalled Chinese intentions of re-arranging the international frontier between India and China. India rejected the basic Chinese argument that the borders between the two countries as they existed in 1947-49, were artificial, and an arbitrary colonial and imperial phenomenon, which required alteration taking into account pre-colonial, factual-national, and even socio-cultural jurisdiction and affinities. After giving concessions to China on Tibet, India was not prepared to make further territorial adjustments affecting the metropolitan territories extent of the Indian Union. Apart from the macro-level geo-political anxiety to protect the country's territorial integrity, an equally important consideration taking this stance was sustaining the multi-ethnic, linguistic and religious character of the Indian state. Making territorial adjustments with China which might have resulted in the alienation and separation of population of North Eastern India was not and cannot be acceptable to India.

Mrs. Indira Gandhi's purposive and firm leadership and her Indo-centric world view galvanized trends and processes mentioned above. Programmes of national consolidation and defence preparedness were being implemented untramelled by other domestic political controversies (like the crisis and split of the ruling party in 1969, the devaluation of the Rupee earlier in 1966, the nationalisation of banks, the province of Punjab being divided into two parts, etc.), when India was confronted with the fall out of the East Pakistan crisis. The Indo-Pakistan War, as a constituent phenomenon of Bangladesh's freedom struggle however, affected Indian policies in the ensuing years. Analyses of the 1971 war by Pakistani authors have asserted over the years that the freedom struggle of Bangladeshis was either a pre-planned conspiracy by India, or that India took unscrupulous and opportunistic advantage of a domestic political crisis in Pakistan to fragment that country. Only a marginal section of Pakistan's decision making elite accepts that Bangladesh's creation was primarily the result of Zulfiqar Ali Bhutto's obstinacy in not accepting the electoral verdict of the people of Pakistan at the general elections of November, 1970 and the inability or unwillingness of the military regime of General Yahya Khan to compel Bhutto to respect the verdict of the elections and to allow Sheikh Mujibur Rehman to become the Prime Minister of Pakistan.

To move to a survey of the shift in emphasis, and orientations in India's foreign policy from 1964 to 1984, First, Lal Bahadur Shastri, despite his short tenure as Prime

Minister and then Mrs. Indira Gandhi ushered Indian foreign policy into channels of political realism away from the romantic illusions and moral idealism which characterizes the foreign policy of India during the Nehru era. This shift in orientation was epitomized by Lal Bahadur Shastri destroying the smug predications on which Pakistan attacked Kashmir in September, 1965. The Pakistani predication was that India would only respond militarily in areas of operations which Pakistan chose in Jammu and Kashmir. Lal Bahadur Shastri scattered this calculation to the winds by ordering the Indian armed forces to attack Pakistan across the entire international border, which compelled Pakistan to disperse its armed forces away from Kashmir, ultimately resulting in Pakistan's failure in this third attempt at capturing Jammu and Kashmir.

Indira Gandhi extended the content and range of this assertive and realistic Indo-centric orientations in Indian foreign policy by building up India's technological and defence capacities and giving a clear message to all India's neighbours that while India had no aggressive or hegemonistic intentions towards them, India's response to any threats to its unity and territorial integrity emanating from other countries would receive a prompt and decisive response. The trends in Indian foreign policy of the Indira Gandhi period from 1966 to 1984 (except the interregnum of 1977 to 1979) could be summed up on the following lines:

- She (Indira Gandhi) followed a two track policy to galvanise India's economic development to sustain India's security and consolidated India's position in the international community,

- She expanded defence cooperation arrangements with the Soviet Union and her allies, culminating in the signing of the Indo-Soviet Treaty of Peace, Friendship and Cooperation of August, 1979.

- She initiated successful policies for augmenting India's capacities in the spheres of space and nuclear technology which have resulted in India's nuclear weapons capacities and the satellite and missile capacities both for technological and defence purposes. The nuclear explosion at Pokharan in 1974, the first launching of satellites, missiles and rockets for scientific and technological purposes concretised this policy orientation.

- While continuing to oppose military alliances and security arrangements, under the umbrella of any super power, she initiated the doctrine that having bilateral defence supplies and security arrangements to serve specific Indian predicaments and Indian interests is not against nonalignment. The Indo-Soviet Treaty of 1971 was a source of support and strength during the East Pakistan crisis leading to the creation of Bangladesh.

The conduct of peaceful nuclear explosion in 1974 was a response to the changed Indian geo-strategic environment resulting from China becoming a nuclear weapons power from 1964 onwards and Pakistan commencing its nuclear weaponisation programme in 1972.

The second track was to strengthen the non-aligned movement and to support the United Nations becoming an important factor to stabilise global political and economic arrangements conducive to India's geo-political and economic interests.

The question that arises is whether Indian interests could have been served better if our foreign policy stances had been different in dealing with specific issues affecting us from 1947 to 1984. There are six landmarks of India's failures because of foreign policy and security policy stances that India took during this period.

The first was our taking the Kashmir issue to the United Nations while we were three-fourths on the way to neutralising Pakistani invasion of Jammu and Kashmir.

The second was our not reacting firmly and decisively enough against Pakistan when Pakistan signed its defence agreements with the US in 1954, and then joined the CENTO.

The third was our not being alert enough to the implications of the Sino-Pak nexus at the Bandung Conference in 1955.

The fourth was our accommodating attitude towards China when it took over Tibet.

The fifth landmark was our not nuclearly weaponising ourselves when China became a nuclear weapons power in 1964.

It is interesting to recall that the United States had urged India to become nuclear weapons power in the early 1960s, assuring assistance, but we refused.

It is also pertinent to mention that we could have exercised the nuclear weapons option in 1962 immediately after the Sino-Indian war and in 1965 after the Indo-Pakistan war and the Chinese nuclear weaponisation a year earlier. We could also have followed on our 1974 underground nuclear explosion.

Getting a little ahead in terms of chronology, the sixth landmark was our not reacting decisively to exercise nuclear weapons option when there was confirmed information that Pakistan was becoming nuclear weapons capable power between 1985 and 1987.

This delay was remedied in May 1998, when we conducted the Shakti tests (Pokhran II), confirming our nuclear weapons capacity, as the tests covered experiments both normal nuclear and thermo-nuclear weapons.

Prime Minister Atal Behari Vajpayee, announced on the afternoon of 11 May, 1998 that India had conducted three nuclear tests, including a thermo-nuclear test a little after 3 p.m. on that date. India conducted two more subkiloton nuclear device tests on 13th May. India had crossed the nuclear Rubicon the *Lakshman Rekha,* so to say, of reticences regarding nuclear weaponisation to assert and affirm its position as a nuclear weapons power. The reasons for India's concretizing its nuclear weapons options in my assessment, are broadly the following.

First and foremost, the progressively deteriorating security environment that India faces and has faced since the late 1980s activated the leaders to go nuclear. Secondly, the incremental and definitive prospects of restrictive and discriminatory international regimes being put in place which would have not just stifled but would also have put a complete stop in India realising its potential in the fields of space and nuclear technologies spurred India to exercise the nuclear option. Thirdly, India was averse to adjusting to a new international strategic and technological order in which the existing five nuclear weapons states would remain a dominating factor for a prolonged period of time. Fourth, India required a long-term and sophisticated defence capacity, in the context of its own post-independence experience of its territorial integrity being threatened more than once. Fifth, India took note of the fact that other nuclear weapons capable states, which were subjected to restrictive pressures, either overcame the pressures by becoming nuclear weapon powers themselves, such as France and China, or they succumbed to international pressure and their nuclear technological capacities (in terms of self-reliance) were capped, rolled back and eliminated as in the case of Argentina, South Africa and Brazil. India decided to adopt the first option to overcome these pressures.

The first criticism levelled against India is that by conducting these tests it has abandoned its unqualified commitment not to acquire nuclear weapons and missile capacities. This is not true. New Delhi had noted the discriminatory orientations of the nuclear weapon powers at the time of the very inception of India's own nuclear programmes. Political and technological element of the statute on the establishment of the International Atomic Energy Agency (IAEA) discussed at the conference to finalise the statute in 1957, gave clear indications of its prospective discriminatory orientations. India was alert to the negative prospects and articulated its reservations. India while abjuring the acquisition of nuclear weapons, despite suggestions to the contrary by the US in 1963, took note of the Chinese nuclear weaponisation in 1964, and decided in response that it (India) should build up infrastructural capacities for a nuclear weapons deterrent of its own. India's building a plutonium processing plant in 1964 was the affirmation of this intention. India's refusal to sign the nuclear non-proliferation treaty (NPT) in 1967-68, and India's conducting the peaceful nuclear explosion test at Pokhran on 18th May, 1974 were clear signals that it was aiming at acquiring basic nuclear weapons capacities and that it would create this capacity and keep this option open to be exercised as and when the country's security concerns required it.

The post-1974 reactions of the nuclear weapons powers led by the United States heightened India's alertness and sensitivity about a restrictive non-proliferation policy being evolved to foreclose India's nuclear options. Multilateral technical discussions on safeguards procedures, and transfer of technology policies of nuclear weapons states and the advanced industrial countries changed the very definition of non-proliferation which was initially aimed only at preventing acquisition and proliferation of nuclear weapons. The definition of proliferation was extended to cover all related technologies. So were the objectives of safeguards changed to monitor and supervise nuclear and space technologies being used for peaceful purposes. This approach was embodied in the concept of full-scope safeguards of the IAEA which India consistently opposed. Full-scope safeguards were also going to be discriminatory, as these were not applicable to the facilities and laboratories of the nuclear weapon states.

If one recalls the provisions of the 1978 Nuclear Regulatory Act of the USA, its primary target was to control and diminish India's nuclear, technological and defence capacities. The deleterious impact that agreements on regional and sub-regional nuclear weapons free zones had on the nuclear self-reliance capacities of important countries like Brazil and Argentina (e.g. the Treaty of Tlatlalco) was also taken serious note of by Indian defence and strategic planners. India was also convinced that establishment of regional and sub-regional nuclear-free zones was irrelevant in terms of the objectives of non proliferation, especially when nuclear weapons had a global reach and more so when most of the regions had at least one nuclear weapons power within the region itself.

India also noted that the discriminatory terms of reference governing the NPT remained the guiding principle of all international regimes being put in place, whether it was the missile control technology regime, the comprehensive test ban treaty, or the proposed fissile material cut-off treaty.

In more recent times, since the beginning of the 1990s, the pressure exerted on South Africa to totally give up its nuclear weapons options the moment black African majority government came to power in that country, as also the enormous pressure exerted on, and financial incentives running into over a billion dollars given to Ukraine to give up its nuclear weapons capacities, had a clear political message for India. The end of the Cold War and the end of the US-Soviet confrontation did not change the discriminatory and self-aggrandising attitude of the nuclear weapons powers on non-proliferation issues. This static and self-serving approach of the nuclear weapon states was manifested in all the discussions related to non-proliferation of every category held after the disintegration of the Soviet Union and the end of the Cold War. India, consequently, had to fashion a practical and effective (though reticent and disciplined) deterrent-oriented response to this evolving situation. This was the objective that India sought to fulfil by conducting nuclear tests in May, 1998.

The purpose of recalling these trends in more recent history is to underline the fact that India's nuclear policies have not developed in a vacuum. It was essentially a graduated and measured response to international non-proliferation trends which India perceived as a threat to its long-term security interests. It is the same motivation which made India commence its missile development programme which was given a pronounced impetus by Rajiv Gandhi from 1984 to 1989, a process which has continued to date.

To focus attention on more recent qualitative deterioration in the regional security environment, the threat from Pakistan is of primary importance to India. Conventional wisdom that Pakistan commenced its clandestine nuclear and missile weaponisation programme only after the Indian nuclear test of 1974 is factually incorrect. In their book *Islamic Bomb,* Steve Wiessman and Herbert Krosney (Vision Books, Delhi 1981) assert that right since the mid-1950s, Zulfiqar Ali Bhutto (when he became minister in Ayub Khan's cabinet) was an advocate of Pakistan developing nuclear weapons capacity. Pakistan's defeat in 1971 strengthened Bhutto's conviction. He took the decision to nuclearly weaponise Pakistan two years before India's 1974 tests in Pokhran. His articulated logic was that Pakistan should have such overwhelming superiority in non-conventional weapons that India would never be able to defeat Pakistan in conventional warfare. Pakistan consistently increased its nuclear weapons and missiles capacities from 1972 onwards. By 1987, Pakistan was in possession of a limited number of nuclear devices. During 1987 and 1988, Pakistan improved its missile arsenal with Chinese help, culminating in a situation where, in between 1996 and 1997. Senior Pakistani political and military figures asserted that they were capable of adopting a nuclear and missile posture against India. The firing of the potential IRBM missile, Ghauri in April 1998 and the claims of the creator of Pakistani nuclear weapons programme Dr. Qadir Khan, that Pakistan had an effective military nuclear arsenal, could not be ignored by India.

India's conducting the thermonuclear and nuclear tests has the following implications.

First, India has affirmed to itself and confirmed to the rest of the world its status as a full-fledged nuclear weapons state. Secondly, these tests confirm the sophisticated level of Indian technological capacities in the sphere of high-energy physics and nuclear engineering, with capacities for computer simulation and sub-critical tests in future. Thirdly, India has acquired strategic position as a balancing factor both in regional and international power equations. Fourthly, regardless of the intransigence of the five nuclear weapon powers, objective terms of reference for the future arms control and disarmament processes stand changed with the principle of discriminatory restrictions facing a question mark.

An important question needing an answer is whether India's economic modernisation and development would be affected in an irretrievable manner because of the sanctions imposed in the aftermath of the nuclear tests. The assessment in informed government circles as well as by strategic and economic experts is that the sanctions would create problems for India in the short-term. But India's basic natural and human resources and the inherent strength of the Indian economy would be able to withstand the pressure of these sanctions provided India fulfilled three requirements, that of remaining politically stable and united, that of engaging in constructive discussion with all the important powers of the world to reassure them about their concerns, and that of continuing with its economic liberalisation and reforms purposefully. One speculation was that Defence Minister George Fernandes's critical remarks about China were in preparation for these nuclear tests. There is no such linkage as far as one has ascertained.

On the whole, India's acquiring the nuclear bomb is justified first on the ground of its national security requirements in the present regional context. Second, as a continuing basis for technological self reliance for defence purposes. Third, to structure a strategic balance in its neighbourhood given the weapons capacities and deployment of super powers in the region. Fourth, to avoid being subjected to restrictions and punitive international regimes by being categorised as a non-nuclear weapons State (whatever the legal squabbles, *de facto,* India's nuclear weapons status cannot be questioned). Fifth, the Indian objective is to change the discriminatory terms of reference governing negotiations on non-proliferation, arms control and disarmament which are sought to be perpetuated by the existing nuclear weapons states. This is precisely why India may not be inclined to sign the CTBT in its present form, much less the NPT. Sixth, and the most important of all, India's nuclear weaponisation is motivated more by political and strategic purposes than operational military intentions. India will only opt for the latter under compelling and unavoidable circumstances.

On the issue of imposition of sanctions, our response should not be confrontationist. It should be patient, sober and rational. There should be no element of jingoism in our political and diplomatic postures. We will have to undertake a concerted and stable campaign aimed at multilateral financial institutions to head off any excessively negative decision being taken by them against India. Initial assessments are that we can survive the sanctions, if there is political unity and stability and if we carry on with our economic restructuring and reforms in a purposeful and dynamic manner, not allowing partisan politics to affect the process. We would also have to bear the brunt of restrictions on transfers of technology to us. Our own technological and infrastructural capacities and trained manpower resources should enable us to survive this particular pressure to some extent. If over a period of the coming year or two, the world gets convinced about our rationale and responsible behaviour, sanctions may diminish. We must utilize the influential non-resident Indian communities in the advanced countries to remove suspicions and doubts about us and to generate positive points of view in the establishments of these countries regarding India.

The broad question being raised is: what has India achieved by taking the radical and internationally unpopular decision of becoming a nuclear weapons state? The achievements could be summed up as follows: The first point to be made is that it is the capacity and capability of the country and its people to go down a lonely path alone in its own interests which is the ultimate test of its will to survive and to safeguard its independence and territorial integrity. The tests perhaps affirm this capacity or capability. Secondly, the people of India, leaving aside the experts and the pillars of power structure, were quite uncertain about our scientific ad technological capabilities. They were getting a little bemused about the theory of nuclear options being kept open. The tests confirmed to the people, India's potentialities in a definite manner. Thirdly, the tests have infused a sense of confidence and decisiveness in India's foreign and defence policies. A positive psychological and emotional repercussion has been felt in India though the phenomenon cannot be quantified. Fourth, we have sent clear and unambiguous messages to the international community that we are a nuclear weapons power and we have indigenously developed our capabilities to a satisfactory level. This is a ground reality which the world would have to come to terms with, whatever be the legal quibbling about our status as nuclear weapons state because we did not acquire the capacity before 1 January, 1968. Fifth, the achievement has sent out a signal to the world as well as to our own public that our restraint and discipline, despite provocations and restrictions lasting for 24 years, were not a result of inabilities or lack of technological capacities. Our restraint was voluntary and was based on knowledge about our own strength and our potentialities. Sixth, we have laid the foundation for a credible response to the strategic security environment around us Seventh, we have profoundly changed the strategic balance between nuclear weapons powers in the political sense. We have also changed the strategic equations in Asian power relations. Eighth, the technological spin off of this confirmed capacity of ours would serve peaceful purposes and contribute to economic development. And lastly, in any new global arrangement, India would be a force to reckon with.

India cannot be ignored in international calculations for global security in the future.

In many ways India's nuclear tests and nuclear weapons status balance off the critical impact that our hesitations and reticences made on our foreign and defence policies during the last fifty years. It is appropriate that we have redressed the balance in the international order in favour of developing countries and in India's interests by the momentous decision that we implemented at Pokhran on 11 and 13 May, 1998. Pokhran II will stand out as an appropriate watershed from which we can evaluate the past and plan the future after more than 50 years of independence.

Getting back to the main chronological narrative, Rajiv Gandhi's government, when it came to power in December 1984, perceived the following factors and trends as affecting India's foreign and defence policies:

(a) The cold war was disappearing. US-USSR consensus on international issues would require adjustment by India and other developing countries, whose policies were predicated on the leverage available to them due to the Cold War.

(b) Soviet Union's withdrawal from Afghanistan would increase US and Pakistani influences and options for them in the Gulf and West Asian regions.

(c) Pakistan itself would emerge as an assertive and self-assured entity in the South Asian region.

(d) Changed leadership in the Soviet Union and China would result in a thaw in their attitudes towards each other.

(e) China would adopt a more practical approach towards India, as indicated by Deng Xiaoping to the then Indian Foreign Minister, Atal Behari Vajpayee during latter's visit to China in 1979.

(f) While older multilateral organizations and arrangements were losing their unity and sense of purpose (like G-77, UNCTAD, the Non-aligned Group), new centripetal forces were at work resulting in regional and sub-regional groupings being formed for technological, economic and commercial cooperation, their objective being to fashion durable framework for peace and security in their respective regions.

(g) The potentialities of mechanisms of socio-economic management and development conceived and operated since the Nehru era had levelled off. Comparative inadequacies of somewhat similar systems in the Socialist countries—particularly in the Soviet Union and China, were noted. India had to change gear and reorient its methods of socio-economic management to overcome internal socio-economic stagnation.

(h) Regardless of the factual situation of Indian commitment to principles of non-interference and peaceful co-existence, regional perceptions of India were about India harbouring hegemonistic and regional power ambitions.

(i) At the end of the fourth decade after independence, India was facing potent centrifugal pressures in Punjab and the North Eastern States. There was a tangible emerging internal threat to India's internal stability and security.

(j) Pakistan's acquisition of nuclear weapons capacities changed the South Asian military balance.

(k) Apart from Pakistan, India's neighbours like Nepal, Bangladesh and Sri Lanka were forging political and defence relationships with US, China, Israel and other countries due to their perceptions about India.

Rajiv Gandhi initiated clear-cut policies and a measured response to these challenges and trends. He opened up lines to the US and Western countries, while sustaining requisite levels of relations with the Soviet Union; he embarked on the path of greater diversification of sources for supplies and technologies for the defence section. Signals were sent to China indicating India's willingness to normalise relations and resume discussions on the boundary issue. He established personal contacts with Zia-ul-Haq and Jayawardene, Presidents of Pakistan and Sri Lanka, respectively, with whom India's relations were passing through a critical phase. He proposed a new time-bound initiative for nuclear disarmament, arms control, and reduction in strategic arms, aimed at their elimination by the first decade of the 21st century. He started liberalisation of the Indian economy. He expedited the creation of South Asian Association for Regional Cooperation (SAARC), proposed by Bangladesh while participating in its first summit at Dhaka in December, 1985. He was prompt in visiting Pakistan to meet Benazir Bhutto after the restoration of democracy in that country in 1988, and then again in 1989, resulting in the signing of the important Indo-Pakistan agreement not to attack each other's nuclear facilities. He put forward a number of proposals to enhance economic and cultural cooperation, and people to people contact between India and Pakistan to build an atmosphere of mutual trust and confidence. He assured the Sri Lankan President that India's support to Tamil aspirations was matched by an equal commitment of India to Sri Lankan unity and territorial integrity. His last significant contribution to safeguarding India's security was his visit to China in December, 1988, where the discussions with Deng Xiaoping commenced the important and gradual process of normalisation of relations between China and India.

The continuing concerns of the foreign policy are:

(i) India's territorial integrity remains under threat from Pakistan due to Pakistani claims on Jammu and Kashmir, and from China due to the still-unresolved boundary dispute. In the latter case, the threat is not operational, as it was till the late 1980s. It remains so, nevertheless, till Sino-Indian agreement is reached on the subject;

(ii) Internal centrifugal forces continue to affect India's geo-political unity. There are demands for secession from segments of population in Jammu and Kashmir and the North Eastern States of India. Incipient separatist aspirations have been expressed by some groups in Tamil Nadu, Punjab, Orissa and North Bengal on and off since late fifties and early sixties.

(iii) Adversary relations with Pakistan and China, and military conflicts with these countries have resulted in India having to divert its scarce financial, material and trained manpower resources for defence purposes, thereby reducing Indian capacities to formulate and implement social and economic policies for national consolidation and reconstruction.

(iv) Foreign countries, foreign think tanks questioning the practicability of India's survival as a united polity because of the religious, ethnic and linguistic diversities in India, has been a recurrent refrain which India had to and has to counter.

(v) Foreign military bases and foreign military presences, including the deployment of strategic and tactical nuclear weapons systems in India's neighbourhood, in the Northern reaches of the Indian Ocean and in the Arab and African littoral countries, have been a matter of apprehension to India. End of Cold War has not discontinued this force deployment posture whether it is at Diego Garcia or seaborne or airborne forces.

(vi) China's overwhelming nuclear capacities and the presence of nuclear weapons in the Asian and Indian Ocean region have influenced India's foreign policy planning since 1964.

Since 1991, India is adjusting to the rapidly changing international and internal security environment. Constituent factors and elements of these environments at two levels will determine the content of India's foreign policy and the direction which it will take. Detailing these elements is therefore relevant.

First, the objective ground realities. The end of the cold war and the disintegration of the Soviet Union resulted in transforming the two fundamental predications in India's foreign policy. The relevance of nonalignment as manifested in the nonaligned movement, since its evolution required a re-examination.

Second, the leverage which India had due to its security linkages with the Soviet Union to safeguard its national security and to calibrate the geo-strategic environment around India for this purpose was lost.

Third, the process of globalisation and information revolution necessitated India having to qualitatively reorient its economic, social and developmental policies, to be in step with the mainstream of international development in this respect.

Fourth, India had to cope with a new agenda on international concerns which the world powers commenced generating pressures, not taking into account the diversity of individual pressures and the diversity of individual concerns of developing countries, namely, the issue of human rights, environment management, unilateral social conditionalities stipulated by world powers governing the processes of developmental cooperation.

Fifth, the cold war was not replaced by an harmonious world order but by new patterns of competitions and incipient impulses for world domination by the advanced countries through expansion of security and economic arrangements dominated by United States and by unilaterally stipulated discriminatory regimes on transfer of technologies, international trade, flow of investments, controlling the biological mineral and genetic resources of the world, and so on.

Sixth, India had to define its position and find its place in the new regional groupings and politico-strategic security arrangements being put in place after the end of the Cold War.

Seventh, India had to develop new equations with the emerging power centres of the world like North America, Western Europe, Japan, China, Russia and ASEAN.

Eighth, India had to forge relations with newly emerging countries like South Africa, Central Asia, the former European and Eurasian Republics of the Soviet Union.

Lastly, India had to diversify its defence and economic cooperation with various countries in conformity with new power equations emerging in the world in the context of orientation of policies of different important countries. Over and above all, India had to cope with comparatively volatile and uncertain political and economic situations in its immediate neighbourhood in South Asia.

On balance, the failures and achievements of our foreign policy during this first fifty years of our existence can be summed up as follows:—

The failures were during the first decade and a half of our independence; our foreign policy was imbued with idealism and an unrealistically positive vision of the world order. This approach resulted in our not meeting our national interests on some specific issues. Our going to the

UN to neutralize the Pakistan invasion of Kashmir, our acquiescing in China's take-over of Tibet, our gradualistic and then suddenly assertive approach on the evolving boundary dispute with China from 1956 onwards, leading to our military defeat in the 1962 war confirmed this assessment.

We acquired an influence in world affairs quite disproportionate to our economic, political and military strength because of Pandit Nehru's moral stature and international influence. As far as Nehru lived, India's leadership could be sustained. His passing from the scene should have adjusted as to political realities, making us play a more realistic role in international affairs. What actually happened was that we acquired a mindset from Nehru legacy which hankered for an international leadership role, regardless of whether the rest of the world was willing to accept India in this role and regardless of whether India had the necessary resources and power to lay claim to this role. Our desire to play such a role also became a limitation on us to act decisively in our national interests at time. We also landed ourselves in contradictory predicaments because of our claim that we deal with international issues from a high moral ground and not on the basis of real politik. Our actions willy nilly had to be based on real politik, whether it was police action in Hyderabad, the military operations against the Portuguese in Goa, and the contradictory manner in which we reacted to the Soviet invasion of Hungary and Czechoslovakia and the British-French invasion of Egypt or the Arab invasion of Israel in the late 1960s and 1970s. The same contradictions were manifested as late as in 1980s and 1990s in relation to US military operations in Libya, Grenada and Panama on the one hand and Kuwait's invasion by Iraq on the other.

There are perfectly acceptable reasons why India acted in the manner in which it did on developments in terms of

India's national interests but we were to be on the defensive because of our reluctance to get down from the artificial moral pedestal which we had built for ourselves. An example of foreign reactions to this predicament of ours was a conversation which I had with one of the seniormost State Department officials on the USA's unfair criticism of India's human rights records, when I was Foreign Secretary. This US official neutralised my assertive questioning of US judgements by saying: "India faces this problem because India has itself defined high moral standards about its socio-political behaviour on issues of international concern like human rights. We are only judging you by the standards which you claim yourselves. You do not see us as critical about countries like China, Egypt or Indonesia because they do not speak to us from a moral high ground which you do."

Another self-created shortcoming (not a failure) in our foreign policy mindset is the desire to get good conduct certificates from other countries about ourselves, namely that we are a great country, that we desire to be leaders of developing countries, that because of our virtues we must automatically become permanent member of the UN Security Council. That other countries should look up to us as an important regional, and if possible global entity. This Narcissim results in unrealistic ambitions, hypothetical plausibilities and petulent frustrations in our foreign policy. This mindset can and should be assiduously avoided.

The following can be considered the successes of India's foreign policy:—

1. Despite the enormous diversities and centrifugal forces affecting India, we have remained a united country.

2. We have safeguarded our territorial integrity despite external threats and pressures which we have faced through subversion, military threats and political challenges.

3. Despite negative perceptions about India amongst India's neighbours, howsoever unjustified they may be, we have maintained a working relationship with our neighbours in overall terms, whatever the interim ups and downs might have been. In more recent years, we have managed to stabilise our relations even with Pakistan and Bangladesh with whom we have some fundamental disputes to resolve.

4. We have retained our foreign policy, our nuclear, our space, our technological options, despite continuous negative pressures on us to fall in line with arrangements which would have been detrimental to our national interests.

5. We have managed to structure a working relationship with all the major power centres of the world on a continuous basis over the last 50 years whether it was during Cold War period or during the enormous transitions witnessed by the world after the end of the cold war.

6. We are an effective and credible member of all the multilateral for a dealing with global issues, even if we are not given the role and position due to us because of power politics.

7. We have managed our defence and foreign economic relations with sufficient imagination and flexibility to meet our interests and to ensure the security and well-being of our people in a complex world in constant ferment and change.

8. That we have achieved all this as a democracy subjected to contradictory pulls and pressures of a pluralistic society characterized by enormous diversities is a remarkable achievement, if one were to indulge in a comparative evaluation. What India has achieved in foreign policy terms is something which all the countries of Europe are still in the process of achieving after nearly three

centuries of experience as nation-states, with a lesser population and endowed with much greater resources.

At this juncture of our passage past more than half a century milestone of existence as a Republic, we must be capable of critical introspection about these matters. But there is every reason for us to be imbued with hope, provided we remain united as a country and do not succumb to the forces of fragmentation and divisiveness.

II

It is time to undertake a critical introspection as to how we have been dealing with the world around us, what has been the pattern of our relations with other countries, what has been our position in the international community as an independent and sovereign political entity. It would also be relevant to examine as to how far we have been able to safeguard our country's basic interests.

If India was to find an appropriate place in the international community, it would have to define its geo-political identity and cultural individuality in terms of India's own history and politico-social traditions. Secondly, India's multi-cultural, multi-religious, multi-ethnic civilisational identity would have to be transmuted to a political identity as a nation state and that this identity had to be consolidated. Thirdly, the long experience of foreign invasions and colonial rule imbued India with a firm conviction that India should zealously guard its independence and its freedom of options to fulfil the aspirations of our people. Fourthly, India being conscious of the dangers to its own independence from the ramifications of international power politics, there was the thoughtful decision that India would not get involved in such power politics on its latest emerging manifestation, the cold war. The consequence was the national leadership consciously adopting a pacific and rational approach to international relations. The objectives of this approach were quite different from the motivations of aggrandisement, acquisition of military power, creating equilibrium in such power equations in a competitive framework. India articulated interest even for a cooperative, but not competitive, and just world order. This vision was first articulated by Jawaharlal Nehru in India's first exercise in international diplomacy at the Asian Relations Conference held in Delhi in March 1947. India followed this approach in its foreign policy assiduously for nearly 15 years upto 1962, untramelled by the alarms of a world ferment which was subject to the pressures of the cold war.

In terms of India's own foreign policy and national security concerns, India's interests were to consolidate its territorial integrity, to create a state structure based on democratic institutions, to organise a polity responsive to the Plural multidimensional nature of Indian society, to prevent internal or external centrifugal forces from disrupting the above processes and to ensure the economic well-being of the Indian people on the basis of scientific and technological modernity and social justice. Externally, in its external dimensions, India's foreign policy objectives were to eradicate colonialism and the remnants of imperialism, to end apartheid and racial discrimination, to advocate peaceful political negotiations to resolve political dispute and military conflicts to ensure non-discriminatory treatment and to create an international economic order ensuring distributive justice to the majority of the people of the world who were poor. India sought the achievement of these aims not through acquisition of military might or exploitative economic power. India desired to influence, and through whatever small influence it could, public opinion in other countries. The signposts of this influence were India's harnessing international public opinion against imperialism and colonialism which resulted in practically all the developing countries following India's line.

The period from 1947 to 1962 was a period of creation of India's foreign policy and its success in meeting India's objectives mentioned earlier. The military defeat of India in the Sino-Indian conflict in 1962 and the manner in which the world refused to help India resolve the Kashmir conflict on the merits of the issue brought about shifts in India's foreign policy. These events taught India an important unpalatable lesson that international relations are governed by power equations and real politik, that they are an amoral phenomenon. From 1962 to 1971 India translated this lesson, which she learned, into her foreign and security policies. India focussed attention on improving its defence capacities and on its technological and economic development. India created equations with Eastern Europe and the Soviet Union for this purpose in view of the fact that compared to Western democracies, these countries were responsive to India's needs. The security and strategic interests of the US and the Western democracies did not mesh with India's concerns and interests. India adopted a two-dimensional strategy to safeguard its interests. It activated entities like the UNCTAD, the Group of 77, and it strengthened the non-aligned movement to counter the negative pressures generated on developing countries by the Western powers for their own purposes. Secondly, India strengthened and expanded its technological, economic and defence relationships with the socialist countries led by the Soviet Union to safeguard India's specific interests in terms of defence, development and security. The period between 1963 and 1984 witnessed the continuation of this dual strategy which generally met India's interests and India's foreign policy objectives.

Shri Lal Bahadur Shastri briefly and Mrs. Gandhi for nearly a decade and a half, introduced the necessary realism and purposiveness in our foreign and national security policies, the most significant manifestation of which was noticed, successfully dealing with the East Pakistan crisis and defeating Pakistani armed forces in 1971. India became as self-reliant as it could in its defence and technological capacities. It successfully structured political and economic equations with the different important powers in the world. It withstood international pressure on accepting discriminatory and unequal disarmament measures like the non-proliferation treaty. India became a nuclear weapon capable power and developed an entirely new and beneficial pattern of relations with important countries like Iran and countries in South East Asia.

In the post Cold War period the United States has emerged as the supreme in the world order. In more general terms, the eight industrially advanced countries, who form the Group of 8, dominated the world affairs. Most importantly, India's conducting nuclear tests on May 11th and 13th and Pakistan's following suit on May 28th and 30th have changed the strategic balance and affected the non-proliferation agenda of the five nuclear weapons powers.

It is in this context that we in India have to assess our major challenges and security concerns in the first decades of the 21st Century.

Our first and foremost concern should be to ensure our political stability within the framework of democratic political processes. Our stability has been under pressure due to various political impulses affecting our society since the mid-80s. Our second and more immediate concern should be to preserve our nuclear weapons status and our technological capacities for defence without getting too isolated from the international community which views critically our acquiring nuclear weapons. The objective should be to sustain our capacities while rejoining the mainstream of efforts to achieve a genuine, comprehensive, non-discriminatory disarmament and non-proliferation.

India's territorial integrity remains under threat from Pakistan due to Pakistani claims on Jammu and Kashmir and, from China, due to the still unresolved boundary dispute. In the latter case, the threat is not operational, as it was till the late 1980s. The threat shall, nevertheless, remain till a Sino-Indian agreement can be reached on the subject.

Barring Bhutan and Maldives, India's relations with its other neighbours, namely, Nepal, Sri Lanka, Myanmar, Bangladesh and Pakistan (which falls into a special hostile category) have remained problematic for one reason or another. This pattern continues. With Nepal, the points of worry have been:

(a) its trying to play China against India,

(b) differences of opinion regarding trade and transit issues (which crop up periodically), and

(c) differing views on water resources utilisation for agricultural purposes and power generation.

With Sri Lanka, first there were the issues of the citizenship of Tamils of Indian origin who migrated to Ceylon in the nineteenth century to work in the tea plantations there, and determining the jurisdiction of the two countries on coastal islands off India's peninsular coast without disrupting the traditional fishing rights of fishermen of both countries. Then, from the late seventies, the Tamil-Sinhalese ethnic conflict impacted on the politics of Tamil Nadu. Though relations are normal now, the ethnic crisis casts a shadow on these relations. With Myanmar, the memory of the expulsion of the Indian community in the 1960s and 1970s still rankles in the Indian mindset. India has forged a working relationship with the SLORC military regime in Rangoon, but Indian public opinion has not yet reconciled to the non-fulfilment of the democratic verdict of the people of Myanmar. This attitude has been existent since General Ne Win's assuming power in the country. Finally, Myanmar's economic and defence relations with China remain a matter of interest to India. With Pakistan and Bangladesh, the points of dispute are too well known to need elaboration, particularly since both these countries were one political entity till 1971. The point to be noted is that Bangladesh's creation and India's support to the process have not made much of a difference; in fact, on many issues Bangladesh has reverted to the former "East Pakistan" adversarial posture towards India.

Pakistan's attempts to influence the attitude and policies of India's other direct neighbours and also the Islamic countries, with a view to generating apprehensions amongst them against India, have posed a continuing challenge to Indian security interests.

Foreign military bases and foreign military presence, including the deployment of strategic and tactical nuclear weapons systems in India's neighbourhood, in the northern reaches of the Indian Ocean and in the Arab and African littoral countries, have been a matter of apprehension to India. The end of the cold war has discontinued this force deployment posture, whether it was at Diego Garcia or whether the forces were sea-borne or air-borne.

China's overwhelming nuclear capacities, and the presence of nuclear weapons in the Asian and Indian Ocean regions, have influenced India's defence planning since 1964.

Late in 1991 the US Department of Defence circulated a policy note on "Forward Defence Planning for the US" in the aftermath of Gulf War. The US Defence Department, while referring to prospects and policy objectives in South

Asia, held the view that one of the most important tasks of the US would be to prevent India from dominating its neighbours, especially Pakistan. Consequently, Pakistan's economic and military capacity was to be built up to balance Indian regional ambitions. This was the view of the US Department of Defence. Jerrold Elkin, faculty member of the US Air Force Academy is more direct. He declares that "the government of India maintains three principal strategic objectives: consolidating its position as hegemon in South Asia (grounded on military superiority over Pakistan and lesser regional actors); achieving military paramountcy throughout the Indian Ocean, and accrediting sufficient armed power to press successfully status elevation demands upon the international community."

Thus the first perception is that India has hegemonistic ambitions in South Asia and also that India desires status elevation in international arrangements. Presumably, this implies India's claim to and desire for a permanent seat in the UN Security Council. The assertion that India has hegemonistic ambitions is irrational. This is because given India's own internal problems, resource constraints and preoccupations with national consolidation (in the face of continuing domestic centrifugal challenges), it would be foolish for India to harbour hegemonic or expansionist tendencies. India wanting to become a regional power is begging the question—India's physical size, demography, resources, technological capacities and the size of its defence forces make its regional power status an existentialist reality. India has intervened in neighbouring countries—Bangladesh, the Maldives and Sri Lanka-only on the basis of requests from these countries themselves, and only when developments in these countries had a direct fallout on India's own security and stability. Indian forces were withdrawn as soon as they had completed their mission, or when the country which had called on their services asked for their withdrawal. It is only motivated imagination which can describe India's track record in regional relations as hegemonic. The rationale for propagating India's hegemonic, on the other hand, is and could be the calculated objective of ensuring the political and economic influence of countries propagating this image in the South Asian region with a view to preventing solidarity and cooperation of the countries there. This is a process in which India will emerge as the dominant factor. India aspiring to a blue-water Navy to safeguard its economic and maritime interests is logical; to allege that India wishes to achieve military paramountcy throughout the Indian Ocean region is an unrealistic exaggeration. Naval capacities and naval forces deployment of the USA and China in the Indian Ocean and with the expanding navies of Australia and Indonesia, attributing this motive or capacity to India is a deliberate exercise in generating groundless apprehensions about India. India's naval fleet cannot challenge or defeat any major naval battle group of an external power.

The second perception is that India poses a nuclear threat to the South Asian region. In fact, the late President Zia-ul-Haq of Pakistan and the Foreign Minister of Pakistan, Lt. General Yakub Khan, had put forth the contention to India's other neighbours that Pakistan's acquiring nuclear weapons capacity would guarantee the security of not only South Asian but also South East Asian (Muslim) countries against any Indian threat. Benazir Bhutto has repeated this line of thought. This is a patently self-serving argument which has not made any impact on India's neighbours. They would much rather have both Pakistan and India abjure the acquisition of nuclear weapons capacity. Even otherwise, China and the US, individually or together, are capable of countering such threats if India were inclined to adopt any such insane nuclear posture towards her neighbours.

A third perception amongst India's immediate neighbours is that India, with its larger resources and larger technological and economic capacities, desires to capture and dominate the economies of other South Asian countries. This apprehension has manifested itself in Pakistan refusing to establish trade relations with India; in Bangladesh being reluctant to allow transit facilities for Indian goods to the North-Eastern States of India or through its port of Chittagong; in Nepal and India engendering frequent controversies about bilateral trade and transit relations; and in Sri Lanka being cautious about Indian investment in its economy. The attempt to overcome this apprehension, under the umbrella of the SAARC through the South Asia preferential trade arrangements (SAPTA) mechanism, has not succeeded so far, primarily because of delays being caused by Pakistan. This imagined acquisitive and domineering image of India stands contradicted by the simple instance that India had participated in developing economic relations with its neighbours upto the level and extent to which they sought such cooperation. Such is the Indian policy stance on economic interaction in the bilateral framework as well as in the SAARC.

The fourth perception is that the increasing population of India will generate demographic pressures leading to Indian migration to neighbouring countries backed up by Indian political and military power. This apprehension would stand to reason if the countries neighbouring India were underpopulated, with space to spare with respect to land-to-people ratios. This is not the case with any of India's neighbours; each one is densely populated and short of space. In fact, it is people from neighbouring countries, particularly from Bangladesh and Nepal, as well as

Mohajirs (former residents of Indian States of Uttar Pradesh and Bihar) from Pakistan, who have been migrating into India over the last two decades. The prospect is not of Indian migration into neighbouring countries but of coping with the collective population explosion in South Asia.

The fifth negative perception about India is that it has adopted a static rejectionist stance on non-proliferation issues, related to nuclear weapons, missiles, arms control and arms reduction measures. The point to be pondered is whether India has behaved in a more responsible manner in meeting non-proliferation objectives, despite not being a party to various non-proliferation regimes, compared to a number of countries which have attracted punitive measures for violating non-proliferation commitments which they had undertaken under international agreements. Even otherwise, India has had bilateral discussions on these matters with a number of countries, including the super-powers, in which it has indicated a willingness to expiore areas of agreement on these vital subjects.

The sixth perception, entertained particularly by its neighbours, is that India is not willing to compromise or grant any concessions on any matter of dispute between them and India. Their feeling is that India being the larger and better-endowed country, should not only be fair but also generous in responding to the demands of her neighbours, whether the issue be Kashmir, distribution and utilisation of water resources or trade and transit facilities. This critical perception is shared by other foreign countries, depending on their interests and inclinations at given points of time. India is faced with a Hobson's choice in such a critical evaluation. Being bigger and better endowed with resources, the advocacy for generosity and concessions on the part of India appears reasonable. But each of the issues on which such an accommodating attitude is demanded affects India's vital territorial or economic interests; compromises are just not possible on such issues (e.g. Kashmir, accepting Bangladesh's demands on Farakka waters, and granting trade and transit facilities to Nepal and Bangladesh) in a short time span. The gradual approach, spread over a period of time, is the practical solution to this criticism.

The seventh external perception pertains to the impression that India is given to pontification on norms for international behaviour, the inclination of India to preach on topics such as non-alignment, peaceful co-existence and non-violence is viewed with scepticism, even exhaustion, by a large number of countries. There is some validity in this viewpoint. This trait in Indian policy pronouncements and postures, however, is diminishing after the end of the Cold War and consequent lowering of rhetoric and public postures in politics and diplomacy.

The eighth critical perception, though generally shared by a number of countries, found articulation in an article published in the political journal of the Chinese Army (in 1992). In a manner, it was an elaboration of Professor J.K. Galbraith's thesis of India being the largest functioning anarchy in the world. The Chinese article put forward the contention that India's society and policy were fragmented due to religious, caste, ethnic and other factors. Consequently, the article further states, Indian society lacks cohesion and unity of purpose for national consolidation and this results in India not having any structured strategic doctrines to ensure its defence, and, therefore, the Indian armed forces suffer from the handicap of ineffective command and control systems. While the centrifugal forces affecting the Indian state are not to be denied, the Chinese assessments about India's vulnerability in terms of national security are exaggerated.

India has been sensible of, and sensitive, to the foregoing views. Some specific initiatives have been taken to counter-balance the aforementioned perceptions wherever possible. These initiatives have been reflected both in foreign and defence policies. India has undertaken negotiations with each one of her neighbours, since the middle of 1991, to remove misunderstandings, to stabilise economic and political relations, and to formulate and implement confidence building measures. India detached itself from the ethnic conflict in Sri Lanka, preferring to focus attention on building up bilateral relations. Trade restrictions against Nepal were removed; the controversies affecting bilateral relations were overcome.

The transfer of territories and enclaves to Bangladesh (*Beru Bari* and the *Teen Bigha* corridor) was done by 1993. The Prime Minister of India pledged that Bangladesh would not be deprived of requisite water supplies from the Gangetic river system during the lean season. Despite continuing large-scale illegal migration of Bangladeshis and Chakma tribals into India, the latter agreed to negotiations to control such transborder movement, delaying punitive action by the Indian Border Security Force (BSF), which would have been ordered otherwise.

Even in the case of Pakistan the high-level political contacts at the prime ministerial level were continued right upto April 1993, despite their being inconclusive each time. Various Indian Prime Ministers met their Pakistani counterparts nine times between December 1988 and April 1993. Eight rounds of Foreign Secretary-level talks were held between May 1989 and January 1994. Similarly, the Home Secretaries and Defence Secretaries, as well as military commanders of both countries, met several tim during the period 1989-94. Though none of the major political problems was resolved, a number of important confidence building measures were agreed upon and also implemented. Agreements have been signed to keep respective military forces at stipulated distances from the border and to give advance notion of army, air force and navy exercises being undertaken by each country to the other. Direct and regular institutional contacts have been stipulated and hotline telephone connections established between the Directors-General of Military Operations of the two countries and between field commanders at lower echelons. An agreement was signed in 1991, not to attack each other's nuclear installations. In January 1994, India made important suggestions to Pakistan—that a bilateral agreement be signed by both sides not to attack each other's economic and populous centres and not to use their respective nuclear capacities against each other under the "no first use" doctrine. Pakistan has rejected this suggestion.

III

There is a general impression that our Ministry of External Affairs and the Foreign Service are mostly involved in the ceremonial and cosmetic aspects of India's relations with other countries, that the most serious thing that our missions do abroad is to prepare general political assessments and function as liaison offices for the Central and State Governments of India and that they do not do anything more tangible. The highlighting of political and structural initiatives taken by the government in foreign relations in the media and the criticism that despite more than half a century having passed after our attaining independence and half a century of diplomatic and foreign policy experience, we have still not evolved institutional mechanisms and operational arrangements to periodically review the results of our foreign policy operations. There is still no effective means to assess "foreign policy operations and target achievement ratios". The political elements in foreign policy operations because of the very nature of political work remain intangible and nebulous, but there are three aspects of foreign policy operations which are capable of being assessed in terms of concrete results, namely, the economic, security and cultural aspects of the implementation of our foreign policy.

It is significant that while monitoring and review mechanisms have not evolved, there has been a gradual evolution of institutions and coordinating arrangements within the Government of India for initiating new orientations, proposals and projects in external relations. The apex institutions for these purposes are the 'Cabinet Committee on Political Affairs' and the 'Cabinet Committee on Economic Affairs'. (It is a different matter that the CCPA has not been reconstituted since the cabinet reshuffle of January, 1993, due to various political reasons.) Below these Cabinet Committees, we have the Cabinet Secretary heading an informal sort of a National Security Advisory Group, in which the Foreign Secretary, the Home Secretary, the Defence Secretary, and in more recent years the Finance Secretary are members, alongwith the Chiefs of our intelligence organisations.

The Principal Secretary to the Prime Minister and the Foreign Secretary take meetings and have discussions with Secretaries and officials concerned of other government departments as well as representatives of economic organisations to adjust the details of bilateral relations with different countries to changing and emerging realities. Specific agreements, proposals and projects emerge from these arrangements, constituting the content of our relations with different countries from time to time.

The Foreign Office is also represented on the apex committee of Secretaries on economic matters in the 'Foreign Investment Promotion Board'. During the last ten years, the Cabinet Secretariat has been obtaining statement of objectives which the Ministry of External Affairs expects to achieve and fulfill each year. The statement is required to be sent at the beginning of each year and is expected to cover in detail both general and specific objectives, and the activities which would be undertaken by the Ministry to fulfill that.

These arrangements led to concrete results in terms of new orientations in India's foreign policy: its paying more attention to technological, economic and security aspects of our relations with other countries, particularly since the Congress Government came into power in June, 1991. The requirements generated by the emergence of new countries with the break-up of the Soviet Union, the new economic focus of our foreign policy and the transformed strategic environment with the end of the cold war necessitated the fashioning of new arrangements, the formulation of new proposals and the creation of new security equations between India and other countries. The institutions and mechanisms mentioned above served these purposes well, as manifested in the opening of new missions, the signing of a series of new agreements with various countries covering a wide spectrum of areas of cooperation with them and new defence cooperation arrangements with other countries.

While the annual reports of the Ministries of External Affairs, Defence, Commerce, Finance and Industry give some idea of the results achieved from these initiatives, proposals and projects, the Consultative Committee of Parliament on External Affairs, the Standing Committee of Parliament on External Affairs plus the debate on demands for grants for the Ministry each year also provides some idea of the results achieved. This is, however, not a structured or systematic exercise which provides the Government or the public a clear and precise idea of our successful or unsuccessful foreign policy. Some thought has to be given to monitor first the content and results of the foreign policy initiatives that India has taken; secondly how far have these results met the interests and objectives which we had in mind while taking new steps and initiatives at a given point of time. It would be relevant to take note of what happens in the Foreign Offices of other countries in this respect. The Japanese are the most methodical in assessing results. Their policy planning cell or its equivalent body and the Japanese Self-Defence Agency and the important technological departments take follow-up action on foreign policy decisions and their results. A quarterly assessment is made within the Japanese Foreign Office itself about the results and impact of foreign policy moves and adjustments are made to meet the targets. I understand that an assessment of foreign policy resources and achievements is sent to the Japanese Cabinet and by the end of each year the next year's planning process commences, based on this continuous monitoring exercise. The Germans and the French may not have as precise and systematic arrangement as the Japanese but their policy planning division and foreign service inspectorates jointly undertake an evaluation of the impact and achievements of their respective foreign policies, reportedly once every six months. Particular attention is given to specific cooperation projects and proposals which are initiated to see whether they are progressing within a definite timeframe allocated for them.

The Indian Ministry of External Affairs had essentially adhered to the procedures and practices of the old British Indian Foreign and Political Departments which were modified on patterns being followed in the British Foreign Office. The Indian debacle in the Sino-Indian war of 1962 awakened us to the need for forward planning and assessment. The result was the creation of a Central Research Division which ultimately evolved into the Policy Planning Division of the Ministry of External Affairs, but its essential terms of reference was that of foresight; no hindsight assessment role was specifically allocated to it.

In contrast, the British woke up to the need for post facto evaluation and assessment of foreign policy moves after the Suez crisis of 1956 and the result was that a series of changes have been introduced in the British Foreign Office based on recommendations of the Plowden Report of 1964 and the Broomfield Report of 1983. These recommendations included suggestions for forward planning by a trust in the Foreign Office not subject to the daily pressures of work in a territorial division. The British Policy Planning Division is supposed to be both foresighters and hindsighters, as mentioned in an informative book entitled *Inside the Foreign Office* by John Dickie, a veteran diplomatic correspondent who perhaps was commissioned to write the book to ensure greater transparency about the British Foreign Office to the British public.

The State Department in the United States has its Directorate of Policy Planning, which has similar responsibilities, but has the added pressure of having to send its representatives to the Congressional Committees of the US Legislature to give testimony about the rationale of changing elements in US foreign policy from time to time and to give assessments about the results these initiatives have achieved, an arrangement derived from the separation of powers in the US Constitution, inherent in which is a very influential role for the legislature in the conduct of US foreign policy.

It is time that we in India also devise mechanisms and institutions by which we can evaluate the impact and results of our foreign policy in tangible terms. To take just two examples of the imperative need for such arrangements: India signed a series of agreements of cooperation on economic, technological and cultural subjects with the Central Asian Republics of the former Soviet Union between the middle of 1991 and the end of 1994. There has been no precise monitoring of the follow-up action on these agreements and programmes and projects which have been put in place in consequence. Secondly, with the end of the cold war India has diversified its defence cooperation arrangements with a number of countries. These include arrangements for technological cooperation, joint military exercises, defence training programmes on a bilateral exchange basis, and so on. One reads occasional reports in the media about some aspects of these arrangements if they have visibly fallen short of original objectives or something similar. But there is no structured institutional mechanism of interaction between the Ministry of External Affairs, and the Ministry of Defence to assess the progress of these cooperation arrangements and its likely implications on India's national security. Consultations and coordinations exist to the extent that the senior officials of the External Affairs Ministry and the Defence Ministry are willing to share information and interact with each other in terms of the human chemistry that exists between these officials from time to time. A suggestion which could be considered is that the Policy Planning Division of the Ministry of External Affairs which is mostly engaged in theoretical or speculative work at this stage should be given the specific responsibility of preparing a report every three months about the results achieved in the light of objectives envisaged and defined in our foreign policy. An inter-departmental committee on foreign relations should be established at the Joint

Secretaries level from the Policy Planning Cells of the Ministry of Defence, the Ministry of Home Affairs, the Ministry of Commerce, the Ministry of Industry, the Ministries of Power and Petroleum and the Ministry of Finance. The Joint Chiefs of Staff Committee and our intelligence agencies should also be asked to nominate a representative each on this core group or coordination committee.

This committee should prepare a consolidated assessment report on the impact of India's foreign policy in all spheres once every six months, which in turn should be submitted to the concerned Cabinet Committees through the Cabinet Secretary's Office or the Office of the Principal Secretary to the Prime Minister. If such an arrangement comes into existence despite the perambulations of our administrative system, hopefully the Cabinet Committee headed by the Prime Minister would have concrete information about the results of the policies that they have adopted and direct adjustments to be made to meet the changing patterns of India's interests. Structuring of operational hindsight exercise will contribute positively to our foreign policy, both in terms of effectiveness and accountability.

2

CHALLENGES FACING INDIA'S FOREIGN POLICY

After witnessing more than half a century as an independent country, India faces a transformed world. The terms of reference of India's interaction with the international community stand profoundly changed. Great power ideological confrontation has come to an end. National sovereignty and national insularities are being subsumed by processes of economic globalisation. The information and technology revolutions are progressively reducing the relevance of international frontiers between nation states. The strategic equations and the chemistry of power which underpinned international relations for about half a century since the end of the Second World War have been replaced by new equations. India and many developing countries have lost the leverages which they exercised in foreign policy and strategic matters over the last 50 years because of the disappearance of the Soviet Union and the centripetal qualities characterising the relations between the five great powers, the permanent members of the Security Council. It is in this context that one tries to perceive the challenges to India's foreign policy into the first decades of the 21st century.

International relations, like general processes of history, defy attempts to force their flow into predetermined theoretical patterns or preconceived logical grooves.

Prognoses in foreign policy cannot be strait jacketed in *a priori* generalisations. When discussing the future of international relations or challenges to our foreign policy, we are dealing with the complexity of human emotions, the involutions of human motivations and the ambiguities and uncertainties of the political and socio-economic impulses which underpin them. Foreign policy's eternal challenge is to deal with the unpredictability of interstate and intersocietal relations. International relations will remain involuted, subject to wayward human behaviour. They are baroque, in a manner of speaking.

It is with a profound awareness of this limitation that I undertake the speculative exercise about the tasks facing India's foreign policy in the twenty-first century and the challenges that we would face.

At the most fundamental level, the challenge that India as well as other members of the international community face is to resolve a basic contradiction affecting prospects of human survival. This contradiction is best expressed in the debate between philosophers and socio-economic theoreticians about the perfectibility of human beings. Such a debate and its repercussions marked the end of the eighteenth century. On the one hand was Thomas Robert Malthus, who posited that power of populations is indefinitely greater than the capacity of the earth to produce sufficient subsistence for human beings. According to Malthus, while population increases by geometrical progression, productive capacities increase only in arithmetical progression. Social upheaval and instability, therefore, are the predetermined future predicament of mankind. As opposed to this theory, scholars such as Antoine Condorcet and William Godwin argued that the growth of human understanding, the increase in the capacity for self-improvement and the break throughs in technologies and knowledge would one day lead to a more equitable world where people would live free from crime, disease, war and want. Developments over the last 200 years have proved Malthus's analysis of the population to productivity ratio right but his dire prophecies to be wrong. At the same time, the prognosis of Godwin and Condorcet have proved to be right, while their questioning of Malthus's theory about imbalances between population growth and productivity have proved to be wrong. Populations have increased in a geometrical progression, while productivity has been increasing at lower rates, but there has been an increase in the human capacity for self-improvement, unexpected break throughs in knowledge and technology have made the world progressively a relatively more equitable and comfortable place to live in.

As the future inevitably originates in the impulses of the past, it would be pertinent to confirm the preceding positive assessment through some specifics. Trends since the middle of the nineteenth century till now, when we are on the threshold of the twenty-first century, clearly indicate that the world is more egalitarian. The information technology revolution and the consequent increasingly expeditious access to information combined with the emergence of user-friendly technologies, have resulted in the increasing empowerment of individuals. The levers of power are increasingly in the hands of average human beings all over the world, compared to their being a monopoly of oligarchies or plutocratic elites in different societies and states. Political colonialism has disappeared, so has slavery. There is a universally greater shared concern about human right. There is also an increasing awareness that the natural resources of the world should be exploited and utilized in a more equitable manner while, at the same time, being subject to the imperatives of ecological balance and environmental protection. Discrimination based on ethnicity, language and race, which characterised the attitudes and policies of different states and societies, depending on their military and technological strengths, are now subject to the moral pressure of international public opinion and the political and legal pressures of the norms of international law. The power structure of nation-states is going through a metamorphosis. Nation-states as they evolved since the Treaties of Westphalia, signed in 1648, are now subject to the pressures generated by the economic and technological globalisation of the world. Their relevance in the conventional sense of the term (nation-state) and their claim to unqualified sovereignty are now in question. Socio-economic interdependence between different countries, the democratization of international politics, the disappearance of the cold war antagonism and the incapacity of national boundaries to compartmentalise the flow of ideas and information have resulted in the requirement of nation-states redefining their respective identities.

There are also certain strands of emerging conventional wisdom in international politics, the logic and validity of which must be examined when determining the problems and challenges that India would face in fashioning its foreign policy and structuring its external relations. The first of such strands is the theory that the world has become unipolar and that there is going to be "Pax Americana" for the next hundred years or so. One does not question the fact that the United States will be the most dominant factor in world politics for quite some time to come, but in terms of technological capacities, access and control of natural resources, population strengths and economic determinants of investment opportunities and markets, the world is bound to be multipolar with other power centres being Western Europe, the Russian Federation, China, Japan, India and some strong regional arrangements if they were to emerge in South America and Africa. A major task for India would be to nurture its economic and technological capacities and to increase its political stability and military strength to levels where it can elevate itself to a position of strength to network an equilibrium with the new power centres of the emerging multipolar world. Indications are there that an atmosphere and an opportunity for such networking now exist.

Then there is the theory about the world facing confrontation based on religious and civilisational identities of different societies. I am referring to the Samuel Huntington thesis about the clash of civilisations which has become a fashionable reference point to speculate on the future of interstate relations. This theory is of particular relevance to India because Huntington visualises our country being in a state of isolation because it is neither Islamic nor Christian. He visualises an India without allies or natural external political support systems. His theory is of intriguing interest because while he talks about India's potential isolation, he prognosticates that there would be a collusion between confucian and Islamic civilisations, against the Western, Christian and Judaic civilisations.

One has to deeply ruminate on the predicaments envisaged by Huntington. Though one disagrees both in fundamentals and in detail with Huntington's theory about the clash of civilisations, one would agree that he has contrived and presented a challenging framework to evaluate some of the emerging realities of global politics into the twenty-first century. He has certainly succeeded in being provocative and, to that extent, his book has some relevance. Looking at the statistical tables and the political interpretations of Huntington's thesis, one gets the impression that the provocation for this work perhaps originated during or immediately after the 1991 Gulf War in which the United States' military assertiveness against Iraq was perceived as a religious confrontation by segments of US academia.

The reason for my lengthy critical evaluation of the Huntington thesis is that inherent in this thesis is one of the overarching and fundamental challenges that India's foreign policy will face in the coming century. While the Huntington thesis is definitionally flawed and based on *a priori* confrontationist motivations, it brings out in relief the fact that India, the South East Asian countries (such as Thailand, Burma, Vietnam, Laos and Cambodia), China and Japan are not part of the broad religio-cultural categories which may dominate the power equations. India particularly, because of its plurality and its being a composite of practically all the major religions and cultural groups of the world, does not easily fit into the Christian-Judiac camp or the Islamic camp. Indian foreign policy, therefore, would have to facilitate our country's integration with one of the camps visualised by Huntington, if his thesis is correct. This is not going to be easy because the Hindu majority in India is a very India-specific phenomenon. The millions of Muslims in India, would generate pressures for developing equations with the Islamic world. The other religio-ethnic identities of India may generate contradictory pressures towards the other camp. The prospect to be alert about, and to be consistently monitored, is that such pressures are not generated. The concretisation of this prospect occurred in the break-up of Yugoslavia on ethnic and religious lines. The break-up of the Soviet Union was the result of other impulses, but the phenomenon of ethno-religious separation afflicting the Russian Federation and Georgia provide warning signs to be taken note of by India.

Another dimension to this challenge is that the sanctity of maintaining state structures of plural societies, characterised by diversity, stands eroded, with the disintegration of the Soviet Union and Yugoslavia. If such societies do not have the inner discipline, the required levels of economic and technological development endowed with social justice, and if they do not have the defence capacities to sustain themselves, the other power centres of the world would not be supportive of their unity and integrity. In fact, a disintegration of such state structures could be perceived as making the world a more manageable place by the more powerful, more cohesive and economically advanced countries in the international community. India's foreign, political, economic and national security policies should be pre-emptively responsive to this challenge.

Before turning to the specific tasks on which Indian foreign policy should focus, it would be pertinent to analyse broad trends which would characterize international relations in the coming decades and the motivations of the important powers of the world which would underpin them.

Emerging trends make it obvious that international relations would be dominated by the industrially and technologically advanced countries led by the United States well into the twenty-first century. The first objective of these countries would be to create an international political system in which states and civil societies would be structured on the basis of political and economic terms of reference acceptable to the US and those world powers which would be responsive to their interests. State systems governed by democratic trans-Atlantic terms of reference would be sought to be established. The individual social requirements, traditions and cultures of the countries of Africa and Asia will be questioned and they are likely to be diminished. Political and economic pressures, even coercive pressures, may be generated for this purpose. Secondly, regardless of the claims regarding an emerging equitable and fair economic order, the orientations would be to create a globalised free market economy in a manner in which the advanced industrial countries would remain dominant and influential. Controversies which have arisen after the signing of the Marrakesh Agreements in March 1995 and the additionalities regarding social clauses, intellectual property rights and the time frame for speeding up the implementation of the WTO's export and import regimes confirm this prospect. The third phenomenon characterizing world politics would be the orientation of the foreign policies of the important powers to maintain and to acquire access and control over the raw material and the natural resources of the world, especially of infrastructural, economic and strategic importance such as oil, natural gas and minerals. The alertness and the speed with which this objective is attended to was first indicated in the promptitude with which the former US Secretary of State James Baker visited Kazakhstan to negotiate his country's entry into the Kazakh economy, even before the revised arrangements of relations between the CIS (Commonwealth of Independent States) and the Russian Federation were finalised in the aftermath of the break-up of the Soviet Union (in 1991-92). Another example was the alacrity with which a consortium of businessmen from the USA visited Congo in the summer of 1997 when Mobutu was about to be ousted from the presidentship by a military coup. These businessmen entered into negotiations with leaders of the anti-Mobutu forces and paid an advance of 3 billion dollars to them for long-term access to the natural resources of Congo. The basic aim was clear; that advanced countries should not fall short of essential raw materials nor should their pre-eminent economic position be eroded.

The fourth characteristic of international relations which India would have to cope with is the objective of the Western industrially advanced countries to maintain long-term exclusive control over sophisticated technologies. Regimes governing the transfer of higher technologies being put in place since the beginning of the 1980s have sent out a clear signal that the industrialised advanced economies consider unrestricted transfer of technologies to the developing countries a threat to their capacity, i.e., of the industrially advanced countries to maintain the competitive edge over the majority of countries of the world. The emphasis on the concept of "dual use technologies" and the anxieties that such technologies should be made available to the developing countries under restrictive and discriminatory disciplines and subject to strict safeguards establish the validity of the assessment regarding the acquisitive motivations of the more important powers. This restrictive approach has manifested itself in the export policies of the advanced countries regarding supercomputers, computer hardware, higher electronics, lasers, robotics, genetic engineering, and technologies related to the management and utilisation of biodiversities. This acquisitive competitive approach goes beyond the transfer of technologies originating in these countries. The manner in which certain aspects of intellectual property rights and international standards for the patents clause are sought to be structured militates against the traditional capacity as well as the self-reliance of developing countries. The struggle which India has to engage itself in preventing Western entrepreneurs from patenting the use of neem and turmeric for medical and health purposes is a case in point. These items have been used as ingredients of traditional medicines and health care in India for hundreds of years. The move to claim royalty rights and economic returns on the use of these items under new names and new packaging patented in the West was a blatant attempt at intrusive exploitation. This phenomenon is not going to abate. The processes of globalisation will be used as an excuse for such purposes. The discriminatory and restrictive approach regarding the transfer of technologies will fundamentally affect the capacity for self-reliance, productivity and the ability to produce quality goods of the developing countries. The competition generated by free market economy can be useful and relevant only if it ensures fair play, equity and justice in international economic transactions. Though this is the declared rationale for adhering to the mainstream of international economic trends, in certain dimensions, the actual developments indicate intentions to the contrary.

That meeting the aforementioned macro-level, political, economic and technological objectives necessitates the US and other important powers of the world to maintain their military and technological superiority over the majority of the countries of the world is not just an undeclared objective; it has been articulated. Statements made by President George Bush and President Bill Clinton and by leaders of the European Union, and to some extent, even of the Russian Federation since the end of 1991 and beginning of 1992, have expressed the following views:—

The new world order should aim at preventing the emergence of militarily powerful countries (except those which are already militarily powerful and nuclearly weaponised) as regional or subregional hegemonies.

A corollary of the preceding view is the insistence on discriminatory non-proliferation of various kinds of weapons of mass destruction and insistence on reduction of conventional forces and conventional armaments.

The national and regional export control policies of the advanced countries back up this objective of multifaceted restrictive regimes controlling the transfer of technologies.

The introduction of the concepts of "irresponsible" states and "rogue" states into the lexicon of international law and foreign policy is part of this exercise. To be candid, except the United States and Iraq, no other country has used weapons of mass destruction without provocation on civilian populations. The inclination to apply this label to other countries on the basis of political motivations other than the objective criteria developed by the UN should be noted.

The policy of restricting the military and technological capacities of countries which do not fully conform to the stipulations of the great powers is not just a political stance. This stance has found operational expression in the last three decades of the twentieth century. The attack on Ossirak nuclear facilities in Iraq by Israel, the fulfilment of Henry Kissinger's warning to Zulfiqar Ali Bhutto that his nuclear weaponisation policies would lead to disastrous consequences for him (for Bhutto), the US's coercive stance on Iraq in 1990 and 1998 and the air strikes on Libya in the 1980s prove this point.

It is also significant that US officials, while mounting military pressure on Iraq in January/February, 1998, articulated the view that the policies towards that country were not just aimed at Baghdad, but they were also a signal to other countries which may have inclinations to acquire weapons of mass destruction, whatever their security concerns of justifications may be.

These US officials further expressed the view that those countries which do not abide by stipulated international disciplines on non-proliferation matters should be ready to forfeit their sovereignty, if necessary under pressure of superior military force.

The expectation that, after the disintegration of the Soviet Union and end of the cold war, the UN would become stronger, would become more democratised and would play a more effectively impartial role in ensuring world peace and stability, has not been fulfilled. The UN, at least during the 1990s, has become more of an instrumentality of foreign policy objectives of the five permanent members of the United Nations Security Council and particularly that of the United States. The UN has been used either as a cosmetic umbrella, or a fig leaf, for the USA's political and military moves in reordering the world with the support of the other important powers. The manner in which the crises in Yugoslavia, Somalia and Iraq were handled leads one to this conclusion. If we add to this list the powerful multilateral financial institutions operating on the policy orientations of Western advanced countries, it becomes obvious that the emerging world order would remain subject to the overarching influence of the United States and that it will remain unfairly competitive and acquisitive.

While countries such as the Russian Federation, Japan, China and, to some extent, France and Germany may be able to counter the aforementioned trends on specific issues related to their respective national interests, the rest of the world would have to succumb and adjust, unless new patterns of strategic understandings emerge and new power equations are established between some of these powerful countries and the more important developing countries such as India.

One must also mention, in paranthesis, the likely framework of UN reforms. While the Security Council may be expanded with the addition of some more permanent members, it will be dominated by the European powers. The existing five members will retain their veto while the new permanent members are unlikely to be given this power. The advocacy for abolishing the veto will not get a positive response. The developmental and economic role of the UN will progressively shift away from it and will be concentrated in the International Monetary Fund (IMF) and the International Bank for Reconstruction and Development (the World Bank).

International commercial and technological arrangements will not only technically, but also politically, fall within the jurisdiction of the World Trade Organisation. A beneficial development in some respects, it could, however, be disadvantageous if the WTO were to toe an entirely Western line.

The increasing empowerment of peoples worldwide, generating democratic political impulses, combined with the speedy facility of obtaining almost unrestricted information, will generate significant centrifugal forces in those societies which cannot cope with the rising social and economic aspirations of their peoples. These centrifugal forces will find expression in ethno-religious or linguistic movements within state structures, threatening their very stability and unity. On the other hand, countries which are successful in economic management, and in creating a satisfactory quality of life, would become part of the centripetal arrangements of the type exemplified in the European Union and the NAFTA (North American Free Trade Association). I would have mentioned APEC (Asian Pacific Economic Cooperation) and ASEAN (Association of South-East Asian Nations) also, but given the economic upheavals that have affected ASEAN, since the middle of 1997, I exclude them from these centripetal orientations for the present.

These then are the broad trends in the international situation, that India's foreign policy would have to deal with well into the twenty-first century. The capacity of our foreign policy to cope with the complexities which I have mentioned is inextricably linked with our current politico-economic and social predicament. The positive ingredients of this predicament during more than fifty years of our existence as an independent country are that we remain committed to carrying on the processes of national consolidation and government through democratic means. We have ensured food security for our unmanageably vast population. Despite our intensive diversities, we have managed, though just barely so, to maintain our political cohesion and unity. Barring the loss of territory at the end of the 1962 Sino-Indian war, we have sustained our territorial unity and integrity. We are endowed with natural resources and technologically qualified manpower though the latter has not been developed to its full potentiality, nor has it been utilized as judiciously or as effectively as we could have. We have had a general consensus in regard to perception of our national interests and our foreign policy orientations. Despite the shortcomings in our foreign policy and critical perceptions about us in the countries of the region, and in the international community at different points of time, we have sustained a practical working relationship with most of our neighbours and with the majority of the countries of the world. Even where there are abiding adversarial relations with one or two of our neighbours, we have managed to prevent them from degenerating into military confrontation at least over the last two and a half decades of 20th century.

On the negative side, first of all, we have to acknowledge that the quality of politics in India has declined in many vital respects. Secondly, the efforts at national consolidation and reconstruction have made very slow progress. We have failed to achieve the minimum required standards in the fields of education, public health and infrastructural economic capacities. We rank rather low if we apply the international "quality of life" index to our society. We are subject to a rising curve of ethno-linguistic and religious fissiparous and secessionist tendencies. Despite being conscious of the imperative requirement of national security, our defence capacities remain inadequate. Over and above all, we have not been able to cope with the unmanageable increase in our population. The most optimistic estimate is that the year 2050, India's population will stabilise around 1.5 billion. If we add to this figure demographic pressures that may be generated on us by a population of nearly 300 million in Bangladesh and between 270 and 320 million in Pakistan, at that point of time, the consequent political ramifications are daunting.

While we have managed to maintain a normalcy in our relations with most of our neighbours, they remain subject to undercurrents of tensions related to specific issues or the perceptions about us in our neighbourhood regarding our hegemonic intentions. We are afflicted by a general ambience of indiscipline and lack of national purpose. We are generally considered a soft state with the additional problem of our exaggerated sense of self and our unrealistic desire to be acknowledged as a leading nation unrelated to the perceptions about our political stability, or the substance of our economic, technological and military power. This listing of inadequacies is necessary as they constitute a barrier of limitations on our capacity to structure a foreign policy capable of meeting the challenges ahead. What then are the tasks ahead? And what can we do to fulfill them.

First, the short and medium-term objectives to be attended to. Ensuring the continuity, unity and territorial integrity of the Indian Republic is a matter of the highest priority in this respect. The certainties which animated our national struggle for freedom and the initial idealism about India's national unity stand eroded with the passage of time. Ethnocentric, linguistic and religious centrifugal tendencies have challenged the unity of India, be it in Jammu and Kashmir, Punjab or the North-Eastern States. These tendencies, combined with territorial claims of neighbouring countries such as Pakistan and China, remain a threat to be coped with. Though we have generally preserved our territorial integrity and we are structuring equations with these two countries to prevent territorial alienation, fissiparous forces, undeniably, exist. The foreign policy dimension of the problem is that such forces find encouragement from foreign countries and foreign sources. The threat is not limited to claims articulated by neighbouring states such as Pakistan or China, but this threat forms the undercurrent of orientations in strategic policies of important countries such as the United States and the more cohesive nation-states and regional groupings. Maintaining durable peace and equilibrium in power equations would be easier if the international state system did not have to cope with large geopolitical entities or states endowed with economic power and military strength competing with each other.

Whatever the superficial analysis and arguments about the disintegration of the Soviet Union and Yugoslavia may be, one substantial dimension of their fragmentation was the strategic planning and political encouragement rendered to the process by the Western powers led by the United States. Breaking up two pluralistic states with a sense of self, one of which was a super-power, was the practical application of the objective of politico-strategic domination or pre-eminent influence of the Western camp. The same motivation is reflected in the foreign policy approach of the United States and Russia in containing China and getting it subjected to multilateral international disciplines and regimes. The deeper motivation in generating pressure on Iraq, as well as in keeping it isolated and in questioning the long-term viability of India remaining united is the same. Our foreign policy would have to assiduously create a regional atmosphere and equation with important power centres of the world which would prevent external encouragement to the inherent centrifugal tendencies affecting our polity. This step would involve an imaginative responsiveness to the aspirations of different segments of the Indian people and nurturing at least a non-adversarial, if not friendly, relationship with our neighbours and establishing a patter of relations with important power centres of the world within the framework of which they will perceive a united India serving their broad economic and strategic interests. There will have to be decisive, even coercive, resistance to separatist forces originating from other countries and foreign agencies. This is not an *a priori* predication that India will continuously face a confrontationist situation with the international community. It is only emphasising that we must be aware of undercurrents of political realities in evolving international equations.

The second important objective of India's foreign policy would be to ensure an atmosphere of peace and stability in which India can focus on its economic development and can also cope with the complex problems affecting the well-being of our people. This process would involve not only the fashioning of an appropriate domestic economic policy, but also the formulation of a "foreign economic policy" which would ensure the necessary financial, technological and foreign trade inputs to meet India's developmental requirements in the broadest sense of the term. In terms of present calculations, India needs an investment of roughly 80 billion US dollars per annum in the infrastructural sector of its economy (energy, surface transport, ports, power generation, telecommunications and so on). Moreover, foreign policy has a vital role to play in creating peace and stability in our region and ensuring India's image as an attractive economic partner in the process of global cooperation to meet the aforementioned objective. The technological dimensions of our foreign economic policy should particularly focus on enhancing technological potential and on increasing India's capacity for self-reliance in science and technology.

The third objective to be aimed at would be to create national defence capacities to protect India's unity and territorial integrity, a capacity which should primarily rely on our resources and our own technologies, but which should also be based on a balanced and sufficiently diversified pattern of external inputs in a manner wherein India does not become excessively dependent on one country or the other or one group of countries or the other. This precautionary step would involve calibrating our nuclear weaponisation and missile policies and policies related to the structuring of the three wings of our armed forces on lines which would be responsive to changing international power equations and technological developments. The overall aim should be to nurture and develop our strengths without going in for confrontation and without being isolated to the extent possible. This exercise would involve diplomatic skill, tact and flexibility of the highest order, in the context of the developing international situation, where the more important powers are aiming at fashioning a world order which will perpetuate their pre-eminent position.

The fourth objective would be to strengthen regional cooperation and to work for mutually beneficial equations between the South Asian and other regional groups and associations, so that regional cooperation becomes and instrumentality not only for peace and stability but also for long-term security and economic well-being.

The fifth objective would be to strengthen the UN, its organs and its specialized agencies keeping in mind two goals; First, to enable the UN to truly reflect the interests and aspirations of the majority of its membership and, second, to restrict to the extent possible the UN's becoming an instrumentality of superpower policies. All issues affecting UN reforms should be dealt with, keeping these goals in mind. This task is not going to be easy, given present indications of UN reforms being undertaken in a selective and elitist manner based on the orientations of the more influential powers. India beseeching a permanent seat on the Security Council is not the solution. India should become strong enough in every respect and should attract sufficient voluntary support from the general membership of the UN and, based on this strength it should become an influential voice at the UN. As this process would take time, in the interim phase, India should use its influence to make the UN more democratic by advocating the cause of greater representation for the smaller countries in the important organs of the UN and its agencies.

The sixth task would be to undertake the necessary organisational and institutional reforms in the Ministry of External Affairs and in the Indian Foreign Service to enable the foreign policy establishment of India to fulfil its required advisory and executive role to meet the following objectives. This initiative would involve the modernisation of recruitment methods, concentrating on area and functional specialisation, and facilitating lateral inclusion of specialists of different categories in the Foreign Service. These steps would also involve the creation of institutional mechanisms for interdepartmental coordination and consultation within the Government of India and between the Central Government of India and the State governments to meet foreign policy objectives at given points of time. Creation of a National Security Council and the post of a National Security Adviser with clearly defined responsibilities and powers should be an essential part of this exercise.

The seventh short or medium term task would be for India to focus on managing its relations with Pakistan and China, so that the inherent tensions in its relations with these countries do not affect our vital interests. Also, a special relationship with the United States, Russia and Japan should be fashioned in the context of their undoubted political influence and economic clout which is likely to last into the twenty-first century.

Having speculated on the short and medium term objectives and the required responses to meet them, it has to be emphasized that the nature of the challenges and India's responses to them would evolve in the context of broad trends in international relations. The next obvious question would be : on what lines would these trends evolve in the first years of the 21st century? One can only speculate. The possibilities are that nation-states would have to reluctantly give up some aspects of their sovereignty, thereby facilitating international supervision and monitoring of economic, political, technological and military phenomena. The system of monitoring would be determined by the important powers and managed by them. The United Nations would be marginally strengthened and democratized, but it would function mostly under the influence of the United States and the Western democracies. But nation-states would still need their own economic and technological capacities as well as armed forces for safeguarding their vital national interests. The nuclear weapon states may agree to some kind of time-bound nuclear disarmament and, consequently, they would be more assertive in generating pressure on conducting inspections against countries which would not abide by their non-proliferation agenda. This possibility would be subject to the limitations that none of the nuclear weapon states would place their nuclear forces under UN supervision. None of them except China would be willing to commit themselves to "no first use" of their nuclear capacity. Most nations of the world would have signed the Comprehensive Test Ban Treaty (CTBT) and the Fissile

Material Cut-off Treaty (FMCT). There would be progressive pressure to eliminate the military missile systems and to prevent countries from missile development. Clinical and biological weapons would have been effectively banned. Some regional groupings, specially the NAFTA, the NATO and the European Union, would become more influential and effective instrumentalities of the foreign policies of those countries.

Russia and China would not be entirely happy with the aforementioned scheme of things and may be looking for new strategic equations to counter the unidimensional influence of the United States on international affairs. The US response may be to contain China through equations with Russia and/or India, while China and Russia may be interested in a similar equation with India to counter the USA's strategic pre-eminence.

If India remains united, becomes politically stable and economically and technologically strong, it could acquire a leverage in playing an important role in international relations.

What should be India's responses to the aforementioned trends? First and foremost should be a focus on dealing with macro-level problems such as population control, environment management and economic development. Creating a strong Indian economy in the mainstream of international economic trends would lay the foundation for resisting intrusive international pressure or competition. India should acquire limited nuclear weapons and IRBM capacities to a level where regional or global powers would accept that generating pressure on India would not be worthwhile. The Indian army, air force and navy should be modernized, strengthened and endowed with sufficiently advanced weapons systems which would prevent military actions of the type which Iran and Iraq faced in the 1980s and 1990s. India should retain the freedom of option to adjust to external strategic threats and economic challenges detrimental to its interests.

India, therefore, would face a complex world in the twenty-first century in which it has to survive with just a little over 50 years of experience as a modern nation-state. This survival has to be ensured in the context of the abiding reality in international relations that governments of great and influential powers command resources and military strengths that they use primarily to fulfil their perceived interests. As far as the international order consists of nation-states, which act in terms of their institutional strengths, economic resources and technological capacities, foreign relations will remain a competitive phenomenon, occasionally prone to confrontations. India's foreign policy, therefore, has to predicate itself on real politik rather than on purely moral considerations or an idealistic world view, however desirable that latter may be.

Foreign policy experts towards the end of the twentieth century have asserted that the future of foreign relations depends on how countries and their leaders will cope with five new imperatives in the international situation. First, a nuclear war is unthinkable. Second, everything must be done to dispel suspicion and nurture international trust and security, even when confronted with profound hostility or radical contradictions. This implies a willingness to maintain communications and nurture cooperation at every possible level, to the extent possible. Third, despite the requirements of adjusting to real politik, states should have sufficient faith in moral values to be convinced that they do not need war and military conflict to survive and flourish. Fourth, while deterrence or balance of terror provides temporary peace and stability, in fundamental terms, the arrangement is questionable. And fifth, the collective commitment to evolve an international mindset which will endeavour to create a fair and just world order should animate the foreign policies of all countries. A principled and moral response to these unexceptional imperatives should be the overarching purpose of India's foreign policy in the twenty-first century, but it is not entirely possible. So in the interim phase, Indian foreign policy will have to deal with continuing contradictions between the amoral ground realities of world politics and the moral norms which we and the international community aim at. The endeavour would remain that of reconciling responses to the international situation, as it is likely to be, and the aspirations of what the situation should be in moral terms. Cohesion and purposiveness in our foreign policy in dealing with this multidimensional dilemma would depend entirely on the creation of a national consensus based on enlightened public opinion responsive to our changing national interests in a continuously changing world.

Indian Foreign Policy-Desirabilities of Polycentric World

It is refreshing to note that India's foreign policy acknowledges the reality of other states. And it has a tangible influence on global political and economic equations. Indian diplomacy has moved beyond the acknowledgement of this reality to affirm an approach of encouraging a poly-centric dynamics in international relations. The Government of India undertook specific initiatives with three countries. Recently we received the French Foreign Minister HubertVedrine, we had the Japanese Deputy Foreign Minister, Mr. Royuzo Kato and a high-level Indian economic delegation led by our Minister for Commerce, Mr. Murasoli Maran, visited Beijing and signed bilateral agreements on expanding Sino-Indian economic and technological cooperation. In the process, India strengthened linkages with Japan, France and China, three important centres of regional and global influence covering Europe and the Asia-Pacific region.

Before assessing the impact and results of these interactions, it must be noted that there is a certain parallelism in the world view and perceptions regarding the evolving strategic environment amongst these important countries.

While the pre-eminent position of the United States in military and technological terms is accepted and it is acknowledged that the agenda on global issues is profoundly influenced by the United States, there is a consensus that the approach of the US may not necessarily be responsive to the concerns and interests of other countries or other regions of the world. The need to conserve and expand the economic capacities and political influence of other countries is felt by a number of important countries, as in their opinion, the development of such capacities and influences would counter-balance asymmetrical and excessive domination by just one country on world affairs. The region-specific security concerns of important countries in Europe, South Asia and in the Far East do not entirely mesh in with the strategic perceptions and evolving security doctrines of the United States. This is particularly so in the case of India, China and to some extent France. The deliberations preceding the aborted WTO Conference at Seatle as well as post-Seatle discussions clearly indicate the dichotomy and competitive complexities affecting the management of international trade under the WTO regime. There is agreement among a number of countries that international trading arrangements should evolve on the basis of consensus, taking into account the varied concerns and differing requirements of countries in different regions, and at different levels on the scale of development, technological and resource mobilization capacities. There is also a question of unilaterialism in the formulation and implementation of non-proliferation and arms control regime.

It is the general similarity of perceptions on some of these issues and trends which affirms the need for consciously structuring a world order based on an equilibrium between important countries balancing off each other's inclinations and capacities to influence world affairs. Discussions between Indian Ministers and senior officials and the Foreign Minister of France, the Chinese and Japanese leaders in a manner, were aimed at furthering the processes of establishing such an equilibrium. The twin objectives of this diplomatic exercise were to sustain and expand poly-centricism in interstate relations on macro-level issues, and secondly to expand the content and range of bilateral cooperation in specific areas of mutual interest. Which would underpin macro-level processes mentioned above. A network of bilateral relations and regional cooperation mechanisms will temper and to some extent counter hegemonistic tendencies which may originate from one part of the world or the other.

The outcome of the recent interaction between India on the one hand, and Japan, China and France on the other is to be assessed in this context. The visit of the French Foreign Minister, and Japanese Deputy Foreign Minister is to be followed by the visit of a former Japanese Prime Minister Ryutaro Hashimoto. It is interesting that these visits were preceded by high level seminars of the Indo-French forum and another one jointly organized by the Centre for Policy Research and Japan Centre for International Exchange. Scholars and analysts who participated in both these seminars, endorsed the validity of the political trends and the resulting needs described earlier. Though Japan still remains firmly critical of the sub-continent's nuclear weaponisation, there was agreement that economic and technological cooperation between India and Japan is desirable to ensure Asian security. There was a consensus that since the end of the Cold War, economic growth has been accepted as the pre-eminent priority in the economic policies, not only in India and Japan, but also in most Asian countries. Discussions with the Japanese resulted in an agreed assessment that the following factors profoundly affect the political stability and security environment in the Asian region, viz. the emergence of a strong China as an economic, political and overarching military power in Asia, the continued tensions between India and Pakistan and the tensions affecting the Korean Peninsula and the Straits of Taiwan, the economic crisis in East and South East Asia, has disrupted the economic dynamism of the region, resulting in political uncertainties, particularly in an important country like Indonesia. The territorial disputes and competition for energy resources in South China Sea, the nuclearisation of the Indian subcontinent which has profoundly changed the strategic and security environment, the rise of Islamic extremism in West and Central Asia, and the dangers posed to state structures by terrorism and narco-terrorism. There is a gradual, nevertheless, incremental acknowledgement that despite the geographical diversity and different implications of these factors for India and Japan, the two countries with their respective geostrategic and economic capacities could structure cooperative relations could lessen tension and increase stability in the Asian region because there is convergence of interests in balancing off China's power potential, in enhancing the economic interests of the peoples of the Asia Pacific and Indian Ocean region, in cooperating within the framework of the ASEAN, specially in the Asian Regional Forum, and by evolving a joint approach to counter-terrorism, narco-terrorism and piracies in the South

China Sea, Straits of Mallaca and the Northern reaches of the Indian Ocean.

External Affairs Minister Jaswant Singh's discussions with French Foreign Minister Hubert Vedrine, were of particular significance in that France, at the bilateral level showed sensitivity to Indian security concerns and nuclear weaponization policies. France and India agreed that excessive US domination of world politics would be unhealthy for a stable world order. They echoed the conclusions reached in the discussions at the Indo-French Forum which preceded the Jaswant Singh-Vedrine exchanges, that the US has today, as no country before it, concentrated all forms of power and influence from the conventional hard forms such as military power and advanced technologies to soft but much more impactful forms of influence in terms of cultural and informational phenomenon. There was agreement that a multipolar world requires the nurturing of alternative power centres like Europe, Russia, China, India, Brazil and South Africa. France shared India's approach towards the democratisation and reform of the United Nations.

Commerce Minister Murasoli Maran's visit to China is an interim but a significant watershed in the revival of the process of normalisation of relations with China, after the setbacks post-Pokhran II of 1998. India endorsing China's admission to the WTO and the agreement reached in substantially expanding bilateral economic and commercial relations, signals Sino-Indian relations coming back on track.

The structured diversification of our policy orientations towards important power centres like Paris, Beijing and Tokyo indicates an acknowledgement of realities and a clear sense of priorities in our foreign policy, a process which merits support from the media, Parliament and public opinion.

India and the Post-Cold War World

The latter half of 1980's witnessed the disintegration of established international power equations, ultimately leading to the disruption of individual State structures the simplistic assertions that the Cold War has ended the world has become unipolar and the apparent failure of socialist, political and economic policies should now lead on to a more orderly democratic, market economy oriented world order, should not become the predication on which the future can or should be fashioned as far as the countries of Asia, Africa and Latin America are concerned.

The only incontrovertible virtue or benefit which the end of the Cold War can claim is the reduction or elimination of the chances of a nuclear holocaust between the nuclear Super Powers. All the other positive trends being analysed and adumbrated upon are debatable.

Disintegration of the Soviet Union and the Gulf War are watersheds from which more recent developments have emanated. These portend a more complex, more involuted world with which we have to deal with. While clear cut patterns of conflict and rivalry have disappeared, the world is perhaps unipolar only in the military sense. There are other centres, of power and influence, emerging apart from the United States. We will see a world engaged in multi-polar competition in all spheres of international relations. Discernible trends in policies and postures, actions and operations in the international arena are a desire on the part of what one would call the "new alliance" led by the United States, with Western European countries constituting participant elements to consolidate and continue the post-Cold War status quo. The West aspires to create a new world order of economic and political relations with the objective of long-term strategic dominance of the world scene.

This evolving approach has twin origins, first the rational and liberal idealistic view of the world with a slightly calvinistic tinge which results in advocacies of "good governance, adherence to human rights—norms as conceived and stipulated by the Western democracies, the rule of law, generally based on norms and principles of equity evolved in the Western legal system, and the insistence on transparency in the functioning of State institutions and agencies. The new world order should conform to these political concepts now that the communist evil empire has been eliminated."

The second origin is the motive to back up the terms of reference of the idealistic and spiritual framework mentioned above with appropriate temporal and material inputs. So all countries, all the peoples of the world should restructure their economies on the basis of principles of free market forces. This stipulation must be accepted and implemented regardless of the factors of demography, requirements of distributive justice, social fairplay, or the need to attend to the elemental requirements of human existence of poorer sections of people in different countries.

Good government, justice, and a decent quality of life will be ensured by the mysterious osmosis of social and economic arrangements, which have led to current levels of prosperity and peace in the developed world.

The point to note is that in the current world situation the stronger and richer countries have a happy opportunity of adopting policies and postures which while claiming a high moral basis also serves their aspirations. What countries like India face is the problem of adjusting to the critical predicament, with many of our interests being questioned and challenged.

Realistically speaking, the situation has become more difficult for India, more complex to deal with. At the micro level, there is an emerging convergence of policies amongst more powerful countries to acquire increasing control over natural resources and natural raw materials in different parts of the world. The derivative politico-military strategy adopted for this purpose is to engineer security arrangements and strategic presence for themselves to influence the political systems in developing countries, specially important countries like India. Inherent in this approach is a tendency to control economic and the technological potentialities of countries like ours by creation and imposition of international control and monitoring regimes affecting nuclear and space technology, environmental management, trade and investment policies.

This approach extends not just to questioning but even attempting to manage and influence the security and defence arrangements of countries by advocacies of unilateral norms for defence expenditure and defence arrangements. The more powerful countries with their undoubted equity in the multinational financial agencies and in the UN are orienting even the policies of these agencies to serve the above purpose. Initial suggestions for the expansion of the Security Council, the structuring of the UN, and the conditionalities being stipulated for future flow of investments and technologies to developing countries confirm this assessment. Another significant phenomenon managing India's interests and the interests of countries in a similar situation is centripetal trends in inter-State relations. There is a growing trend towards regional integration amongst countries in different parts of the world irrespective of different economic conditions and different levels of development characterising countries within each region. Leaving aside the established regional groupings new groupings have come into being, like the

APEC, the NAFTA, the EAC, and the aspirations for the expansion of the ECO are manifestations of the phenomenon. Our own South Asian region remains tension-prone and problem affected slowing down the pace of South Asian regional integration through SAARC. There are many and oft-analyzed limitations of our region. India has to find a place of prominance in these emerging arrangements to safeguard its economic and political interests.

This process is progressively affecting transcontinental and transregional cooperation between developing countries with similar problems and similar unfulfilled aspirations. The collective introspection being undertaken by countries on the relevance of non-alignment, the conceptual framework for North-South dialogue and South-South cooperation reflect the dilemmas, which we face in the post-Cold War era. There are also explosive and de-stabilising forces of ethno-religious identities and sub-regional competitiveness affecting the stability of existing states and the cohesion of plural, multi-linguistic, multi-ethnic, multi-religious nations; a phenomenon of imperative concern for India. Useful leverages which developing countries like India had for stemming pressures and attempts at intrusive influence by powerful countries have disappeared with the end of the Cold War. All major powers have a convergence in policies and their objectives towards managing international relations. The advantage of one Great Power balancing off the competing intrusiveness of the other has disappeared.

More complex equations have to be evolved and put in place till a stable pattern of international relations emerges providing a durable safety nets to meet the essential interests of India in particular and developing countries in general. These are the challenges that India faces in fashioning its foreign, defence and economic policies. Withdrawing into a shell and adopting an insular approach will be self-defeating. An impractical assertiveness about one's own importance based on illusory confidence about our resources and strengths will not serve our purposes. A confrontationist approach towards more powerful groupings will also be counter-productive because there is no and there can be no unity amongst the developing countries, which was somehow managed during the 1950's and upto the 1970s. India's political and strategic policy planning necessarily has to be a thoughtful and measured exercise. We must deal with individual powers as well as collective groupings of such powers in an issue based framework. We must painstakingly evolve cooperative interaction while not succumbing to any pressure which affects any of our vital interests in the political, economic or security categories.

As mentioned we must not predicate our policies on any false sense of self-importance or illusory perceptions about our resources and capacities, but equally we must not go by general impressions being generated about India's vulnerabilities. At times this is done deliberately to make us prone to accepting pressures on issues which are important to us. So the most important effort in our thought process should be to carefully assess our strengths and weaknesses and then to create our foreign and domestic policies in a rational and practical manner, where our interests are served, where we do not get isolated and where the external and environmental inputs to safeguard our territorial integrity, unity and our development objectives are met.

3

INDIA'S FOREIGN POLICY : NATIONAL SECURITY CONCERNS

The last decade of 20th century was characterised by many momentous events, namely, the disappearance of the Soviet Union, the end of ideological confrontation and the Cold War, the beginning of a uniform market-oriented global economy and the appearance of new forms of competition for influence to control natural resources and political processes. In some respects, the United States has emerged winner in the world order. In more general terms, the eight industrially advanced countries, who form the Group of Eight, dominated world affairs. Most importantly, India's conducting nuclear tests on May 11th and 13th and Pakistan's following suit on May 28th and 30th have tilted and strategic balance and affected the non-proliferation agenda of the five nuclear weapon powers. It is in this context that we in India have to assess our major challenges and security concerns from now onwards into the first decades of the 21st century.

Our first and foremost concern should be to ensure our political stability within the framework of democratic political process. Our stability has been under pressure due to various political impulses affecting our society since the mid 1980s. Our second and more immediate concern should be to preserve our nuclear weapons status and our technological capacities for defence without getting too isolated from the international community which critically views our acquiring nuclear weapons. The objective should be to sustain our capacities while rejoining the mainstream of efforts to achieve a genuine, comprehensive, non-discriminatory disarmament and non-proliferation. Apart from these macro-level and high priority concerns we have to cope with the following challenges and concerns in the coming decades.

India's territorial integrity remains under threat from Pakistan owing to Pakistani claims on Jammu and Kashmir and, from China, due to yet to be resolved boundary dispute. In the latter case, the threat is not operational, as it was till the late 1980s. The threat shall, nevertheless, remain till a Sino-Indian agreement can be reached on the subject. Internal centrifugal forces continue to affect India's geopolitical unity. There are demands for secession from segments of the population in Jammu and Kashmir and the North-Eastern provinces of India. Incipient separatist aspirations have been expressed by some groups in Tamil Nadu, Punjab, Orissa and North Bengal on and off since the late 1950s/early 1960s.

Adversary relations with Pakistan and China, and military conflicts with these countries, have resulted in India having to divert its scarce financial, material and trained manpower resources for defence purposes, thereby reducing capacities to formulate and implement social and economic policies for national consolidation and reconstruction.

Barring Bhutan and Maldives, India's relations with its other neighbours, namely, Nepal, Sri Lanka, Bangladesh and Pakistan (which falls into a special hostile category) have remained problematic for one reason or another. This pattern continues. With Nepal, the points of worry have been, (a) its trying to play China against India, (b) differences of opinion regarding trade and transit issues which crop up periodically, and (c) differing views on water resources utilisation for agricultural purposes and power generation. With Sri Lanka, first there were the issues of the citizenship of Tamils of Indian origin who migrated to Ceylon in the nineteenth century to work in the tea plantations there, and determining the jurisdiction of the two countries on coastal islands off India's peninsular coast without disrupting the traditional fishing rights of fishermen of both countries. Then, from the late seventies, the Tamil-Sinhalese ethnic conflict had impact on the politics of Tamil Nadu. The ethnic crisis continues to cast a shadow on our relations. With Myanmar, the memory of the expulsion of the Indian community in the 1960s and 1970s still rankles in the Indian mindset. India has forged a working relationship with the SLORC military regime in Rangoon, but Indian public opinion has not yet reconciled to the non-fulfilment of the democratic verdict of the people of Myanmar. This attitude has been existent since General Ne Win's assuming power in the country. Finally, Myanmar's economic and defence relations with China remain a matter of interest of India. With Pakistan and Bangladesh, the points of dispute are too well known to need elaboration, particularly since both these countries were one political entity till 1971. The point to be noted is that Bangladesh's creation and India's support to the process have not made much of a difference; in fact, on many issues Bangladesh has reverted to the former "East Pakistan" adversarial posture towards India.

Pakistan's attempts to influence the attitude and policies of India's other direct neighbours and also the Islamic countries, with a view to generating apprehensions amongst them against India, have posed a continuing challenge to Indian security interests. Foreign military bases and foreign military presence, including the deployment of strategic and tactical nuclear weapons systems in India's neighbourhood, in the northern reaches of the Indian Ocean and in the Arab and African littoral countries, have been a matter of apprehension to India. The end of the cold war has discontinued this force deployment posture, whether it was at Diego Garcia or whether the forces were sea-borne or air-borne.

China's overwhelming nuclear capacities, and the presence of nuclear weapons in the Asian and Indian Ocean regions, have influenced India's defence planning since 1964.

Late in 1991 the US Department of Defence circulated a policy note on "Forward Defence Planning for the US" in the aftermath of the Gulf War. The US Defence Department, while referring to prospects and policy objectives in South Asia, held the view that one of the most important tasks of the US would be to prevent India from dominating its neighbours, especially Pakistan. Consequently, Pakistan's economic and military capacity was to be built up to balance Indian regional ambitions. This was the view of the US Department of Defence. Jerrold Elkin, faculty member of the US Air Force Academy is more forthcoming. He declares that "the government of India maintains three principal strategic objectives: consolidating its position as hegemon in South Asia (grounded on military superiority over Pakistan and lesser regional actors); achieving military paramountcy throughout the Indian Ocean, and accrediting sufficient armed power to press successfully status elevation demands upon the international community".

Thus the first perception is that India has hegemonistic ambitions in South Asia and also that India desires status elevation in international arrangements. Presumably, this implies India's claim to and desire for a permanent seat in the UN Security Council. The assertion that India has hegemonistic ambitions is irrational. This is because given India's own internal problems, resource constraints and preoccupations with national consolidation (in the face of continuing domestic centrifugal challenges), it would be foolish for India to harbour any hegemonic or expansionist tendencies. India wanting to become a regional power is begging the question - India's physical size, demography, resources, technological capacities and the size of its defence forces make its regional power status an existentialist reality. India has intervened in neighbouring countries— Bangladesh, the Maldives and Sri Lanka— only on the basis of requests from these countries themselves, and only when developments in these countries has a direct fallout on India's own security and stability. Indian forces were withdrawn as soon as they had completed their mission, or when the country which had called on their services asked for their withdrawal. It is only motivated imagination which can describe India's track record in regional relations as hegemonic. The rationale for propagating India's hegemonic, on the other hand, is and could be the calculated objective of ensuring the political and economic influence of countries propagating this image in the South Asian region with a view to preventing solidarity and cooperation of the countries there. This is a process in which India will emerge as the dominant factor. India aspiring to a blue-water Navy to safeguard its economic and maritime interests is logical; to allege that India wishes to achieve military paramountcy throughout the Indian Ocean region is an unrealistic exaggeration. Naval capacities and naval forces deployment of the USA and China in the Indian Ocean and with the expanding navies of Australia and Indonesia, attributing this motive or capacity to India is a deliberate exercise in generating groundless apprehensions about India. India's naval fleet cannot challenge or defeat any major naval battle group of an external power.

The second perception is that India poses a nuclear threat to the South Asian region. In fact, the late President Zia-ul-Haq of Pakistan and the Foreign Minister of Pakistan, Lt. General Yakub Khan, had put forth the contention to India's other neighbours that Pakistan's acquiring nuclear weapons capacity would guarantee the security of not only South Asian but also South East Asian (Muslim) countries against any Indian threat. Benazir Bhutto also repeated this line of thought. This is a patently self-serving argument which has not made any impact on India's neighbours. They would much rather have both Pakistan and India abjure the acquisition of nuclear weapons capacity. Even otherwise, China and the US, individually or together, are capable of countering such threats if India were inclined to adopt any such insane nuclear posture towards her neighbours.

A third perception amongst India's immediate neighbours is that India, with its larger resources and larger technological and economic capacities, desires to capture and dominate the economies of other South Asian countries. This apprehension has manifested itself in Pakistan refusing to establish trade relations with India; in Bangladesh being reluctant to allow transit facilities for Indian goods to the North-Eastern States of India or through its port of Chittagong; in Nepal and India engendering frequent controversies about bilateral trade and transit relations; and in Sri Lanka being cautious about India investment in its economy. The attempt to overcome this apprehension, under the umbrella of the SAARC through the South Asia Preferential Trade Arrangements (SAPTA) mechanism, has not been successful thus far, primarily because of delays being caused by Pakistan. This imagined acquisitive and domineering image of India stands contradicted by the simple instance that India had participated in developing economic relations with its neighbours upto the level and extent to which they sought such cooperation. Such is the Indian policy stance on economic interaction in the bilateral framework as well as in the SAARC.

The fourth perception is that the increasing population of India will generate demographic pressures leading to Indian migration to neighbouring countries backed up by Indian political and military power. This apprehension would stand to reason if the countries neighbouring India were underpopulated, with space to spare with respect to land-to-people ratios. This is not the case with any of India's neighbours; each one is densely populated and short of space. In fact, it is people from neighbouring countries, particularly from Bangladesh and Nepal, as well as Mohajirs (former residents of Indian States of Uttar Pradesh and Bihar) from Pakistan, who have been migrating into India over the last two decades. The prospect is not of Indian migration into neighbouring countries but of coping with the collective population explosion in South Asia.

The fifth negative perception about India is that it has adopted a static rejectionist stance on non-proliferation issue, related to nuclear weapons, missiles, arms control and arms reduction measures. The point to be pondered is whether India has behaved in a more mature manner in meeting non-proliferation objectives, despite not being a party to various non-proliferation regimes, compared to a number of countries which have attracted punitive measures for violating non-proliferation commitments which they had undertaken under international agreements. Even otherwise, India has had bilateral discussions on these matters with a number of countries, including the superpowers, in which it has shown a desire to explore areas of agreement on these vital subjects.

The sixth perception, entertained particularly by its neighbours, is that India is not willing to compromise or grant any concessions on any matter of dispute between them and India. Their feeling is that India being the larger and better-endowed country, should not only be fair but also generous in responding to the demands of her neighbours, whether the issue be Kashmir, distribution and utilisation of water resources or trade and transit facilities. This critical perception is shared by other foreign countries also, depending on their interests and inclinations at given points of time. India is faced with a Hobson's choice in such a critical evaluation. Being bigger and better endowed with resources, the advocacy for generosity and concessions on the part of India appears reasonable. But each of the issues on which such an accommodating attitude is demanded affects India's vital territorial or economic interests; compromises are just not possible on such issues (e.g. Kashmir, accepting Bangladesh's demands on Farakka waters, and granting trade and transit facilities to Nepal and Bangladesh) in a short time span. The gradual approach, spread over a period of time, is the practical solution to this criticism.

The seventh external perception pertains to the impression that India is given to pontification on norms for international behavior, the inclination of India to preach on topics such as non-alignment, peaceful co-existence and non-violence is viewed with scepticism, even exhaustion, by a large number of countries. There is some validity in this viewpoint. This trait in Indian policy pronouncements and postures, however, is diminishing after the end of the cold war as is seen in lowering of rhetoric and public postures in politics and diplomacy.

The eighth critical perception, though generally shared by a number of countries, found articulation in an article published in the political journal of the Chinese Army (in 1992). In a manner, it was an elaboration of Professor J.K.

Galbraith's thesis of India being the largest functioning anarchy in the world. The Chinese article put forward the contention that Indian society and polity were fragmented because of religious, caste, ethnic and other factors. Consequently, the article further stated, Indian society lacks cohesion and unity of purpose for national consolidation and this results in India not having any structured strategic doctrines to ensure its defence, and, therefore, the Indian armed forces suffer from the handicap of ineffective command and control systems. While the centrifugal forces affecting the Indian state are not to be denied, the Chinese assessments about India's vulnerability in terms of national security are definitely exaggerated.

India has been sensible of, and sensitive, to the foregoing views. Some specific initiatives have been taken to counter-balance the aforementioned perceptions wherever possible. These initiatives have been reflected both in foreign and defence policies. India has undertaken negotiations with each one of her neighbours, since the middle of 1991, to remove misunderstandings, to stabilise economic and political relations, and to formulate and implement confidence building measures. India detached itself from the ethnic conflict in Sri Lanka, preferring instead to focus attention on building up bilateral relations. Trade restrictions against Nepal were removed; the controversies affecting bilateral relations were overcome. By September/October, 1992, relations has been normalised.

The transfer of territories and enclaves to Bangladesh (*Beru Bari* and the *Teen Bigha* corridor) was done by 1993. The Prime Minister of India pledged that Bangladesh would not be deprived of requisite water supplies from the Gangetic river system during the lean season. Despite continuing large-scale illegal migration of Bangladeshis and *Chakma* tribals into India, the latter agreed to negotiations to control such transborder movement, delaying punitive action by Indian Border Security Force (BSF), which would have been ordered otherwise.

Even in the case of Pakistan the high-level political contacts at the prime ministerial level were continued right upto April 1993, despite their being inconclusive each time. Various Indian Prime Minister met their Pakistani counterparts nine times between December 1988 and April 1993. Eight rounds of Foreign Secretary-level talks were held between May 1989 and January 1994. Similarly, the Home Secretaries and Defence Secretaries, as well as military commanders of both countries, met several times during the period 1989-94. Though none of the major political problems was resolved, a number of important confidence building measures were agreed upon and also implemented. Agreements were signed to keep respective military forces at stipulated distances from the border and to give advance notion of army, air force and navy exercises being undertaken by each country to the other. Direct and regular institutional contacts were stipulated and hotline telephone connections established between the Directors-General of Military Operations of the two countries and between field commanders at lower echelons. An agreement was signed in 1991, not to attack each other's nuclear installations. In January 1994, India made important suggestions to Pakistan-that a bilateral agreement be signed by both sides not to attack each other's economic and populous centres and not to use their respective nuclear capacities against each other under the "no first use" doctrine. Pakistan, however, rejected this suggestion.

These initiatives and approaches on the part of India should have set at rest the doubts regarding our alleged hegemonic intentions.

As far as the charge of dominating the entire Indian Ocean region goes, *TIME* magazine, in the summer of 1989 had published a cover story depicting India as the emerging military giant or power or some such hyperbole. While some sections of Indian public opinion were smugly pleased about *TIME's* certificate to growing power, the coverage was a calculated, perhaps even an engineered and orchestrated, exercise in arousing apprehensions about India in the entire Asia-Pacific region. As a result, anxieties about India's evolving military potentialities were expressed in Australia, Indonesia, Malaysia, and other countries of South and South East Asia.

The end of the cold war gave Indian opportunity to remove these anxieties. By 1991 India had commenced a dialogue for defence cooperation with the USA. Similar contacts were established with Indonesia, Malaysia and Australia. Exchange of visits between armed forces personnel went up. Joint naval exercises were undertaken with the US and other countries. India showed greater transparency about its military and strategic intentions. Cooperation in the Indian Ocean region, rather than domination of the region, has been the Indian objective. The other external perceptions about India, enumerated earlier, overlap with India's current threat perceptions and security concerns. These emanate from the changed international situation. The manner in which India has been adjusting to these changes and has been coping with resultant pressures is now described.

Conventional wisdom has it that the disappearance of the Soviet Union and USA's victory in the Gulf War have led to three major trends which will govern international relations in the foreseeable future. First, the world has become unipolar with the US as the power centre. Secondly, there would be consensus among the great powers on important international issues in the UN under the leadership of the USA. Thirdly, the international community will have to conform to economic and technological regimes which are considered necessary by the great powers for ensuring a stable new world order. There is some validity in this prognosis, but in is not entirely accurate. The world might have become unipolar in military terms, with the US as the focal point of power, but other centres do exist and are likely to emerge in terms of economic and technological capacities. Western European countries, Japan, the Russian Federation and China cannot be written off as second class powers in global equations.

India's main security concern is to be cope with a more complex and competitive international situation. Now, without the leverage of a stable political equation with one of the superpowers, new political relationships need to be established. New strategic and defence equations need to be forged. Diversified economic and technological links have had to be established with a number of countries due to the erosion of arrangements which existed earlier, particularly with the Soviet Union and the Eastern Bloc countries.

The threat to, and restrictions on, India, as well as other developing countries, emerge from the new concept of the "danger of dual technologies falling into the hands of irresponsible states". The Iran-Iraq war and Iraq's invasion of Kuwait created this concern among the advanced industrial countries. Simply put, the apprehension regarding dual use technologies, material or equipment, is that such technologies can be used for peaceful as well as military purposes. Let me illustrate this point : the metallurgy processes used for manufacturing milk containers can also be used for making gun barrels. So the logic is that such technologies should not be exported to "irresponsible" countries such as Iraq, Iran, or Libya, or tension-prone areas such as South Asia, and if such technologies are exported or transferred at all, they should be under arrangements which ensure strict monitoring and transparency. India has faced problems on this count regarding the import of a number of items for industrial and research purposes from the USA, the UK and Germany. It is obvious that a recurrent handicap in sustaining and updating India's technological capacities is a significant hurdle to ensuring Indian security. Needless to add that India cannot quite reconcile itself to the idea of being categorized with Libya or Iraq. Renowned institutions such as the Indian Institutes of Technology and the Council for Scientific and Industrial Research as well as a number of research and industrial organizations have come up against problems of non- availability as well as non-supply of equipment and technologies from advanced countries in spheres such as lasers, fibre, optics, genetic engineering biochemistry, computers and electronics. Since 1991, India has had to undertake a series of separate bilateral negotiations with different countries to resolve these problems.

In the above context and against this backdrop, Indian foreign policy concerns and objectives in the coming years would be as follows:—

1. To structure suitable equations with the emerging centres of influence and power in the world, which will secure India's unity, territorial integrity and well-being. India does not perceive the world as unipolar. (While the USA is important, Europe, China, the ASEAN region and Japan are equally significant areas for Indian interests.)

2. To ward off externally supported political movements and insurgencies threatening India's territorial integrity and unity.

3. To manage the continuing adversary drift in Indo-Pakistan relations and not allowing it to degenerate into a military conflict.

4. To establish a pattern of a stable and friendly working relationship with India's other neighbours to ensure a positive security environment in the South Asian region. This has to be done by forging reasonable compromises on points of differences with them. Relations with China and resolving the boundary dispute with that country remain matters of priority in this context.

5. To ensure access to sophisticated technologies of all categories to meet India's economic and defence requirements and to resist pressures by big powers against this Indian interest by political and diplomatic means.

6. To establish relations with Islamic countries in order to ensure their not becoming a party to Pakistani strategies threatening India.

7. To strengthen the UN and to support the reorganisation of its major organs so as to make the latter more representative and, more importantly, prevent the UN from becoming an instrument of superpower policies and objectives. (Though politically unrealistic, this should remain an Indian objective, nevertheless.).

8. To gain admittance to newly emerging regional and sub-regional economic and security arrangements, particularly those in the Asian region, and those involving the Asian region, as this would subserve and consolidate India's political existence, territorial integrity and defence as well as economic security. India's aspirations and expectations in relation to the ASEAN and APEC are cases in point.

9. To recast the terms of reference and orientation of the Non-Aligned Movement and make it relevant to transformations in the international situation. If this

objective is not achievable, India should remain non-aligned to retain its freedom of options in foreign and defence policies, but should be realistic enough to detach itself from the Non-Aligned Movement as such if it remains a shibboleth and a shell.

10. To oppose all forms of religious and ideological extremism - both internal and external.

11. To continue its efforts for bringing about non-discriminatory universal disarmament in all categories, nuclear to conventional, but not to accept discriminatory arrangements which affect India's security.

12. To pay particular attention to countering domestic centrifugal trends, as they pose a more potent threat to India's unity and security. India's historical experience of foreign invasions and colonialism and the reasons for their success should make the country concentrate on negating internal threats and divisiveness by political, socio-economic and constitutional means.

13. India is, and should remain, unperturbed by deliberately motivated and pernicious strategic image as a self-opinionated hegemony being projected by certain think tanks and academic circles. Compared to the USA, China and Russia (even after the break-up of the Soviet Union), India does not have any ambitions or greater capacities to create an area of influence in Such Asia. The USA's involvement with creating a new world order, China's general approach towards South East Asia and Russia's continuing policies of intrusive influence in East Europe and Central Asia merit the term " hegemony" more than Indian policies. India interprets such inclinations and accusations as motivated by a desire to keep it under pressure and ensure its not achieving a status in the international community commensurate with its size, resources, capacities and commitment to democracy.

4

INDIA—A CANDIDATE FOR UN SECURITY COUNCIL

India held a non-permanent seat in the Security Council in 1991-92. But for 1997-98 period it lost out to Japan in its bid for the temporary seat. Of late, the US have shown inclination to expand the membership of Security Council from 5 to 10 to make it more representative. There are clear signals that two of these five seats will go to Germany and Japan. The remaining there would be allocated one each to Africa, South and Central America and Asia. The additional members are unlikely to have the veto power with which the existing permanent members are equipped. What are then India's prospects on getting a permanent seat in the UN Security Council, let us examine.

Anticipatory fever of optimism about India now being given a new opportunity to become a permanent member of the UN has afflicted sections of our media and political circles. There is reliable information that the Ministry of External Affairs has initiated a fresh assessment about India's prospects for permanent membership in the Security Council. The State Department's announcement in favour of expanding the permanent membership came in the wake of Secretary General Kofi Annan's detailed statement making a number of suggestions for reforming the UN to the special meeting of the General Assembly on reform on the 16th of July 1997. The United States might advocate the immediate induction of Japan and Germany into permanent seats in the Security Council arguing that it is already willing to give three more seats to developing countries as soon as there is a consensus on thc three countries which should represent the Asian, African and South American region permanently in the Security Council.

Though an expanded permanent membership of the Security Council has been a matter of continuous discussion for the last so many years since the Security Council summit on UN reforms held in New York on the 31st of January, 1992, certain questions demanding a response and analysis merit repetition. Is the expansion of the general membership and specially the permanent membership of the Security Council necessary? If so, what would be the criteria for designation of countries which would be part of this expanded representation? Thirdly, what are the criteria being articulated or hinted at by the influential powers in the UN for such expanded membership? Fourth, if the veto power remains restricted to the present five permanent members, is there any point in nominating additional permanent members without such powers? Fifth, what are India's prospects and more importantly would any vital interests of India be served by India becoming a permanent member without a veto?

Several working groups of the UN membership, the UN Secretariat itself and a group of eminent experts appointed by Secretary General Boutross Ghali have discussed the first four questions in some detail, a number of suggestions are in circulation in UN circles and in the Foreign Offices of member countries. No definitive set of recommendations have emerged so far. Only one point is clear. Any proposal for the expansion of the Security Council for it being made more representative will succeed only if it has the endorsement of the United States. That the views of the

United States will get the general support of its allies on the final count is a foregone conclusion even if there are some differences of opinion between the US and its allies. That the Security Council membership should be expanded to make it more democratic and representative is axiomatic. The UN has 185 member states today compared to the 52 members which it had at the time of its establishment. If a 52 member organisation had a 15 member Security Council, in terms of notional mathematical calculation, the Security Council should perhaps now have 50 members representing various regions. That is neither practical nor desirable. But the membership has to expand at least by 10 more seats to give a representative character to the Security Council. The logic by which the permanent membership of the existing Security Council was determined was based on the Allies' victory in the Second World War. The five permanent members were the major Allies who defeated the Axis. China was included notionally as part of the victorious Alliance, but more importantly because of Chiang Kai Shek's close relations with the United States. UK, France and Russia, permanent members of the Security Council representing Europe account for only about 8 per cent of the world's population, whereas Asia accounting for nearly 60 per cent of the world's population has only one permanent member, China. Africa, with 13 per cent of the global population, and South America with between 10 to 11 per cent of the population of the world, have no permanent representation. If the present US suggestion of inducting Germany and Japan into permanent seats goes through, then Asia would have two permanent representatives, whereas Europe with less than 9 per cent of the world's population will have four members, UK, France, Germany and Russia. Asia will have two permanent members despite being inhabited by 60 per cent of the world's population. The normative conclusion, therefore, should be that both the permanent and non-permanent membership of the Security Council should be expanded. Secondly, there should be proportionate representation in the Security Council's permanent seats on the basis of demography. If this logic is found acceptable, China, India, Japan and Indonesia should get permanent seats in the Security Council taking into account their populations, their resources, their technological capacities and potentiality for political influence. Europe at the most should have three members and if the above criteria are applied, the United Kingdom should certainly relinquish its permanent membership. Africa should be represented on the permanent membership by Nigeria, South Africa and Egypt. South and Central America should be represented by Brazil, Argentina and Mexico, North America by the United States. To give proper representation in the membership of the Security Council to those areas which do not have permanent membership, there should be 14 non-permanent members. The Security Council, therefore, should have 25 members, 11 of whom would be permanent and 14 would be non-permanent members. The permanent membership would have to be expanded by 6 seats and the non-permanent membership by 4 seats. The tenure of the non-permanent members should be increased to three years to provide greater continuity in the Security Council membership. This kind of arrangement would fulfil the criteria of demographic representation, regional representation and an appropriate reflection of the technological and economic capacities of different parts of the world. One quite realises that this is purely theoretical proposition which would not be acceptable to the powers that be (though there is no harm in working at it through purposive diplomatic activity and political discussion). The actual criteria being advocated for permanent membership of the Security Council and its general expansion are quite different. These criteria are : first, political acceptability for the Western powers led by the United States. Secondly, political, economic and social conformity with the new world order which the United States and its allies are structuring. Three, military power, specially nuclear and strategic capacities, economic resources and reliability as a political ally of the West. Fourth, the capacity to financially support UN activities.

The answer about denying the veto power to the new permanent members is simple: that either the veto power should be abolished altogether or it should be given to all the permanent members of the expanded Security Council. Permanent membership of the Security Council without the veto power, while the five older permanent members retain this power, would make the whole exercise meaningless except it being a cosmetic gesture to some countries. Such an arrangement would in no way make the Security Council more representative or strengthen the UN.

If one takes into account the criteria on the basis of which the United States is advocating the expansion of the Security Council, India's prospects of becoming a permanent member of the Security Council are very limited because:

(a) It is unlikely that we would be the consensus choice of the Asian region.

(b) India cannot conform to the politico-strategic agenda of the new world order being stipulated by the United States in terms of nuclear nonproliferation, space technology, disarmament and arms control.

(c) We do not fall in the category of reliable political partners of the West in their judgement.

(d) Our financial capacity to contribute to the UN is much less than countries like Japan and Germany or of the countries of the ASEAN region collectively.

(e) Most importantly, even if we overcome the above hurdles and manage to become a permanent member of the Security Council, such membership without the veto power in no way enhances our political clout to influence the working of the UN or to safeguard India's interests on which UN activities may impinge.

There is, therefore, no reason for us to get euphoric or enthusiastic about the latest offer of three permanent seats to developing countries in the Security Council made by the United States. We should avoid facing the type of debacle which we underwent when we lost to Japan the contest for election for a Security Council seat in 1996. Our endeavour should be to create a consensus among the general membership of the UN and a cohesive strategy to ensure that the more objective and normative criteria become the basis for the expansion of the Security Council rather than the political criteria based on the chemistry of power equations which are advocated for the expansion of the Security Council and related UN reforms.

India's Point of View

China's relations with Myanmar are particularly close now. China has given defence assistance to Myanmar, to the value of two billion dollars over the last decade. The Chinese have given some visiting facilities to the Coco Island naval base in South Eastern Myanmar. China has established a politico-strategic equation with Myanmar which impinges on the security environment of both South and South East Asia. The relations of China with the countries of South East Asia, and the ASEAN region, have been complex and turbulent. The Chinese had supported the communist movements in Malayasia and Indonesia, which evoked a firmly negative political and military response from these countries over the last four decades. In a manner, the creation of ASEAN, with a general security and political umbrella provided by the US, Japan and Australia could in fact have been a reaction to Chinese assertive postures vis-a-vis the region.

In more recent years, the Chinese territorial claims on coastal seas and islands have been a cause of apprehension as well as tension between China and some of the South East Asian countries. The Chinese invasion of Vietnam in March 1979 was the first signal of Chinese acquisitive postures vis-a-vis the region. In the decades of the 1990s, China has laid claims to areas to the South China Sea, islands adjacent to Vietnam and stretching down to Indonesia and even the Philippines. While China has a normal political and economic relationship with all the countries in the region, there is an undercurrent of apprehension about China's undoubted military might and the traditional collective nationalistic and assertive mind-set of the Chinese regarding peoples and territories which they claim as integral to the Chinese collective identity. This is a logical apprehension given the Chinese stance on Hong Kong which has been brought to a successful culmination from the Chinese point of view and China's declared intentions regarding Macao and Taiwan.

Some interesting perception about China's Asian vision merits being mentioned. First, China has a sense of destiny about being a pre-dominent Asian power in the 21st Century. Within the framework of this aspiration China considers South and South East Asia has a potential area of Chinese influence. China perhaps does not have the same intensities about Central Asian Republics of the former Soviet Union which due to ethnic and religious characteristics seem more related to other cultural and civizational groups in China's eyes. China does not consider India or Indonesia as challengers of the role which it desires, though it is conscious that China should sustain its position at a higher level of political influence, military strategic and technological capacities, compared to India and Indonesia. China would also like to develop equations with Asian countries further a field like Iran and in the Gulf to nurture its position as a balancing centre of power vis-a-vis the power centres of the US, West Europe and the Russian Federation.

PART—II
INDIA'S NEIGHBOURS

5

PAKISTAN : INDIA'S MOST IMPORTANT NEIGHBOUR

Nearly 30 years ago, in the introduction to his three volume classic on Asian development *Asian Drama—An enquiry into the poverty of nations,* Dr. Gunnar Myrdal wrote: "Many of the concepts and theories regarding South Asian relations analysing the problems of South Asia broke down when examined in terms of their adequacy to realities." This is a succinct description of the underlying characteristics of India's relations with its South Asian neighbours.

India and its Neighbours

As we move into the 21st century, it would be pertinent to undertake an introspection about the state of our relations with our neighbours and to review more recent developments in this regard. First, the abiding existentialist overarching realities affecting India's relations with its neighbours. These are : first, barring Maldives, Bhutan and Nepal, the remaining four countries, Bangladesh, India, Pakistan and Sri Lanka were united under the British imperial regime in one form or other at given points of time, during the British rule of this region. The three major countries of the South Asian region, India, Pakistan and Bangladesh were part of one political entity which divided itself into three sovereign countries through the forces of more contemporanous history. Secondly, there is a qualitative asymmetry between the size, the demography and the resources of India on the one hand and India's South Asian neighbours on the other. Thirdly, though India has six immediate geographical neighbours who constitute separate sovereign countries, the social, cultural, religious and linguistic ethos of these countries do not only have strong links with India, but in fact they are part of a composite sub-continental socio-cultural phenomenon in which India's neighbours perceive India as the dominent institution. Fourthly, India has frontiers with all its six neighbours. None of the other six are geographical neighbours of each other. Fifthly, the history of the creation of Bangladesh and Pakistan and the disparity between India's economic and military resources on the one hand and their capacities of this category on the other generates a pattern of apprehension and threat perception, which affects India's relations with its neighbours. The bitter heritage of the partition of British India in 1947 and the subsequent role that India played in assisting Bangladesh to break away from Pakistan had profoundly affected India's relations with these two major neighbours of the country. In addition, a number of problems have afflicted our relations with these neighbours because of the contradiction resulting from the fragmentation of what was a naturally unified geo-political region. This statement is made only in terms of a generic value judgement and not arguing for any reversal of the processes of history suggesting any reunification of Bangladesh or Pakistan with India. This is neither desirable nor possible. In fact, India should consciously avoid any such prospect. The problems of Kashmir, the demarcation of certain sections of the boundary between India and Pakistan, the fundamental difference of opinion between India and Pakistan about the two nation theory and a number of other minor issues have affected Indo-Pakistan relations over the last 50 years.

Despite India having supported Bangladesh's liberation, the apprehension of the Muslim majority population of Bangladesh about possible revival of Hindu domination remains a factor in Indo-Bangladesh relations. The issue of Farakka, massive migration of Bangladeshis to India, the mutual difficulties of India and Bangladesh in granting each other full transit facilities for trade purposes, and the adverse balance of trade which Bangladesh has with India are matters which have to be resolved if Indo-Bangladesh relations have to be stable and have to contribute to durable friendship between the two countries. India's smaller neighbours like Nepal and Bhutan have incipient apprehensions about India's cultural, religious and ethnic linkages with them, resulting in cultural and socio-economic hegemony, even if it is not direct political domination. The crises which affected Indo-Nepalese relations in the late 1980s and Indo-Sri Lanka relations between 1983 and 1990 reflected this phenomenon. While there is not a single instance of India doing anything aimed at territorial aggrandisement to the detriment of the interest of these neighbours, and while Indian interference in neighbouring countries whenever it occurred was due to unavoidable circumstances and despite India pulling back from such interference the moment India's concerns were resolved or the moment when the neighbours concerned asked India to pull back, the subconscious worries of our neighbours and derivatives are there. India has to acknowledge this perception even if in reality India has no negative intentions towards its neighbours (which, in fact, is the reality in Indian policies).

It is in this context that we have to assess the prospects of India structuring better relations with neighbours and contributing to an integrated process of cooperation in the South Asian region. Ethno-cultural affinity or similarity provides an intellectual, emotional and social impetus to regional cooperation. There are both positive and negative elements affecting this dimension of South Asian relations. Linguistic, ethnic, religious and cultural affiliations in South Asian transcend the national frontiers of the seven member countries of SAARC. The same religions are to be found in many of these countries. All this should be a potent impulse for cooperation. Paradoxically, it is the very commonality of the ethno-cultural and religious heritage which has created problems of national political identity among India's neighbours, especially in Pakistan and Bangladesh. Despite the shared socio-cultural and religious inheritance, the assertion of a separate political identity necessitates and results in— countries of the region pulling back from processes of economic and socio-cultural interaction. Their apprehension of being merged or marginalised by India remains an obstacle in the process of consolidating regional cooperation.

Cohesiveness in terms of the institutional framework of the power structures of the states in the region, shared ideas about the organization of government and shared values shaping the political systems of countries in the region, add to the prospects of cooperation. South Asia has to strive towards such cohesion, although there is some distance still to be covered before the objective can be realized. At the time of SAARC's inception member states were a disparate group in these respects. There were two monarchies (Nepal and Bhutan), two military dictatorships pretending to be democracies (Pakistan and Bangladesh) and three democracies (the Maldives, Sri Lanka and India). At that time one of the democracies was, in essence, a one party state (Sri Lanka). Since 1989, however, the landscape has changed. Notwithstanding tensions and uncertainties, all SAARC countries have democratic governments with elected legislatures and ministries conducting affairs of state, with the exception of Pakistan. This is a positive trend which should encourage regional cooperation. Having said this, one would expect elected governments to be subjected to increasing domestic political tensions, if the choice is between ensuring the survival of the government in power and contributing to regional cooperation. However noble the latter objective may be, it is the former objective which will often find favour. It is, therefore only the stabilization of democratic institutions which will overcome this interim hindrance.

Last, but also the most important consideration impinging on regional or subregional cooperation is the commonality of perceptions concerning the manner in which regional stability is to be achieved. To put it differently, is a shared approach to strategic and security issues affecting the region possible? Objectivity requires that India clinically analyze the attitudes of its neighbours towards it, while deciding on the manner and extent of its participation in cooperative diplomacy. While Bhutan, Nepal and the Maldives have no discernible strategic or security concerns in relation to India, Pakistan, Bangladesh and Sri Lanka do harbour serious doubts and reservations whether these are valid or justified is beside the point. It follows, therefore, that until a number of complex bilateral political issues between India and its neighbours are resolved, these countries will (a) continue to look for balancing equations with other countries outside the region; and (b) to that extent their willingness to participate in regional cooperation will be both limited and inhibited. In the foreseeable future, the processes of cooperation will of necessity be gradual.

India's approach until 1991 was to steer SAARC towards projects and programmes which were practical, feasible and devoid of political controversy. It was also opposed to SAARC expanding its activities to areas which would create political problems, or which would encourage extraneous non-regional interference and presence in regional affairs. While India's basic stance remains the same, its position became somewhat more nuanced in November 1991. It decided and conveyed to other member countries that it would join cooperative efforts at the level, extent and tempo acceptable to other members. It also reiterated that it would not oppose the SAARC Secretariat's efforts to initiate contacts with other regional groupings and countries so as to explore possibilities for additional resources and information inputs for SAARC activities, provided that these conformed with the stipulations of the SAARC Charter, and that the external inputs, so sought and obtained, did not contradict the terms of reference of cooperation within the SAARC region. The poverty alleviation programmes and the establishment of South Asia Preferential Trade Arrangement (SAPTA) were the product of this policy stance.

As for Pakistan, its substantive interest in SAARC is related to the Indian presence. In terms of political ethos, Pakistan has since the partition of the sub-continent sought to establish for itself a West Asian, Arab Persian Muslim identity. It attempts to associate with the Gulf regional grouping and more recently its intensified efforts to consolidate the Economic Cooperation Organisation with Iran and Turkey (and the Central Asian Republics) indicate that Pakistan's participation in the SAARC is attributable mainly to Indophobic political motivations. Indicative of this tendency is its soft-pedalling of the SAPTA arrangement and lukewarm participation in SAARC activities across the board. Pakistan's present political orientation is northwestward in regional terms. Therefore, of late Indo-Pak cooperation in SAARC has improved.

Since Sri Lanka assumed the chairmanship of SAARC in 1991, it has shown a greater interest in SAARC. Its participation in SAARC proceedings from 1985 to 1990, however, has been subject to the ups and downs of Indo-Sri Lankan relations. Sri Lanka could not and did not view SAARC as an instrumentality which could overcome its bilateral political problems with India. It should also be recalled that in the early 1980s the Sri Lankan government made a determined effort to become a full-fledged member of ASEAN, Only after it realized that the proposition was a non-starter did it turn its attention to SAARC. Its desire to join ASEAN was both natural and logical at that time in the context of the liberalized market economy and its links with ASEAN countries like Singapore and Malaysia. It should be mentioned in passing that India was an aspirant for ASEAN membership in the late 1970s, early 1980s, and that it too failed in this respect. Here also things have changed for the better in relation to ASEAN since 1995.

Despite being the originator of the SAARC idea, even Bangladesh had incipient hopes of organizing some sort of a regional arrangement incorporating the Islamic countries of East Asia. Sheikh Mujib articulated such views as early as 1974 after participating in the OIC summit in London. The point to be noted is that four out of the seven member countries of SAARC decided to join the organization for reasons other than enthusiastic endorsement of mutual interests. Perhaps SAARC was and is the option chosen, but only as a second best alternative. This contradiction must be removed if SAARC is to emerge as a purposeful and effective instrument for regional cooperation. The origin and content of this contradiction of India's neighbours looking elsewhere to other regional groupings or countries lies basically in the geopolitical asymmetry between India and its neighbours in terms of territory, population and resources. In addition, there is the socio-historical origin of the post-1945 political structuring of the South Asia region. The first factor arouses strategic and security apprehensions about India. The second factor creates problems of national identity amongst the new states carved out of the British Indian empire. These apprehensions and concerns have to be met. India has a greater responsibility in making this effort. Apart from the issues related to Kashmir, all other politically controversial problems which India has with its neighbours are manageable, solvable.

Here, the political approach should transcend technical and material excessively Indocentric advocacies. India should not, in fact need not, compromise on issues which are of genuine national interest, that is, its security and economic well-being. Subject to this consideration, a willingness for accommodation rather than insistence on reciprocity should govern its negotiations. Even on Kashmir, while on solution based on unilateral claims by either side is feasible, a military adventure or conflict to resolve the problem is not acceptable to public opinion either in India or Pakistan. This is even more so in the case of regional and international public opinion. This factor should contribute to the political will of the power structure in both countries to move towards a purposeful dialogue to resolve the problem, however slow and tortuous the process may be. There is also the difficulty posed by the identity crisis facing India's neighbours, because the more significant components of their collective persona are derived from their old Indian connections. Geography underlines this predicament, as India's land and sea borders about on all the other six countries of SAARC, while none of them is a direct neighbour of any of the others. The solution lies in a conscious, continuous, even repetitious assertion and emphasis by India on the separate political identity of all its neighbours, alongwith the communication of formal assurances, as often as is necessary, that India does not aspire to reintegrate them into any contrived or centralized 'Indian sub-continental political system.'

On such issues as Siachen, Sir Creek, Farakka, trade disputes and illegal migration, India has the capacity to accommodate and find a middle way, provided public opinion is educated, mindsets are changed, and a national consensus is developed, giving structure and strength to the political resolve and decision making processes of the government.

An Overview of Indo-Pakistan Relations

A great Indian political thinker and the Supreme Adviser of the founder of the Maurya Empire, Chandragupta, had articulated the dictum on relations between countries, stating that one must understand one's friends and one's enemies well. One must know their interests, their motivations, their aspirations. Such knowledge about a friend will help strengthen the friendship. Such knowledge about an enemy will ensure that you remain always forewarned about the challenges and threats that may emanate from the enemy.

Since the partition of India creating two countries, India and Pakistan, our two countries have had a continuously adversary relationship. We have gone through four full-scale wars and India is now facing a proxy war conducted by Pakistan in Jammu and Kashmir aimed at separating this Indian State from the rest of India. In public perception and more so in the perception of our armed forces, Pakistan remains identified as an adversary, as an enemy. We all know the events and policy trends which have led to distances between India and Pakistan. In terms of history, culture, language and religions, both countries have much in common. Geography has made us neighbours. No amount of political manoeuvring can wish away the geographical proximity of India and Pakistan.

Let us try to understand why the situation between India and Pakistan remains adrift in adversity when geographical location, historical connections, socio-cultural commonalities, ethnic and linguistic affinity, would have led to harmony rather than confrontation.

To blame Pakistan alone would be irrational and self-righteous. Both the countries are at loggerheads with each other because of lack of communications, mutual apprehensions and deliberately nurtured misunderstandings. Let us first try to understand Pakistan's apprehensions. Pakistanis have a bitter memory of the opposition to the partition from the Indian National Congress which the Muslim League had to face. Consequently, the Muslim League did not get Pakistan of the geographical parameters which it expected. It is one of the ironies of history that many of those who now live in Pakistan did not approve of the two-nation theory. The pro-Pakistan movement drew its main strength from Bengali Muslims and Muslims of North-Central India, even this support did not come from the Muslim masses but from the Muslim elite. We must remember that till Jinnah was eclipsed as a leader of the Indian National Congress by Mahatma Gandhi and Jawaharlal Nehru, he was lionised as an ambassador of Hindu-Muslim unity. The Pakistani view is that the machinations of Lord Mountbatten and the Indian National Congress prevented the emergence of a Pakistan encompassing the entire Muslim population of India. This bitterness still permeates the psyche of the Pakistani power structure.

India's strong action in Jammu and Kashmir, Hyderabad and Junagadh heightened this bitterness and, more importantly, generated a genuine apprehension that India would try to nullify the partition by subverting the state of Pakistan, either by breaking it up or by reabsorbing its territory into what the Pakistanis called the Hindu plans of 'Akhand Bharat'. India's stand on the distribution of military resources and for foreign exchange reserves convinced Pakistan that India had disruptive plans. The disparity in size, population and resources between the two countries fuelled these apprehensions.

India's role in the liberation of Bangladesh only reinforced this Pakistani fear psychosis. If this is so, why did Pakistan indulge in military adventures against India in 1948 and 1965? The answer lies in the artificially nurtured memories of Muslim superiority and a subconscious desire to rectify the unfair arrangements of the partition. The conflict of 1971 tempered Pakistan's inclination towards military adventurism for getting even with India, but short of that its power structure continues to have the same mindset.

What is significant is that the anti-Indian intellectual and emotional mindset is being nurtured from generation to generation. This is to underline that the bitterness and frustration on the other side of the border has affected not only political but also cultural, educational and social dimensions of Pakistani life. It is interesting to note that there are two curious and I would say redeeming dimensions of Pakistani attitude towards India. First, Indians and Pakistanis interact with each other with warmth and spontaniety at the Human and personal level, especially when they meet in some other country. The antagonism and bitterness is just not there, leaving aside hard boiled political and diplomatic types on both sides, of the border. There are mutual lamentations about the irrationality of bad relations between the two countries and mutual urgings that something should be done effectively and quickly to remedy this state of affairs. All this of course, changes to hostility when they meet each other in a collective social milieu in the company of their respective compatriots. Secondly, the attitude of people from different regions of Pakistan towards India is different. The people of NorthWest Frontier Province and Baluchistan, do not have any intense antagonism. The people of Sind because of their old associations with the states of Gujarat and Bombay are also devoid of any intense psychological or emotional hostility. It is only in the people of Pakistan's Punjab state that one finds the bitterness of the partition and pre-partition politics. This is the general attitude of common people. One is not talking about those who are in the decision-making power structure.

Another element in the Pakistani mindset is that of a certain kind of envy which Pakistanis would not acknowledge, but it is there. Both countries achieved independence at the same time. While India despite all its diversities, tensions and problems has gradually consolidated its democratic and administrative institutions. Pakistan has gone through a roller-coaster ride of constantly changing political arrangements. Political institutions have no coherence and stability. Armed Forces remain the ultimate centre of authority. This bothers Pakistanis when they compare themselves with Indians. Instead of taking a practical view of their predicament and being rational about it, they tend to justify the aberrations. They even assert that being different from India in respect of practizing democracy is necessary for Pakistani identity.

The net result of all these trends is of a consistent and continuing policy on the part of Pakistan not to allow normal and easy people to people contact between Indians and Pakistanis. If this was allowed many of the dogmas, myths and misinterpretations of Indian intentions would be exploded and a positive orientation in Indo-Pakistan relations may emerge. But this would not suit the vested interests of the existing power structure in Pakistan. The closure of Indian Consulate General in January 1995 is but one more manifestation of this abiding phenomenon.

The Indian mindset also has its complexes. While there is general cohesiveness in the attitudes and reactions of the Pakistani decision-making groups towards India, this is not so on our side of the border. That people of India have not accepted partition and that there are undercurrents to re-absorb Pakistan back into India is however totally incorrect. They hope that those Muslims who had decided to breakaway from the Indian (not Hindu) political identity and are now in Pakistan should not add to India's problems. In fact, Hindu extremists are of the view that the remaining Muslims in India should also go away to Pakistan, a prospect which Pakistan would not welcome. It is not allowing even its own Muhajir citizens in Bangladesh to come back to Pakistan. That a fair number of Muslims stayed back in India, that they have increased in number and are now an integral part of the Indian polity also generates forces of reason and moderation in the Indian mindset. This approach is however eroded each time Pakistan indulges in provocative pronouncements and acts.

The major section of the Indian power structure as well as the vast majority of Indians are of the view that geography, ethnicity and historical linkages of the sub-continent cannot be wished away. Their attitude is that of detached frustration. They feel that political realities of the partition should not only be accepted but also consolidated for peace and stability in South Asia. They think that efforts to establish a working relationship should continue regardless of the ups and downs in Indo-Pakistan relations. At the same time, any direct subversive activities by Pakistan should be firmly resisted. If an adversary relationship is inevitable because of limitations and compulsions on both sides, this should be managed in a manner which would prevent any further military conflict. This last objective is going to be increasingly difficult in view of Pakistan's belligerance, its nuclear weapons capacities and the resulting arms race in the sub-continent.

The large Muslim citizenry of India is also a factor affecting the Indian psyche and the Indian attitude. Our Muslim citizens who did not opt to go to Pakistan or who could not because of economic and socio-cultural constraints are certainly not happy about the partition. However, when it became a fact, their attitude and mindset confirmed Maulana Azad's prophetic insight that the partition of the sub-continent on communal lines would subject the Muslim community of India to socio-political schizophrenia. Pakistan has taken advantage of the existence of a large Muslim community in India to sow dissension within the polity by arrogating to itself the role of protecting it. That it remains subject to greater economic pressures and resulting socio-political limitations cannot be gainsaid despite India's genuine and deep commitment to secularism. Consequently, some segments of our Muslim leadership are not averse to using the leverage of Pakistan's intrusive policies vis-a-vis India.

The Government and people of India generally know the things that Pakistan is doing in relation to India and how they are doing it. It would be worthwhile to compress these 'whats' and 'hows' of Indo-Pakistan relations. At the time of partition the grouse was that all Muslims areas or Muslim-ruled States did not automatically become parts of Pakistan. Kashmir specially so.

In relation to all major international events impinging on the sub-continent, Pakistan took an anti-Indian stance, whether it was our conflict with China, problems related to East Pakistan, issues related to the Non-aligned movement, problems related to non-proliferation and arms control or the ethnic crisis in Sri Lanka.

Since claims based on the religious argument on Kashmir do not find international acceptability, depending on the fora in which Pakistan wishes to articulate them, its advocacies vary from 'Muslims and Islam being in danger' to emphasising the doctrine of self-determination and ultimately flexible and selective advocacy of human rights. It has gone even further, by crossing the threshold of political and socio-moral arguments to threatening the world at large with possibilities of nuclear holocaust if India is not compelled to accept Pakistani claims.

To substantiate this assessment, it is necessary to recall Jinnah's frustration about the 'truncated' Pakistan which he got. There is also an abiding intellectual and ideological conviction that a successful, plural, multireligious, democratic and united India is a permanent question mark against the logic by which Pakistan was created. The passing of two generations of Pakistanis into adulthood since the partition has not changed this, notwithstanding the fact that Pakistani people in general are objective and rational.

It is the assessment and orientation of the decision-making and public opinion making sections of Pakistani society that Pakistan's leadership of the Islamic community can become unchallenged only by the failure of Indian socio-political experiment. Pakistani cogitations on the state of minorities in India, its concern about Muslims religious places being harmed in India despite a number of such structures having been affected similarly in Pakistan itself over the last 40 years, the selective demand for the application of human rights norms through the prism of the Muslim religious identity are only facets of this basic predilection.

Since 1965, and more so since 1971, defence strategists and the military establishment of Pakistan have cultivated an almost self-inflicted masochistic aspiration that its martial traditions and military credibility can only be retrieved by another conflict with India though for a limited duration, which should result in a decisive victory over India, and that Kashmir provides it catalyst and the opportunity for this purpose. One has only to look through the military doctrines articulated by General Mirza Aslam Beg during his tenure to confirm this. He advocated: "offensive defence", "decisive thrust in depth with elements of surprise", etc. This thought-process forms the undercurrent of thinking among the intellectual and decision-makers in Pakistan.

That general bilateral and international political pressure and, where possible, overt and covert military pressure, should be generated on India to weaken its cohesion and territorial unity, comes through clearly in the official memoranda and policy papers of the decades of the sixties and the seventies. One has only to read through the relevant portions of Stanley Wolpert's biography of Zulfiqar Ali Bhutto, and the revelations regarding policies towards Indian Punjab and Jammu and Kashmir during Zia's time to confirm these Pakistani motivations.

This is the context in which Indo-Pakistan relations have evolved and are likely to continue. Important Western powers by their policies based on their own interests have affected them adversely. The sub-continent, specially the Indian part, puzzels the West. The Indian political experiment should not have continued successfully in terms of their conventional wisdom— a feeling aptly and wittily summed up by John Kenneth Galbraith, when he said: "India is the largest functioning anarchy in the world." They hanker, if possible, in structure a more orderly scheme of affairs in the Indian sub-continent. Instead of comprehending the catholic and symbiotic synthesis that forms the socio-cultural ethos of India, they want to apply terms of reference which are simpler to prevent what in their perception is the "impending chaos in South Asia." The logic of separate ethnicities and separate religions seems easier and clear cut. This inevitably results in what we in India interpret as a tilt by the West towards Pakistan. Pakistan is clever enough to respond to these perceptions and concerns and puts forward arguments which are easily understood by the West. But it is not wise enough to foresee that its responses can affect its own cohesion and unity because despite the tenuous bond of religious unity, it is also a multi-lingual and multi-ethnic state.

Whether the power structure of Pakistan foresees the implications of its sustaining an adversary relationship with India is a moot question. For the present and for the foreseeable future, this is a situation which India has to live with. The question arises that how do we manage it. Different approaches have been articulated by political commentators, media persons, etc. They are:

(i) Decisive and controlled military action against Pakistan.

(ii) India must react with a reprisal mindset initiating subversive activities against Pakistan of the type which it has been indulging in against India.

(iii) Why should India be insistent on its territorial integrity? Why not come to a compromise with Pakistan on Kashmir and other issues accepting its demands? May be, this is the price we have to pay for subcontinental peace and development.

(iv) Remain firm in maintaining our cohesion, unity and territorial integrity while managing the adversary relationship in a rational manner to the extent possible, ensuring that Pakistan does not cross the threshold which might lead to war. There are subordinate strains of suggestions to implement these option, like amending the Indian Constitution, abolishing the special status of Kashmir, changing the demography of Kashmir, and so on.

To the world at large, after the experiences in Somalia, and Bosnia, drastic and violence-tinged solutions would not be acceptable, nor would they conform to the basic principles of our foreign policy or our political and developmental interests. Last option (iv) seems to be the inevitable choice for the present unless Pakistan by some misadventure forces India towards other options, which God forbid.

In the long run the elemental fact of geography cannot be wished away. Even if it takes time and even if there are negative activities and statements from Pakistan, India's commitment to peace and normalization should remain firm. It is for Pakistan to decide how long it can ensure its stability and development with an adversary relationship with India. This is both a practical and logical approach to deal with the present predicament in Indo-Pak relations.

The nullification of the constructive initiative taken by Prime Minister Vajpayee by going to Lahore in February 1999, by Pakistan Military aggression in Kargil, Pakistan deliberately heightening levels of terrorist violence in Jammu and Kashmir, and other parts of India, Pakistan being at the back of the hijacking of the Indian Airlines plane flying out of Kathmandu on 24th of December, 1999, re-affirms the fact that being able to reason together with Pakistan, will require firmness, patience and a great deal of political adroitness. The overthrow of a democratically elected Government of Pakistan in October, 1999, by a military coup does not help matters. Subsequent policy statements made by General Pervez Musharraf clearly show that he has no intention of returning to the negotiating table with any sincerity or in a meaningful manner. The entire objective of

Pakistani policies is to get third party, particularly America involved in mediation with the objective and hope that this will pressurise India to compromise on Kashmir and other issues on Pakistani terms. Clinton's visit to Pakistan and his discussions and public pronouncements there have thrown cold water on Pakistani expectations. The initial reaction, therefore, would naturally be of heightened antagonism against India translating itself into incremental subversion and terrorist violence to destabilise the Indian polity.

Given the present circumstances, it is my considered opinion that Indo-Pakistan relations will stabilise and come back to minimal normalcy only after Pakistan gets exhausted (possibly exhausted by our firm resistance to its machinations), about its belligerancy and antatonism towards India. It is only after being exhausted, would the realization dawn on Pakistan power structure that having some sort of practical working relationship with India is good for both their survival and their well-being as a country and a civil society.

Are India and Pakistan heading towards another war? Given the international pressure on India and Pakistan and the unpredictable dangerous implications of the conflict. I do not see India and Pakistan going to a fulfledged war in the foreseeable future. (Except due to some extraordinary circumstances or accident). The second question being asked, if an Indo-Pakistan conflict occurs, will it take a nuclear dimension? It is obvious Pakistan would be more inclined towards exercising the nuclear option in a conflict situation than India. If Pakistan resorts to nuclear weapons in a conflict, India's deterrent reaction is also likely to be nuclear. But it is reasonable to anticipate that the US and other important powers will decisively and physically intervene if such a war degenerates into a nuclear confrontation. There is discernable and gradual shift in the policies of the US and Western democracies in favour of India because of our economic performance, our military and technological capacities and the responsible manner in which we behaved during the Kargil conflict.

General Musharraf's Views on Indo-Pak Relation

General Musharraf, in an exclusive interview to one of our major dailies, made a suggestion to the Government of India and the Indian people that he should be taken at face value on what he says and does without misconceived prejudices. Second, that India should accept the reality that his government is legitimate and that 130 million people of Pakistan fully supported him. His third suggestion was that the core issue of Kashmir must be addressed by India, without which there is no possibility of normal relations between India and Pakistan. That Musharraf chose to give such a lengthy interview to an Indian newspaper transcends the normal objective of such public relations exercise. His interview was a conscious policy decision to convey a detailed and direct message to India about his views on Indo-Pakistan relations. We certainly must take him at face value in this respect.

It is equally important to assess the implications of his views in the context of most recent developments in Indo-Pak relations, and the manner in which important powers are reacting to Pakistan. There has been a qualitative and quantitative increase in Pakistani subversive violence against India and its military activities across the Line of Control. The concerted attacks on military camps and establishments, terrorist violence against civilian targets, infiltration of terrorists and weapons into India being increased. The hijacking of Indian Airlines Flight 814 and the Kargil conflict are major manifestations of Pakistan's continued policy of covert and overt confrontation against India.

While India faces this predicament, Pakistan is not doing too badly in terms of its credibility with the international community. Important world powers have, within the framework of their own interests, decided to acknowledge Musharraf Government's legitimacy and to deal with him. The three factors contributing to the process are, he is in effective control of Pakistan; he has the general support of people of Pakistan and thirdly, the world considers contacts with him and having leverages with the Pakistan government relevant to containing terrorism and furthering the cause of non-proliferation. (This is leaving aside other factors which make Pakistan strategically important and relevant). General Musharraf has visited countries in West Asia, and the Gulf countries. He has visited China and has had meetings with the highest political leadership of that country. A number of US legislators have visited him which was followed by a visit by the US Commander-in-Chief, Pacific, Admiral Blair and the presidential visit. The British Defence Chief, General Sir Charles Gutherie, has also been to Pakistan. The response to India's *puzzled* and *irritated* curiosity about this flurry of visits from representatives of these countries has been that the objective of these discussions was to convey firm messages to General Musharraf to restore democracy, to abjure terrorism and normal relations with India. There is no doubt that such messages have been given to General Musharraf. Two other dimensions of these diplomatic moves, however, would be more relevant to Indo-Pak relations. First, what are the offers made to Pakistan if it responds to these advocacies. Second, what has been the Pakistani initial response to these messages.

Musharraf's lengthy interview and his public pronouncements contain indications of Pakistani policies and responses. One does not have to be interpretive about taking General Musharraf at face value. It would be sufficient to consider what he states and then relate the statements to ground realities. General Musharraf justifies Pakistani military operations at Kargil, arguing that Kargil occured because India consistently refuses to discuss the Kashmir problem in a meaningful manner and acknowledging it as a core issue. The implications of his remarks is that a meaningful dialogue should result in India accepting a solution to the Kashmir issue within Pakistani terms of reference. He rejects the Line of Control being the basis of any solution. When asked about building up an atmosphere of mutual trust through confidence building measures, this was his response: "Well, again these confidence building measures, as I have stated, start looking as a farce, because we on the side try to develop confidence building measures, we try to open hotlines and there is hotline contact between DGMOs. I have been a DGMO. I have been talking to my counter-parts but these are really cosmetic. They hardly serve any purpose..... hardly ever did it serve a useful purpose, addressing issues which came to some conclusion, other than may be there is a dead body they want to pick up and all that."

What is the conclusion to be reached? The entire processes of putting confidence building measures in place which began in 1989 and culminated in Vajpayee's Lahore visit, are considered irrelevant and cosmetic by the General. He is on record in the interview that he was not in favour of the Lahore Declaration or withdrawal of Pakistani troops from the Line of Control in Kargil. As far as the hijacking of the Indian aircraft goes, he categorically denies Pakistani involvement or connections with that tragic and violent event. He says: "They (the hijackers) are not in Pakistan. I categorically deny that statement. They are not in Pakistan and if they ever come to Pakistan they will be tried under normal law. We do not support hijacking at all. We are against all forms of terrorism and hijacking." The General makes these assertions in face of clear evidence that the hijackers as well as the terrorists whom India released crossed over from Kandahar into Baluchistan. The main terrorist released by India Masood Azhar proceeded to Karachi and then to Bahawalpur, where he made public statements about continuing his terrorist campaign against India. He gets married in Bahawalpur and then travels back to Kandahar, where he is received ceremoniously. Azhar also confirmed that the hijackers who got him released had proceeded back to Jammu and Kashmir. Cassettes of his speech were available for distribution in Jammu and Kashmir and other states of Northern India, within ten days of his speeches. But then General Musharraf says he has no knowledge of any of these developments which have received wide publicity in the Indian and international media.

In another interview to the Pakistani newspaper, *The Nation,* he stated that "India would be taught a lesson if it tries to cross the Line of Control." Then he has the following curious comment on terrorism and violence in Kashmir: "Washington has not issued any warning on terrorism related issues. During talks with the Americans I used the word reciprocity, that should be observed in the case of Kashmir. If India wants an end to Kashmiris' struggle, it should accept that Kashmir is an issue and discussions should be held on it. They (India) should end atrocities and if there is reduction of troops in Kashmir, he will request the Mujahideen." An involuntary acknowledgement of Pakistan's control over terrorists, after all the earlier denials about Pakistan having anything to do with terrorism.

One has only referred to his public pronouncements of policies and not referred to his categorical assertion that tension on the Line of Control will continue, that Pakistan will continue to support the struggle of the Mujahideen, etc. His ultimate appeal in the interview is ingenious. He says: "I would request Indians in the interest of peace, again if they keep harping on what I said and did in Kargil, and this hijacking and that, you are not going to progress". His views are equally revealing about domestic political prospects in Pakistan. He is of the view that Pakistan did not have a democracy between 1989 and 1999. He feels that it is the Pakistani army which would bring democracy but that it will take time. The army will first examine what kind of political structure best suits the interests of people of Pakistan. And then the army will return to civilian rule with some modifications in the interests of the people of Pakistan. And then there is the concluding appeal and demand from Musharraf. He says: "I want to have peace in this region. I want this region to develop economically, but they (Indians) have to take me on face value. They have to trust me that whatever I am saying I mean and they have to come along."

In the context of what has been recounted above, in General's own words, there is no problem in taking him on face value so far as Indo-Pakistan relations are concerned. His approach is: (a) Problem of Kashmir has to be solved on Pakistani terms, otherwise Pak terrorism and proxy war will be continued by him. (b) He does not consider confidence building measures and the past political dialogues to be of any relevance. He wants discussions on Kashmir *de novo*. His India policy is underprinned by an aggressive military stance. His tactic is to continue a confrontationist approach with India while being responsive to the demands of the US about countering terrorism against the US and Western democracies.

One does not see prospects of any reasonable dialogue with Pakistan in the near future but interaction with Pakistan whatever its nature, should be subject to the above policy postures clearly articulated by the General.

Dealing with Pakistan—Dangers of Excessive Assertiveness

After the Cartagena's Non-aligned foreign ministers conference, I asked a senior BJP functionary whether it was really necessary for us to take the lead in trying to get Pakistan expelled from the Non-aligned Movement. His response was: "We should give up this approach of being thoughtful and impartial. Pakistan is on the run. It is isolated; we must keep up the pressure on them. This is the only way they will learn their lessons."

Though we must retain the memories of Pakistani aggressiveness towards us, and we must remain alert about further Pakistani operational antagonisms, there seems to be an additional gung-ho, assertiveness in our more recent policy orientations towards Pakistan. The approach seems to be: "They are politically dead beat, so let us annihilate them atleast diplomatically and politically." We should guard ourselves against an irrational smugness which underpins this approach. The content of this self-satisfaction is the general assessment that the International Community led by the United States is now on the side of India, that India should take maximum advantage of this situation to put Pakistan on the defensive, generating compulsions which would make Pakistan agree to rational and practical solutions to Indo-Pak issues. The rationale of this assessment and approach is rooted in the following factors:

Despite great difficulties the Indian Armed Forces got the better of Pakistani forces during the Kargil War; India managed to avoid a nuclear confrontation; the US gave categorical support to India on the restoration of the status quo *ante-bellum* on the Line of Control; the US ensured Pakistani withdrawals on the Line of Control and announced that the sanctity of the Line of Control should be respected. Pakistan did not get any meaningful support from China and important Islamic countries on the Kargil issue. General Pervez Musharraf's assuming power in Pakistan through a military coup, overthrowing an elected Government, has isolated Pakistan from the International Community. The Commonwealth Summit suspending Pakistan from membership late in 1999, confirms this situation. Pakistan is suffering from economic difficulties and centrifugal pressues. President Clinton took a critical stance on Pakistan's Kashmir policies and about the coup in Pakistan during his visit to India, Bangladesh and Pakistan. He articulated these views in clear enough terms in Pakistan itself, both during discussions and during his TV address, though in a sophisticated manner. The mainstream attitude of the international community on issues of terrorism and narcotics converged with India's policies and attitudes. This mainstream orientation of the International Community on issues of terrorism and narcotics, has put Pakistan on the defensive. While Pakistan's general political credibility has declined, India's credibility and economic potentials is being incrementally acknowledged by the major powers of the world. These trends and events put India in a strong position to generate pressure on Pakistan to make it give up its hostile attitudes and activities against India. There is an amount of factual accuracy and political validity in the above rationale, but it does not reflect the emerging realities or likely possibilities fully. It is necessary to look at the manner in which Pakistan has been dealing with its critical predicament under the leadership of General Pervez Musharraf, with a certain amount of objectivity. We must also take note of Pakistan's perceptions and interpretations of US policies and policies of other important countries.

Taking the outcome of the Kargil war, for instance, the Pakistani High Commissioner in New Delhi Ashraf Jehangir Qazi, told me in a television interview ('TALK BACK' Programme anchored by Karan Thapar) that Pakistan has humiliated India during the Kargil war by surprising the Indian army with its massive infiltration into Indian territory and consolidating their new positions across the Line of Control. Mr. Qazi proceeded to assert that Pakistani troops withdrew only because of USA's insistent pressure. He also implied that the post-Kargil statements of General Pervez Musharraf indicate he did not accept that Pakistani armed forces were defeated and that Pakistan will continue its aggressive and subversive activities in Jammu and Kashmir.

As far as Clinton's visit goes Pakistan has asserted that it was a diplomatic defeat for India because Clinton visited Islamabad despite objections from the Government of India. His short stay in Islamabad did not have anything to do with Indian advocacies, but he was responding to his domestic political constituency. His discussions with Pervez Musharraf as well as his television address, is interpreted by Pakistan as an affirmation of USA's continuing interest of having a close relationship with Pakistan. The critical elements in his visit and remarks were animated by sentiments of friendship for and concern for Pakistan. India is indulging in wishful interpretations of Clinton's interaction with Pakistani leaders and the Pakistani public.

The point is that Pakistan is unfazed about our perceptions and resulting policy stances. It must also be noted that Pakistan has undertaken a structured high level diplomatic initiative to remedy the critical predicament in which it finds itself, not so much because of Kargil but because of the military coup. That the USA wishes to maintain meaningful contacts with Pakistan was proved by the fact that the US government agreed to receive the Pakistani Interior Minister Lt. General Moinuddin Haider (Retd). General Haider's visit was followed by the visits of General Mehmud Ahmed, Director General of the Pakistani Inter-Services Intelligence, and Mr. Javed Jabbar, Political Advisor to General Pervez Musharraf. Reports on the discussions held by these Pakistani officials in Washington indicate that US and Pakistan are in the process of continuing their discussions and cooperation on security matters, on issues related to regional peace and stability, terrorism, narcotics and so on.

We should not be carried away by any impression that substantive distances between the US and Pakistan, will have a tempering impact on Pakistani inclinations towards adventurism against India. General Pervez Musharraf continued his exercise of networking with leaders of the countries from whom he expects political, security and economic cooperation. He has visited Saudi Arabia and other Gulf Countries late in 1999. He has been to Iran and China followed by Brunei/Singapore, Indonesia and Malaysia. March and April Indian media out on its usual binge came to the unilateral conclusions about Pervez Musharraf having been rebuffed in these countries which is not the case. General Musharraf was received by top leaders of these important countries of ASEAN. They, of course, emphasised to him the importance of restoring democracy in Pakistan. But at the same time apart from being a useful public-relations exercise, Musharraf strengthened trends of economic and political cooperation between Pakistan and these countries. He went to the G-77 summit in Havana convened by Fidel Castro. En-route he visited Paris and had high level discussions with the French Government. On all counts he created an impression of being a sober and practical leader.

On his return journey he visited Egypt and Libya, there by covering the Northern Flank of the membership of the Organisation of Islamic countries. Simultaneously, Pakistan Foreign Minister Abdul Sattar undertook a sophisticated exercise to project Pakistan as a responsible state willing to cooperate in matters of global concerns and work for South Asian peace and stability. In an interview to the British Newspaper, *The Telegraph* of April 6, 2000 Sattar promised that Pakistan would act against organisations that encourage volunteers to fight the *Jehad* in Kashmir, and that his government will take disciplinary action against *Madrasas* involved in violent activities. Sattar followed up this interview with a pretended statesmanlike act at the Non-aligned Foreign Ministers' conference. He said South Asia cannot afford dangerous confrontation, we need to build bridges between India and Pakistan, the talks have to be a two-way process and that Pakistan is willing to engage in a dialogue without pre-conditions."

The Pakistani predicament now is that though it has lost some credibility and has economic difficulties, it is not isolated from the international community. It not only retains its contacts with countries which matter to Pakistan, namely the OIC countries, China, the USA and the countries of West Europe, but is engaged in an effort to regain the trust and cooperation of these countries. Pakistan's initiatives in this regard have not been rebuffed with any prior conditionalities by these countries. Pakistan's basic policy objectives are:— to convey assurances about the restoration of democracy to the world, to establish an image of a mature and responsible State; the government of which led by Musharraf has the full support of the Pakistani people; to convey signals that Pakistan wants to join the mainstream of the international non-proliferation agenda, but for its fears of India; and on Kashmir convey that Pakistan is willing to enter into unconditional talks with

India, as soon as India agrees. It is reasonable to expect that Pakistani moves in the framework of these objectives would succeed with the international community. We must remember that the international community only supported India on specific issues related to Kargil, terrorism and so on and not on substantive issues affecting Indo-Pakistan relations. Our getting on too high a horse to put down and isolate Pakistan rooted in our unilateral perceptions of international support is not valid. At the fundamental level, we cannot wish Pakistan away as a neighbour. While remaining firm about our interests and alert and decisive about Pakistani skulduggeries, the basic approach should be to work towards restoring normalcy through dialogue without stipulating impractical pre-conditions.

Resuming a Dialogue with Pakistan

Indo-Pakistan relations have been in adversarial doldrums for about two years now. While there has been no direct interaction at the governmental level, aimed at minimal normalisation of relations, significant developments have taken place, both in Jammu and Kashmir and in terms of external attitudes and assessments which should be taken note of. A static inflexible attitude in tackling Indo-Pakistan relations can serve Indian interests only to a certain point. The determination to oppose Pakistani intervention in Pakistan-sponsored terrorism decisively should not undermine our ability to undertake strategic political initiatives to safeguard our long-term interests. Bringing about a normal, cooperative relationship with Pakistan is an important ingredient of India's long-term interests. Our present policy stance of not resuming a dialogue with Pakistan till Pakistan stops interventionist terrorist violence in Jammu and Kashmir, merits a review in the context of recent developments, internal and external.

The National Security Adviser of the outgoing Clinton Administration Sandy Burger asserted in a speech to the

George Town University, late in October, 2000 that an Indo-Pakistan war, a nuclear confrontation was imminent in 1999 and that President Clinton's direct intervention in the situation could only prevent India and Pakistan from going over the brink. Assistant Secretary of State for South Asia Karl Inderfurth, addressing academic and public audiences in the last week of October and first week of November in the United States clarified certain nuances of South Asian Policies of the United States. He stressed that there was no validity in the general assessment that the US had become pro-India and antagonistic towards Pakistan since the Kargil conflict. He further emphasized that the USA deals with India and Pakistan separately within the framework of US interests and convergence of US-Pak interests. Inderfurth elaborated that in overall terms US has a generic South Asia Policy, the objective of which is to ensure peace and stability in the region, to prevent conflict and confrontation in the context of India and Pakistan nuclear weaponisation and to engage in cooperation which would contribute to the economic development and stability of the countries in South Asia. He emphasised that the USA is a strong advocate of the resumption of an Indo-Pakistan dialogue on issues affecting Indo-Pakistan relations. He implied that Kashmir remain the most important which cannot be wished away. Observing that these views have been expressed by senior representatives of Clinton's outgoing administration, the question to be asked is the relevance of these assessments and orientations to policies which are likely to be followed by the succeeding government in the US. The second question to be answered is why India should be bothered about the US attitudes and policies on Indo-Pak relations which are essentially a matter of Indian national interests.

The answers, the validity of which cannot be questioned are :

There would remain a continuity in US perceptions and policies on Indo-Pakistan relations. The main ingredients of US policies on Indo-Pakistan relations are the conflict-prone, tense relations between India and Pakistan which will impact negatively on stability and peace in South Asia which compounds the tensions which USA faces in the Middle East and Afghanistan. Such instability will also have its impact the security of the Gulf region and the trade routes lying astride it, where the US has vital interests. Indo-Pakistan confrontation also spans religious extremism, terrorism and narcocrimes. The nuclear weaponisation of India and Pakistan is a profoundly dangerous element given the explosive historical and emotional impulses affecting Jammu and Kashmir and Indo-Pakistan relations. The United States, therefore, attaches significance to the restoration of negotiations between India and Pakistan as an imperative objective of its South Asia policies. The US has come round the view that any change of the territorial arrangements in Jammu and Kashmir rooted in the Line of Control, would lead to heightened tensions and military confrontation. So the United States supports the Indian stance on the sanctivity of the Line of Control. This, however, should not be interpreted as US supporting India's stance on the basic and overall issues affecting Jammu and Kashmir. The United States considers Kashmir a dispute between India and Pakistan which has to be resolved bilaterally. The US also holds the view that any solution of the Kashmir problem has to take into account the interests and aspirations of the people of Jammu and Kashmir who live on both sides of the Line of Control. There will be a continuity in this policy approach. The level of political activism on the part of the USA on Indo-Pak relations will be related to levels of criticality in Indo-Pak relations at a given points of time. It is equally pertinent to review developments within India and certain facets of interaction between India and Pakistan outside the framework of formal governmental contacts. Discussions on political compromises based on the grant of more autonomy to the State of Jammu and Kashmir in India have become active and substantial. The two most important dissenting political groups in Jammu and Kashmir, the Huriyat Conference and the Hizbul Mujahideen, seem to be coming around to the view that they should engage in negotiations with the Government of India. Huriat leadership as well as a major segment of the Hizbul Mujahideen seemed to be willing to talk to the Government of India in what they call the first phase of negotiations without insisting on the presence of Pakistan. This change in their earlier stand about the conditionality of Pakistani presence seems to be the result of three factors: Political realism, the people of Jammu and Kashmir being weary of the prolonged violence and suffering in the valley and perceptions about international attitudes and pressures on the necessity of a dialogue. One should at the same time realise and anticipate that Pakistan will remain obdurate about any separate discussions being undertaken between Kashmiri opposition groups and the Government of India. But Pakistan may find it difficult to stick to this negative attitude if the major Kashmiri opposition groups take the stance of agreeing to a dialogue with the Government of India without Pakistani presence in the initial stages. There are reports of Pakistan being advised by the USA not to come in the way of the initiation of discussions between dissident groups in Jammu and Kashmir and the Government of India. It would be reasonable to assume that this advice may make some impact on the Pakistan Government, though there is no guarantee that the mercenary militant groups located in Pakistan and coming from Afghanistan would fail in line with this advice.

The Musharraf Government has adopted a clever public stance that it is willing to resume the dialogue with India at any time, at any place, with Kashmir being the core issue on the Agenda, without any pre-conditions and more importantly without any commitment to stop supporting terrorist intervention in Jammu and Kashmir. This is where one answers the second question about the relevance of India taking note of US reactions, merits an answer. The simple answer is that the US continues to have the capacity to exert some pressure on Pakistan to move towards normalisation of relations with India. Secondly, the attitude of the major powers of the world, in fact most of the international community, would be influenced by the US assessments and US policy orientations. India should therefore anticipate the reactions of the international community from the broader strategic and security dilemmas, rooted in Indo-Pakistan confrontation as perceived by them, and structuring policy stances which would ensure formal support from the international community led by the United States for Indian concerns and Indian interests.

While a stand off between Government of India and Pakistan continues, non-governmental contacts between the two countries have maintained certain active momentum. Delegations have been exchanged consisting of women's organisations, NGOs dealing with human rights, think-tanks, with consistent frequency. These delegations included journalists and former diplomats who have dealt with Indo-Pakistan relations, and even former military commanders, from both countries. Their objective has been to see if the aberrations caused by the Kargil Conflict can be removed and some sort of a dialogue could be resumed. It is evident that these exchanges have had and have the general endorsements of governments of both countries, even if the motivations may be different and contradictory with each other. The conclusion that one draws from these developments is that there is a grounds well of opinion in both countries and Jammu and Kashmir, to resume negotiations, however, tentative and difficult they may be.

In this context, therefore, India needs to re-examine the policy stance that it has adopted of not agreeing to a dialogue with Pakistan till there is complete cessation of terrorist intervention in Jammu and Kashmir, supported by Pakistan. In terms of objective criteria of India's experience of dialogue with Pakistan over the last decade and particularly after the experience of Kargil, the Indian stance is logical and valid at the normative levels. But then there is need for flexibility which would be responsive to emerging political realities. That there is an inclination towards such a flexibility, finds reflection in Government of India's willingness to talk to the dissident groups of Jammu and Kashmir without any political pre-conditions. The other realities which should influence our policies are, even if government of Pakistan decides to stop supporting militant groups based within its territory, these militant groups can continue their activities in Jammu and Kashmir atleast for some more time to come, should talks with Pakistan be allowed to be held hostage by these mercenary and religiously extremist groups. No political compromise negotiated with the dissident groups of Jammu and Kashmir can be durable without a separate discussion between India and Pakistan, leading to an endorsement of these possible compromises. Third, there is an imperative need to discuss confidence building measures to ensure strategic restraint between India and Pakistan in terms of their nuclear weapons and missile capacities, a need which was acknowledged during the Lahore meeting between Vajpayee and Nawaz Sharif. Not resuming dialogue with Pakistan will only strengthen and prolong the military dictatorship in Pakistan, as the military establishment there would use India's stand for validity of its continuation in power to meet the political and military threat from India inherent in its rejection of a dialogue.

Important world powers backed by the international community will move back from the generally supportive attitude that it has taken in favour of India's rational and mature reaction to the Kargil conflict. Beyond a certain point of time. India's refusal to resume a dialogue will be taken as India being obstinate and unreasonable. Our argument that we shall not deal with a military dictatorship particularly a military leader who engineered the Kargil conflict, may find acceptability only for a limited period. Requirements of Realpolitik is to deal with whatever government is in effective power in Pakistan. There is a need to unravel the present logjam and impasse. If the Government of Pakistan could be persuaded to make a two-point public statement that it is willing to resume the dialogue at any mutually acceptable level in Delhi or Islamabad, and that Pakistan as a matter of policy will not support terrorist violence in Jammu and Kashmir, from any quarter, there could be an opening for India to resume the dialogue.

It is time that both countries transcend their insular xenophobic antagonisms and get back to the negotiating table. Kashmir being described as core issue need not give us high blood pressure. We must assert that it is equally core issue for us in terms of our security, unity and territorial integrity. We should also state that the use of covert violence to disrupt our stability and unity should be the high priority item on the Agenda when we resume a dialogue.

Pakistan Re-visited— Predicaments and Prospects

Recently, January 2001, I visited Pakistan to take part in a conference between the Islamabad Policy Research Institute and the Delhi Policy Group on nuclear risk reduction. This was a non-governmental effort though the participants in the conference on both sides were ex-diplomats, Government and military officials. We were also invited to speak at the Department of Defence Studies of the Qaid-e-Azam University in Islamabad and the Institute of Strategic Studies of Pakistan and the Foreign Service Academy of Pakistan. Our group was led by India's former

Ambassador to China, the United States and Pakistan, Ambassador K.S. Vajpayee. Other members of the delegation included Lt. General Raghavan. Director-General, Military Operations, of our Army, Rear Admiral K. Raja Menon, former Deputy Chief of Naval Operations of India, Air Chief Marshal S.K. Mehra, former Chief of our Air Force, Prof. Matin Zuberi, Professor on Disarmament from the JNU and myself.

The primary focus of our discussions in Pakistan was to exchange views with Members of the Islamabad Policy Research Institute (which is the think-tank backed by the Pakistan Government and its armed forces), on methods by which India and Pakistan can reduce the risk of a nuclear confrontation between the two countries. The lectures and discussions organised at the other institutions mentioned above were also focused on specific issues of concern. Our delegation was to discuss developments in Afghanistan at the Qaid-a-Azam University, the phenomenon of cross-border and international terrorism at the Institute of Strategic Studies of Pakistan and to exchange views on the comparative experience of Pakistan and India in their respective nation-building activities, over the last fifty years at the Pakistan Foreign Service Academy.

This visit of particular interest to me because I was returning to Islamabad after a gap of seven years. My last visit was in the first week of January, 1994 as India's Foreign Secretary during Benazir Bhutto's last tenure as Prime Minister of Pakistan. I was curious whether there has been any transformation in the Pakistani world view and Pakistan's mindset about India. There were changes and transformations but I have come back chastened and worried. I must preface this description and analysis of my visit with a rider that my value-judgements may not be entirely accurate in terms of their applicability to all segments of Pakistani public opinion, or civil society. The value judgements are based on views conveyed and resulting impressions by those segments of the Pakistani Government, Academia and think-tanks with whom one interacted.

I must also mention that apart from the conferences and seminars in which we participated, our delegation from the Delhi Policy Group, was received by the Foreign Minister of Pakistan, Abdus Sattar, and Foreign Secretary of Pakistan, Inamul Haq, with whom we spent nearly three hours on the 13th of January 2001. This meeting was preceded by an hour-long briefing by the additional secretary Incharge of Multi-lateral Affairs of Pakistan Foreign Office, Mr. Riaz Hussian. The logic of Mr. Hussain briefing us was because of his being incharge of non-proliferation matters in the Pakistani Foreign Office.

While welcoming the Delhi Policy Group, having a technical discussion with the Islamabad Policy Research Institute on nuclear risk reduction, Mr. Hussain emphasised that efforts of mutual nuclear restraint, is rooted in the removal of the basic cause of tension between India and Pakistan, namely, the Kashmir issue. He stressed that nuclear risk reduction cannot be considered in isolation, as a separate issue affecting regional security. He clearly stated that unless the Kashmir problem is solved based on the right of self-determination of people of Jammu and Kashmir, the necessary atmosphere of mutual trust cannot be created for Pakistan to agree to nuclear confidence building measures. When the Indian sides pointed out that the risk of nuclear confrontation and war is more dangerous phenomenon than Pakistan viewing the Kashmir issue as a territorial dispute, Riaz Hussain indulged in a colourful simili in Hindi. He said both India and Pakistan know that the water in the well of mutual peace is dirty and poisoned. Just drawing out the dirty water will not result in the well being cleaned because the reason for the water being poisoned and dirty is a dead dog in the well, and the dead dog is the Kashmir dispute. Unless we take out the dog and dispose it off we cannot hope to get fresh water from the well. The Indian side could have responded to this bizzare simili by pointing out that it is Pakistan which killed the dog and put in the well when it invaded Kashmir in 1948. But we restrained ourselves because the argument could not have led us anywhere. A substantive political point made in this Pakistani foreign office briefing was that Pakistan considers nuclear risk reduction intrinsically linked with its views on Kashmir and thus an affirmation that Pakistan's nuclear weaponisation in one dimension is an instrumentality to further its Kashmir policies. The full day technical discussions with the Islamabad Policy Research Institute on nuclear matters were characterised by a contrast between the approach of the Indian and Pakistani delegations. The Indian side presented structured and written papers on three aspects of nuclear risk reduction. One on the political and strategic context in which Indo-Pakistan confidence building measures are evolved since 1989 till todate. The second paper was on possible technical proposals and measures which both sides could adopt to reduce prospects of nuclear confrontation or accidental nuclear conflict. The third paper was on whether the contradictions between the Indian nuclear doctrine and the Pakistani nuclear doctrine could be reconciled, given the Pakistani doctrine of retaining the option of first strike and the Indian doctrine of no-first-use of its nuclear weapons. The Indian Papers and Indian presentations focussed on this specific issue for which the conference was organised. The Pakistani delegation in contrast refrained from present any written papers. It would be pertinent to mention that like the Indian delegation, the Pakistani delegation also consisted of former Foreign Secretaries, retired Military officers and academic, while the Indian approach was technical and focussed on the issue, the Pakistani presentations consisted of broader political perspectives from Pakistan's points of view. It was interesting to note that in these intellectual exchanges the Pakistani side reflected the approach outlined to us in the earlier foreign office briefing. They emphasised with greater vigour that nuclear risk reduction is dependent on and intrinsically linked with the solution of the Kashmir issue within the framework of Pakistani terms of reference.

Even when touching upon technical aspects, the Pakistan delegation emphasised that India's no-first-use doctrine and its abjuring the option of first strike has no meaning because a Pakistani first strike may obliterate India's capacity for a second nuclear strike. Alternatively, India's no first use approach is public relations exercise and in a conflict situation what is there to prevent India indulging in first strike. Pakistanis put forward the familiar argument that their nuclear weaponisation was a response to India's nuclear weapons and missile capacities and that it was a necessary measure to safeguard Pakistan's security, including in relation to Kashmir dispute, the Pakistan side was not willing to examine the technical feasibility of the confidence building measures on nuclear risk reduction which India had presented.

The meetings at the other academic institutes mentioned in the beginning of the chapter were more revealing. In discussions on developments in Afghanistan and its fall out on the Indian sub-continent and Central Asia, Pakistani academics assertively justified Taliban's policies and objectives. The Indian apprehension about Taliban exporting or conniving at cross-border terrorism in Jammu and Kashmir and in Central Asian Republics was rejected with the assertion that Taliban was not involved in such activities. It was a flat denial. As far as Taliban's extremist domestic policies, violating human rights, particularly of women within Afghanistan is concerned, the Pakistan view was that external criticism was mis-informed and was based on deliberate misrepresentations. That such views were expressed by Pakistani academics who have had exposure to foreign universities and media, left one wondering about the vigour of conviction of orthodoxy which influenced their thought processes.

The theme for discussion at the Institute of Strategic Studies was the implications of religious extremism and cross-border terrorism on regional peace. Instead of a dispassionate and objective discussion on the phenomenon, the Pakistani academics at this strategic institute, proceeded to argue at great length that the world at large and India in particular, is deliberately labelling the intensively spiritual and religious phenomenon of *Jehad* to malign Pakistan. This argument was further expanded with assertion that the international community led by the United States and the West is deliberate in its opposition to the rise of Pan-Islamic Movements and Islamic religious resurgence in the world which finds expression in the success of Taliban in the Jehadist campaigns in difference countries and continuation of the militants' struggle in Jammu and Kashmir. Indian advocacies that *Jehad* in the religious sense is different from militant separatist terrorism and violence, was polemically rejected.

When these discussions meandered into the ups and downs of Indo-Pakistan relations, the Director of the Institute justified the Pakistani intrusion into Kargil in 1999, stating that India should evaluate the intrusion into Kargil in contextual terms because Pakistani moves in Kargil were justified as retaliation to India's Line of Control at Siachen in 1984. An additional point was made that Pakistan would not have withdrawn from Kargil but for the US intervention.

The comparative analysis of the experience in nation-building and building of institutions of state at the Foreign Service Academy was remarkable because the Pakistani participants questioned the credibility of India's democracy and India's secularism citing the contradictions of Indian civil society in terms of treatment of minorities, the caste system, the fragmentation of political parties, the rise of

Hindu religious extremism in India etc. In contrast, discussions with Foreign Minister Abdul Sattar and his colleagues were of comparative relief to this Indian delegation. Sattar affirmed Pakistan's desire to restore a dialogue with India. In response to specific queries from us, he affirmed that Pakistan is willing to revive the Lahore process and that Pakistan remains committed to the decisions taken at Lahore. But then he neutralised the potential impact of his remarks by saying so are all the previous agreements between India and Pakistan, including the UN resolutions, Shimla Agreement, etc. But it was important to note that one found government representatives more rational and practical than the non-governmental Pakistani interlocutors.

The overall impression that came out can be summed up as follows:

There is no intense anxiety in the Pakistani elite to restore democracy. There is an acceptance of General Musharraf's regime. There seems to be a widespread belief in these circles that India is getting exhausted in Kashmir and that India will not be able to hold on to Jammu and Kashmir for too long; and therefore political and militant pressure should be continued on India. While there is an awareness about dangers of nuclear confrontation, there is a parallel feeling that threat of such confrontation will become an incremental pressure on India on the Kashmir issue. While Pakistan has to be responsive to concerns about cross-border terrorism in the western democracies led by the US, there is no need for such responsiveness towards India. The cease-fire and peace initiatives of Vajpayee Government is an interim phase through which Pakistan can work towards its objectives in Jammu and Kashmir.

One acknowledges that these impressions may not reflect the views of all of Pakistani society but the fact cannot be ignored that these are views of an influential section of the decision-making elite in Pakistan.

6

AN ANALYSIS OF DOMESTIC POLITICAL FACTORS IN PAKISTAN AFFECTING PAKISTAN'S INDIA POLICIES

The basic causation of hostility in Pakistan towards India is Pakistan having to face the fact that the two-nation theory based on religion is fallacious. Even if we leave aside the cross-current of politics in Punjab and the North-West Frontier Provinces at the time of the partition, a large segment of people from Baluchistan and Sind were not enthusiastic about the creation of Pakistan. The final irony was that the political leaders and people of East Pakistan who were passionate advocates of the two-nation theory were the ones who threw it aside, questioned its validity and created Bangladesh. Even today the political and intellectual elite shies away from accepting the fact that Bangladesh came into being because of the discriminatory and unwise policies of the central governments in Pakistan. Zulfiqar Ali Bhutto's role in breaking up Pakistan is swept under the carpet completely or is obfuscated. His refusal to accept the overwhelming electoral victory of Mujibur Rahman was the explosive trigger leading to the East Pakistan crisis in 1971. Benazir Bhutto in her autobiography *Daughter of the East* did not refer in any meaningful manner to this period of her father's career. Nothing more need be added about the incapacity for self-evaluation in the Pakistani political milieu. Instead of acknowledging the self-evident political reality that the remaining part of Pakistan was as much a multi-lingual and multi-ethnic society as India was, the Pakistani power structure only became more irrationally obstinate about consolidating the theocratic basis of the Pakistani state. This process had two manifestations: First, increased persecution of *Shias* and other Muslim religious sects within Pakistan who could challenge the *Hanafi* and *Wahabi Sunni* Muslim majority of Pakistan. This was done on the basis of two principles: preserving the purity of Islamic doctrine and safeguarding what is called in Pakistan "the ideology of Pakistan". The second reaction was the conscious revival of hostility and desire for vengeance against India. India was held solely responsible for the breaking away of Bangladesh from Pakistan. A majority of the decision making elite in Pakistan have this approach even today. This shows a total incapacity for introspection or objective historical analysis of the policies of the military regimes of Pakistan between 1952 and 1971 which ultimately created Bangladesh disproving the two-nation theory. This approach transmutes itself into various strands of Pakistan's India policy. The concepts underpinning these strands are:—

(a) India still does not accept the partition of the sub-continent and continues to conspire first to breakup Pakistan and then to reabsorb it into India or *Akhand Bharat*.

(b) The validity of the two-nation theory can be reasserted and reaffirmed only by the Muslim majority Indian State of Jammu and Kashmir seceding from India and joining Pakistan.

(c) Not only should Pakistani society be put into a strait-jacket of Islamic identity determined by the power structure, but Pakistan should also assume the role of protecting and talking about the safety and future of the Muslim minority in India. It should be mentioned in paranthesis that the strait-jacket of Islamic doctrines fashioned by the Pakistani power structure has nothing to do with the essential humanistic and intellectual teachings of Islam. The first constituent element of the concept mentioned above, namely the strait-jacket of Islamic doctrines, reflected itself in the persecution of *Shias,* certain categories of *Ismailis, Ahmediyas,* etc., not to speak of the miniscule minority of Hindus and Christians who still remain in Pakistan.

(d) The attempt at subverting the Muslim citizens of India is also aimed at confirming the validity of the Pakistani two-nation theory. The exercise is based on the advocacy that the Muslim minority in India had stayed back in India, because they were not able to go to Pakistan or because a number of Muslim majority areas did not become Pakistan or separate Muslim states in the sub-continent at the time of partition.

This is the matrix from which Pakistan's India policies have emanated with differing levels of antagonism, destabilising efforts and violence against India. The matrix is essentially of a domestic political nature in Pakistan, which has impacted on Pakistan's policies towards India. It would be relevant to note some interesting post-partition trends in Pakistani policies towards India originating from domestic political considerations or motivations by the Pakistani establishment. At the time of its very inception, Pakistani leaders like Jinnah, Liaquat Ali Khan and Abdur Rab Nishtar were very keen that the Indian Princely states retain their independent status without acceding to India. If the Indian dominion were to consist only of the fragments of the former British Indian provinces in the subcontinent with larger Indian Princely states retaining their separate identities, it would have proved the validity of the two-nation theory, with only populations sharing the same religion constituting a cohesive state of Pakistan in the subcontinent. Secondly, a cohesive Pakistan with the rest of the sub-continent having fragmented political identities would have made Pakistan the most dominent political and military power in the sub-continent. Sardar Patel neutralised these plans and expectations and the first Indo-Pak war on Kashmir conveyed a clear impression of India's capacity to ensure its security and defend its territorial integrity. This failure of theirs did not faze our Pakistani neighbours. Zulfiqar Ali Bhutto kept writing secret memoranda to President Ayub Khan suggesting military action to separate Assam and the North-eastern parts of India from the rest of India by using East Pakistani territory as a springboard for such military operations. Bhutto's pipedream was that Pakistan, in collaboration with China, can fragment eastern territories of the Indian Republic by a combination of military operations from Pakistan and Chinese aspirations regarding the North-eastern extremities of India. But Ayub being a professional military man and perhaps having better political sense than Bhutto did not act fully on Bhutto's recommendation, though he was not averse to the idea in general. One has only to read relevant sections of Field Marshal Ayub Khan's autobiography *Friends, not Masters* and Z.A. Bhutto's biography written by Stanley Wolpert to get the details of these planned skullduggeries, which ultimately proved to be abortive. The point to remember, however, is that these attitudes and plans arose essentially from an internal identity crisis of the Pakistani polity which, despite years of being in existence, despite getting international acknowledgement and support of every kind, suffered from a deep sense of collective emotional and political insecurity. To compound matters, democracy disappeared from Pakistan from 1952, almost till 1988. The Indian secular, democratic, pluralistic experiment succeeded in contrast: This happened despite the socio-economic imbalances and centrifugal forces which affected the Indian State from time to time. What was particularly galling for Pakistan in terms of its democratic credibility was that the Muslim minority in India not only increased demographically, but was also getting representation in all sections of the Indian power structure—academic to military, political to cultural. The facts of like in India controverted the myth and propaganda about persecution of minorities attempted continuously by Pakistan. Before coming to the contemporary domestic situation in Pakistan impinging on Pakistan's India policies, two other substantive factors have to be taken into account. The first is the nature of the Pakistani power structure which has remained elitist, feudal, militaristic and unrepresentative of the Pakistani masses right uptodate. If one undertakes an analysis of the socio-economic background of the leadership in Pakistan in every sphere, they personify the above characteristics one way or the other. Nobody of the category of a Lal Bahadur Shastri, Lalu Prasad Yadav or Mayawati has figured or could figure in the centres of power in Pakistan. The second factor is the extremist theocracy and militarism dominating the political processes in Pakistan regardless of which Government came to power or comes into power. No government in Pakistan reflects the normal desire for peace, stability and a secure political environment amongst the common people of Pakistan. Even more pernicious is the phenomenon of the entire educational and cultural orientation of Pakistani society being directed and nurtured in an anti-Indian stance. The process starts at the primary or secondary school level itself. Pakistani books on history are a distortion of sub-continental history. It would not be an exaggeration to say that most Pakistani books on history which young people read in their formative years will give them the impression that sub-continental history commenced with only the Muslim-Arab invasion of Sind around the second half of the seventh century A.D. The rest of the period of somewhat mythically and irrelevantly analysed. The syllabus at the Pakistani Military Academy in Kakul has a separate course on Pakistani ideology, elements of which clearly include developing an anti-Indian attitude of mind as an imperative quality of Pakistani patriotism. The fact is that the whole internal dynamics of Pakistani polity stands designed to protect the vested interests of a narrow political spectrum of people who constitute the establishment in Pakistan. It would be pertinent to itemise this assessment with some specificity. Pakistani armed forces would lose their justification to go on acquiring more arms and increasing their coercive clout within Pakistani society if the imagined bugbear of Indian hegemony and hostility is replaced by a rational cooperative approach towards India. Political parties led by rich landlords and industrialists will lose their control over domestic socio-economic processes if there is a free, cultural, social and economic interaction with India. People to people contact between India and Pakistan in the economic, social and cultural spheres will destroy the arguments of antagonism propagated by this power elite. The objection to the free flow of information, ideas and books from India to Pakistan, the continous hurdles being placed in the path of substantive commercial, economic and technological cooperation between the two countries (despite the desire of the trading communities of both countries to have such contact), travel restrictions placed on Pakistanis wishing to travel to India which results in India imposing similar restrictions on Indians wishing to go to Pakistan reflect this phenomenon.

Religious parties and Islamic leaders of Pakistan cannot afford to let ordinary people of Pakistan to come into normal human contact with the people of India, because it will expose Pakistani public opinion to the vigour and vibrance of India's pluralistic democracy despite all its shortcomings. Even more dangerous for the theocratic extremists in Pakistan would be the Pakistani public becoming aware of the fact that the Muslim minority in India is not being victimized and traumatized, as is put out by the *Islam-pasand* parties and leaders in Pakistan. It is inevitable that this logic leads to an abiding anti-Indian stance in Pakistani foreign policy.

The question arises as to how long can the undemocratic Pakistani power structure sustain this drift in hostility towards India to meet their vested interests. The answer, to use a sentence from the lyrics of the peace movement of the 1960s, is "playing in the wind". Developments in Pakistan since Benazir Bhutto's coming to power heralded blowing of compelling winds of change. Ex-Generals, worried about Benazir even accidentally acquiring the courage to convert Pakistan into a genuine democracy, started establishing political parties. Former Chief of Army Staff Aslam Beg has created a political party called *Awami Qaidat.* Former chief of the ISI, the dubious Hamid Gul, established a party called *Tehriq-e-Ittehad,* in which he expected to rope in cricket idol Imran Khan who was showing signs of behaving like the proverbial cat deciding to proceed to Haj after having eaten nine hundred mice. Imran Khan was sprouting Islamic political wings till young Jemima from England put paid to the exercise by committing matrimony with him. Generals forming political parties as "third forces" in Pakistani politics showed sign of their wanting to put mechanisms and institutional arrangements in place to safeguard the hold of the military establishment on Pakistani political processes.

It is in this light that one ruminates on the sad predicament of sane Pakistani thinkers like the late Mazhar

Ali Khan, Mr. Mubashir Hassan and even establishment figures like Mahboob-ul-Haq, Niaz Naik and former Foreign Secretary Shahryar Khan not being able to play any role in the structuring of the internal politics of Pakistan or its policies towards India.

Pakistan Government's conflict with the *Mohajir Qaumi Movement* has Indian implications. Among all the people of Pakistan, *Mohajirs* happen to have the most extensive connections with India at the human, cultural and social levels. These people left North and Central India taking a conscious decision to become Pakistani citizens, acknowledging the two-nation theory. Indeed in the initial years of Pakistan's existence, they dominated the administrative and political institutions of Pakistan. In course of time they became more numerous. They have become an influential demographic and economic factor in Pakistani politics, specially in Sind and to some extent in the southern extremities of Pakistani Punjab. Despite this, their expectations and aspirations have not been met. This resulted in tension and violence affecting Karachi and Sind. Benazir first tried to question the credibility of the MQM leadership and their patriotism by asserting that the violence and agitation in Karachi was engineered by Indian intelligence agencies. She abruptly closed down the Consulate-General of India in Karachi in December, 1994, subjecting thousands of Pakistani and Indian citizens to the hardship of not being able to visit each other easily despite their belonging to the same extended families. unfortunately living on two sides of the border. When levels of agitation and violence continued to rise even after the closure of the Indian Consulate-General, Benazir first reacted with hysterical anger indulging in personal abuse against the MQM leader Altaf Hussain. She then blamed him to be an Indian agent. While doing this, she was referring to a man who in the middle of leading the agitation against the Government of Pakistan had clearly stated to Indian journalists that he was first a Pakistani and then a *Mohajir* and that India should have no hopes of exploiting his differences with his Government in any manner. Benazir Bhutto who called Altaf Hussain an Indian agent was herself so described by Zia-ul-Haq during Benazir's long struggle against the military regime of Zia. Benazir perhaps did not realise the fact that by describing *Mohajirs* as foreigners and foreign agents of India, she erodes the two-nation theory further and this redefines the ethno-social paradigms of Pakistani national identity. In effect, she meant that only *Sindhis, Baluchis, Punjabis* and *Pathans* of the Northwest Frontier Province are real Pakistanis. She cannot carry this argument too far because *Sindhis* remain disenchanted with the Punjabi domination of Pakistani politics. Even within Pakistani Punjab, the *Saraikis* of Southern Punjab clamour for a separate ethno-social identity. Blaming India for all these troubles is temporarily an easy way out which Pakistan is practising. But ultimately the Pakistani establishment will have to reconcile itself to the objective reality of Pakistan being a plural, multi-ethnic, multi-linguistic society. The establishment may even have to acknowledge that Islam itself is not a monolithic religion which can find expression in a uniform politico-territorial identity as a single state. The fact that there are 49 separate Muslim countries and not one Muslim country stretching from Senegal to the Philippines is proof enough of this fact.

One cannot but refer to the hilarious aspects of anti-Indianism in Pakistani politics. Once the Pakistani Minister for Interior Major-General Nasrullah Babar accused India of utilizing the Zee TV to send messages to the MQM leadership in Sind and in England. There were reports from Pakistan that the distinguished Minister had accused the Government of India of sending coded messages to *Mohajirs* in Zee TV's programmes beamed to Karachi and on the ethnic TV channels in England. There is no end to the flights of hostile imagination which the Pakistani establishment can indulge in. When I mentioned this accusation of Minister Babar to an Indian Muslim friend of mine, he promptly dubbed it *parvaz-e-Wahiyat* (unmitigated flight of nonsense). The stirrings in Sind amongst the *Mohajirs* and the pressures on the Pakistani power structure from public opinion in Baluchistan and the NWFP, which is becoming increasingly politically conscious, may have a salutary effect on Pakistani politics, institutions and policies. This will take time, as dismantling the entrenched power structure in Pakistan is not going to be a short-term quickfix arrangement. The growth of democratic politics in Pakistan will ultimately reflect the reasonable and peaceful aspirations of the people of Pakistan towards all their neighbours. This, in turn, hopefully, would remedy the current negative drift in Indo-Pak relations which, in my opinion, will continue for some more time, perhaps for a decade or two.

Domestic Political Dimensions of Pakistan's Evolving Attitude to India

Most of our thought processes in analysing the antagonistic nature of Indo-Pakistan relations concentrate on issues of controversy between the two countries, like Kashmir, other border disputes, interferencs in internal affairs, the position of minorities, armaments race and so on. This focus of attention is natural as these are matters of immediate and continuous concern. We ruminate on how events have occured and are occuring. And on the ramifications of contemporary events. It is time now that we in India discern the domestic political trends in Pakistan which give impulse to Pakistan's adversary attitude and approach towards India.

When Benazir Bhutto came to power in the second half of 1993, observers of Pakistani politics felt that there were reasons to be optimistic about her succeeding in structuring a more stable and modern political system in the country.

Her electoral victory was interpreted as, first: the armed forces (the most influential element in the Pakistani power structure) having taken a decision to be impartial and fair in encouraging democratic processes. The confirmed professional orientation of a Chief of Army Staff Wahid, was perceived as an important contributory factor to this phenomenon. Secondly, her victory was discerned as the people of Pakistan rejecting the extremist and dogmatic orthodox Islamic forces which have become influential in Pakistani politics since Zia ul Haq's time. Third, her coming to power was interpreted as beginning of disintegration of political parties, elite which had entrenched itself in positions of influence in Pakistani politics, economy and administration. Fourthly, her coming to power raised expectations that the competition and conflict between the four provinces of Pakistan which characterized Pakistani politics would be remedied by her in the light of the experience of her first tenure in office between December 1988 and August 1990. Fifth, with the disenchantment of large *Mohajir* population about Nawaz Sharif Government, she might be able to win back the *Mohajir Quami Movement* back into the mainstream of Pakistani democratic politics. Her influence and popularity among the Western democracies were expected to make her most successful in managing involuted intricacies affecting the governance of Pakistan.

Except for the armed forces establishment still standing by in the wings, the other anticipations and expectations went totally off the mark. The socio-ethnic and linguistic balances of the state of Pakistan continue to have their negative impact on the domestic political situation. The arithmetic of the situation cannot be overcome or wished away. Punjab, the population of which now stood between 64 to 67 per cent of the population of Pakistan dominates every aspect of Pakistani life. It provides nearly 75 to 80 per cent of the army and almost 90 per cent of its officers cadre, Punjab also dominates the Senior Civil Bureaucracy constituting nearly 80 to 85 per cent of its cadres. Punjabis also dominate trading, banking, industry and the technological spheres of Pakistani life. A compounding factor has been Punjab's intrusion into ethnically the most self-conscious Province of Pakistan, Sind. During the long periods of military dictatorships, a large number of Punjabi military personnel were settled with land grants and other facilities in Sind. Sindhis already under pressure from the growing population and correspondingly increasing political clout of the migrant *Mohajir* population from India have been progressively allenated due to these twin pressures despite Zulfiqar Ali Bhutto being in power earlier and Benazir Bhutto, later. Discrimination against minorities get extended to important sections of the Muslim population itself of Pakistan like *Ahmediyas* has resulted in an attitude of intolerance on the part of majority *Sunni* religious leaders against citizens belonging to other religions increased in Pakistan. The consequence has been the rising growth of violence between *Shias* and *Sunnis* in Punjab and Sind, which has become another de-stabilising factor.

While Pakistan as a whole suffers from the pernicious impact of drug and *Klashnikov* culture, this has been particularly felt in North West Frontier Province, Sind, and other southern portions of Baluchistan. The Federal Government dominated by the Punjabis always remained apprehensive of losing control over politics and economy of Sind, especially of Karachi and important cities like Nawabshah and Hyderabad (Sind) where the *Mohajirs* are becoming democratically dominant backed by political organisation and illegal acquisition of arms. The daily violence affecting the lives in Pakistan's biggest city and economic power centre, Karachi reflects this reality. The slowing down of US economic and military assistance over the last six years has also had a marginal negative effect on Pakistan's economy.

The ethno-centric frustrations of the *Sindism Baluch,* certain sections of *Pushtoons* and *Saraixis* (the last mentioned in Southern Punjab have added to domestic tensions and pressures. Though the Islamic parties and Zia loyalists received an electoral setback in the 1993 elections, they remained assertive enough to keep Benazir and her government on tenter hooks.

At that time Benazir's primary concern naturally was to survive in power, and for this purpose she interpreted the domestic contradictions in Pakistani politics as a threat to national unity and the next step was to claim that India generated that threat. Now her mindset and attitude changed towards India because of the imperatives of political survival and pressures of domestic politics can be discerned by going back to the period when she was a part of the Movement for restoration of democracy opposing Zia Ul Haq. In a book entitled: *Pakistan—the Gathering Storm* written by her in 1983 she had following to say about her attitude towards India:

"While abjuring major initiatives MRD shall endeavour to normalise and improve relations with all its neighbours especially India. The MRD expects the goal of approchment with India. Therefore, it undertakes actively to discourage an arms race with it. It shall freeze those parts of nuclear research programme that are not directly necessary for power generation. It shall enter into exploratory talks with

India if latter wishes for... our two people's possible cooperation in this field."

"MRD accepts the idea of marrying peace, friendship and cooperation treaty with a no war pact. It undertakes to maximise trade, economic and cultural cooperation with India. It will endeavour to convert Indo-Pakistan border into a soft one like the one between Canada and the United States of America..... ."

Over Kashmir MRD accepts the Shimla Agreement as still valid framework for peacefully resolving this old dispute."

Her later stand on Kashmir disowning the Shimla Agreement asking for UN intervention and supporting terrorist violence in Kashmir was a far cry from her views of 1983. Her government added a nuclear dimension to the confrontation with India. Dr. Abdul Qadir Khan in an interview in Peshawar said that Pakistan had neither capped nor abjured its nuclear weaponization programme. So much for her earlier vision of not having an arms race with India. She did not bring about any positive change in Pakistan's policies towards expanding economic, cultural and technological cooperation with India, though she made some very cautious beginnings in this direction during her interaction with Rajiv Gandhi for a brief period of six months between December, 1988 and July, 1989. The substantive causation of deterioration of Indo-Pakistan relations during 1993-94 had been the domestic crisis in Pakistan which compelled Benazir to divert public opinion to the nonexistent external threat from India. Though she managed to survive as Prime Minister longer in her second tenure, she was not politically strong enough to overcome or discipline the domestic challenges. It was conventional wisdom of experts when she first came to power that she was untrammelled by the burdens of history or the partition of the sub-continent. And therefore she would forge new equations with India. What happened was exactly the opposite. Instead of disarming those burdens she did not just take them on but again made them operational ingredients of her policies towards India. Leaving aside the deep under-currents of our adversary relationship, normalcy between India and Pakistan can be achieved only when Pakistan consolidates and stabilises itself as a responsible State and Society.

Nawaz Sharif's Exile—Ramifications in the Domestic Politics of Pakistan

The Chief Executive of Pakistan General Pervez Musharraf sent Nawaz Sharif and his family into exile in December, 2000, little more than a year after he overthrowing assumed power by Sharif from the post of Prime Minister of Pakistan. This is not the first time that the leader of a military coup has exiled political leaders from Pakistan. Field Marshal Ayub Khan did the same when he exiled the front man of the military coup which he conducted in 1958-59, Major General Iskander Mirza to England. He also generated sufficient pressure on political leaders like Mohammed Ali and Nazeemuddin to go out of Pakistan. It is the inevitable logic followed by military rulers that to establish their credibility they have to neutralise credible political rivals by ensuring their departure from the scene either by exiling them or through elimination as was the case with Zulfiqar Ali Bhutto. Nawaz Sharif being exiled, however, has a unique characteristic of a Prime Minister in office, who was in power on the basis of a general election, being ousted from power and then exiled.

The background of Nawaz Sharif's expulsion from Pakistan is relevant to analysing the ramifications of his departure from scene in Pakistan's domestic politics. It cannot be denied that Nawaz Sharif had come to power with general popular support. His forcible removal was the result of two factors: First, betraying the trust reposed in him by the people of Pakistan, manifested in increasing authoritarianism and the unbridled corruption on his part and secondly, the ineptitude and lack of political judgement which characterised his attempt to dismiss his Chief of Army Staff General Pervez Musharraf, an extraordinary example of his refusing to acknowledge the profoundest reality facing Pakistani politics, the reality of the clout of the Pakistani armed forces, as an institutional entity in the power structure of Pakistan.

It is worthwhile analysing the reasons why General Pervez Musharraf sent him into exile. Sharif and his family members, along with a number of officials who coalesced with him in defying the armed forces were put on trial on charges of corruption, high treason, attempt to murder, disrupting discipline of the Pakistani armed forces and so on. He would have been subjected to long periods of imprisonment, followed by a death sentence. General Pervez Musharraf perhaps judged that the Pakistan of the year 1999 and 2000, was different from the Pakistan of years 1977 to 1979, when General Zia-ul-Haq could get away with the execution of a Prime Minister. General Musharraf was under international pressure from the US and from the influential countries of the Gulf on whom Pakistan is depending, advising him that Nawaz Sharif could be convicted but not subjected to any harsh sentence. Whatever his shortcomings, Nawaz Sharif had extensive rapport and influence with the leaders of the US, and the countries of the Gulf and West Asia. General Pervez Musharraf did not wish himself to be seen as a harsh military figure. His aim is to project himself as a catalytic figure who would bring back genuine democracy to Pakistan after the inefficiencies, corruption and commonalities which characterised democratic governments of Pakistan from 1988 to October 1999.

Historical patterns were repeated in Pakistan between October 1999 and end of the year 2000, after the military coup of General Pervez Musharraf. Just as it happened after Zia's taking over power in 1977, Pakistani political parties were again in disarray after Musharraf's coup. But by the autumn of last year (the year 2000) all the political parties had moved towards creating a United Front against General Musharraf's military regime. The culminating point of this process was that the Pakistan Muslim League of Nawaz Sharif and People's Party of Pakistan agreeing to join each other to launch a collective campaign against the military Government of Pervez Musharraf. The expectation of Musharraf and his colleagues that Benazir Bhutto being exiled and the Pakistan Muslim League being divided after Nawaz Sharif's arrest and incarceration, the political parties in Pakistan will not be able to be an active factor in Pakistani politics, proved to be wrong with the above developments. Earlier the Pakistan Supreme Court had given a verdict that the present military regime should finish its tenure by the middle of 2002 which was accepted by General Musharraf. He, therefore, had two options. Either to voluntarily relinquish power and let the political parties of Pakistan fight an election next year or to initiate arrangements for his continuation in power within the frame work of democratic institutional arrangements acceptable to the judiciary as well as the people of Pakistan. He seems to have chosen the second option mentioned. Regardless of public disappointment about political leaders, both Benazir Bhutto and Nawaz Sharif still have certain stature and charisma in Pakistani public opinion, which Pervez Musharraf could not ignore, nor could he allow them to remain active in Pakistani politics. Benazir has remained outside Pakistan under threat of corruption trials by the

Musharraf Government. The practical solution chosen by General Musharraf was to exile Nawaz Sharif as well after significantly eroding his economic assets and related capacities to have any influence on Pakistani politics. His keeping the leaders of major political parties of Pakistan exiled is in preparation for his continuing in power under new and more domestically and internationally acceptable institutional arrangements. Pervez Musharraf himself gave indications regarding this in a radio and television broadcast to the nation in the second half of December 2000. Interesting points in his speech were: first, that he could not have succeeded in overthrowing Nawaz Sharif's corrupt regime and assuming power without divine support, which according to him entailed his being entrusted with certain profound responsibilities to ensure the well-being of Pakistan. "As a wish of Allah Tallah"; General Musharraf went on to confirm that he is not an escapist and that he will relinquish power only after he fulfills these responsibilities. Secondly, he confirmed that he wants to restore democracy in Pakistan. He exhorted the people of Pakistan not to perceive democracy in terms of an exercise in convential party politics. He urged the people of Pakistan to put up qualified, sincere, honest candidates, dedicated to genuine public service, instead of relying on the corrupt party system in Pakistan. Third, he announced that he would be holding elections for local self-governing bodies and Panchayats in Pakistan, as a first step in moving forward to democracy.

At the formal level, the likelihood of Benazir Bhutto's returning to Pakistan in the foreseeable future is remote. Nawaz Sharif has been exiled for ten years and has been banned from politics and public office for 21 years. Some Pakistani analysts had the view that both Benazir Bhutto and Nawaz Sharif will continue to influence Pakistani political processes and that they cannot be kept outisde the country for more than a decade or so. There have also been reports that General Musharraf had, in his four or five meetings with Saudi Crown Prince Abdullah, worked out the arrangements for Nawaz Sharif's exile and for his being kept out of Pakistani politics. It should also be noted that Benazir's residential base is between London and Dubai. There are unconfirmed reports that Musharraf Government has persuaded the Governments of the Gulf not to allow these political leaders to get back to Pakistan so that General Musharraf can prolong his tenure in power.

The speculation is that General Musharraf will incrementally move towards making his government a civilian government once the Panchayat elections are over, moving up from the district to Provincial levels. One is reminded of Field Marshal Ayub Khan's experiment with what he called *Basic Democracies* in the 1960s. There are also reports from Pakistan that General Musharraf will appoint some civilian Prime Minister before he organises general elections next year. The names of the Speaker of the suspended National Assembly Allahi Bux Soomro and Pakistan People's Party Vice President Amin Fahim, are being mentioned for this post.

In the meanwhile, none of the political parties of Pakistan want the national and Provincial assemblies which were suspended by General Pervez Musharraf, to be revived or restored. Indications are that General Musharraf will complete the process of giving his government an incremental but partial civilian identity between now and the middle of the year 2002, by which time he may have created a political platform for himself. In this process he is likely to re-designate himself as President of Pakistan, relinquishing the title of Chief Executive Officer. There is no likelihood of General Musharraf and the Pakistani armed forces relinquishing power and shifting away from the scene in the near future. What is likely to happen is Musharraf continuing in power in some form of democratic and civilian identity, thereby legitimising his position in Pakistani politics. It is obvious that it would be impractical for India to refuse to deal with General Musharraf on the basis of our arguments regarding the means by which he came to power. Practicality demands that we move on to deal with him atleast during coming three to five years. This is the only way that India can hope to manage the current difficult and complicated phase in Indo-Pakistan relations.

7

MUSHARRAF-VAJPAYEE SUMMIT : PERSPECTIVE AND PROSPECTS

The dates for the Vajpayee-Musharraf summit have been announced, 14th to 16th July at Agra. Musharraf has changed his designation declaring himself President of Pakistan on the 20th of June, thereby endowing himself with a more formal political status before coming for a dialogue with Vajpayee. There have been statements from Vajpayee and Musharraf between 16th and 20th of June, indicating that there is no basic change in their negotiating stances on Kashmir; Vajpayee saying that Jammu and Kashmir is an integral part of India and that the issue of Pakistan Occupied Kashmir has to be on the Agenda of the summit. Musharraf on the other hand has stated that resolving the future status of Kashmir is an unfinished task of the Partition. This is the broad political and cosmetic contexts in which a summit would be held.

Analysts and commentators have indulged in speculations, critical assessments of the reasons for Vajpayee's invitation and Musharraf's positive response, some have even gone further to give prescriptive advice that given the allegedly dire straits in which Pakistan is, Pakistan should come to a rational compromise with India to get out of its difficult predicaments.

One would begin with the proposition that there is no place for euphoria or optimism about India entering into these negotiations from a position of strength or a presumption that General Musharraf is coming for this summit under tremendous pressure. A clinical assessment of the perspective and the motivations impinging on the forthcoming summit is necessary. The Vajpayee Government came to the conclusion that their peace initiatives which originated in the declaration of a unilateral ceasefire in November had reached saturation point without any concrete results. Given India's stand that there are two facets of issues related to Kashmir, one the domestic dimension which has to be sorted out with our own Kashmiri dissident groups and second, relating to Pakistan's intrusive involvement in Kashmir in all its dimensions, the Government nominated Mr. K.C. Pant to deal with the first aspect and in a bold gesture invited General Musharraf to come for a meeting with Mr. Vajpayee. The invitation to Musharraf clearly states India's willingness to discuss the Kashmir issue with the chief executive of Pakistan. Despite the contradictions and ambiguities in the response from the Hurriyat and other separatist groups, India has not moved back from its willingness to enter into discussions with them to find a possible solution of issues related to Jammu and Kashmir. However, in the context of these separatist groups not abjuring terrorism and violence, Government of India ended its decision to maintain a unilateral ceasefire, timing it with invitation to General Musharraf. The objective of this exercise seems to be to convey a three-point message. First, the Government of India had not suggested the ceasefire because of exhaustion or lack of political will to resist terrorist violence. Secondly, India is willing to remain patient till the separatist groups come round to having a meaningful discussions with the Government of India. Third, that in the larger interest of peace and stability, India is modifying its stand to have negotiations with Pakistan represented by General

Musharraf. The termination of the ceasefire was also a response to feeling in the Indian public opinion that violent elements in Jammu and Kashmir were taking advantage of the ceasefire. The non-sub-continental dimension of this initiative is the Indian concern at regarding the reactions of important powers and international community about the situation in Kashmir. The Indian assessment is that to sustain international understanding and support for Indian concerns on Kashmir, a resumption of a high-level and multi-pronged dialogue is necessary. There are segments of Indian political circles and public opinion which do not anticipate any concrete results from the dialogue but the majority of people are supportive of the Vajpayee initiative. Trends and impulses which resulted in the positive response of General Musharraf to Vajpayee's invitation are: first and foremost is Musharraf acquires legitimacy both in the regional and international context with Prime Minister of India engaging him in a dialogue. Secondly, from his point of view, General Musharraf can say that he has persuaded India to have a summit meeting specifically on the Kashmir issue. Third, a meeting with Vajpayee will remedy the image of Pakistan as a state supporting Islamic extremism and terrorism. The dialogue with India combined with some tentative steps taken by Pakistan to place restrictions on organisations like Harkat-ul-Ansar, Jaisih-e-Mohammed and even Jammat-e-Islami could be used by Pakistan to claim that Pakistan is responsive to critical and negative perceptions in these matters in the international community particularly amongst the western democracies. It must also be noted that Pakistan Foreign Minister Abdul Sattar was in Washington during third week of June with Secretary of State Colin Powell and President Bush, he would no doubt have utilised the opportunity to convey not only Pakistani concerns about Jammu and Kashmir but expectations of dialogue with Vajpayee. In a manner the speech given by

General Musharraf at the National Seerat conference in Islamabad on June 6, it was remarkable. He admonished leaders of Islam-pasand parties and extremist organisations to refrain from adventurist and irresponsible statements about their militant intentions regarding India. He emphasised that their activities tarnished the image of Pakistan and contradicted their claims that they are committed to Pakistan's identity and dignity. This speech of the 6th June perhaps signifies that General Musharraf has consolidated his position in the power structure of Pakistan and he feels secure enough to take on and resist irrational orthodoxies which have permeated Pakistan over the last two decades and more. The virulent reaction to his acceptance of Vajpayee's invitation from these extremist groups was in consequence to be expected. What is important is that this opposition has not made any impact on the orientations of Musharraf's attitudes regarding the forthcoming summit.

Preparatory consultations and exchange of informal documents between the foreign offices of the two countries has been underway since the beginning of June. Indian High Commissioner Nambiar has been in Delhi for discussions and briefings with Brajesh Mishra, Principal Secretary to the Prime Minister and the Foreign Secretary Ms. Chokila Iyer. He has also briefed the Prime Minister and Cabinet Ministers constituting the National Security Council. Principal Secretary Brajesh Mishra is visiting Washington and some other capitals en route before this summit to apprise the governments concerned of India's general approach on the summit meeting. The United States and other important powers, the UN Secretary General as well as important countries in the Asian region have welcomed Vajpayee's initiative of inviting General Musharraf and there is expectation that the summit meeting will initiate processes for a possible agreement between India and Pakistan on Kashmir.

What then are the prospects of the summit in specific terms. A limited achievement would be the revival of the Lahore process in some sense. There are possibilities of the two leaders deciding on follow up action to be taken, the Memorandum of Understanding on avoidance of nuclear conflict and working on nuclear risk reduction. Though the other issues like the military stand off at Siachen, the border demarcation on Sir Creek and the need to enhance mutual confidence building measures, may be discussed, the central issue would be Kashmir. It is significant that the Pakistani High Commissioner in New Delhi, Ashaf Jahangir Qazi has made special effort not only to interact with the BJP and its associates in the rulling coalition, he has contacted Opposition parties, including the Communist Party leaders to persuade them to accept that the future status of Kashmir should be discussed between the two heads of Government. One understands that he has achieved marginal success. Prospects of any qualitative breakthrough in the immediate future post-summit in July, however, is not possible. Indian public opinion and political circles are firmly opposed to any territorial alienation of Jammu and Kashmir from India. As far as Jammu and Kashmir is concerned, the people of Ladakh and Jammu share the above view. Political groups and people in the Kashmir valley are subject to ambiguities and contradictions about what the solution should be which is responsive to their aspirations. As far as people in the valley go, there are some who want to join Pakistan, there are others who want Jammu and Kashmir to be an independent State with appropriate security guarantees from India, Pakistan and the UN. There are some who advocate trifurcation of Kashmir into three territorial entities, Ladakh, the Kashmir valley and Jammu, with the valley having one kind of connection or the other with Pakistan. One has also come across a radical suggestion by the Kashmiri Hindus who have become refugees in India, who suggest that Kashmir should be divided into four entities (a) Ladakh, (b) Jammu, (c) the valley west of Jhelum to be given to Pakistan and (d) the valley east of Jhelum to become homeland for Kashmiri Hindus. Then there is the domestic political dimension of the debate on a solution between enhanced autonomy or continuation of stronger linkages with the Centre.

As far as Pakistan is concerned, there has been no nuance in their policies or any signal that there is any change in their basic stand on the Kashmir issue. General Musharraf in an interview to M.J. Akbar of the Asian Age published on the 8th of April stated that a solution is possible if both India and Pakistan become flexible enough to move away from their stated positions. Musharraf felt that once a dialogue starts, a movement forward could be possible. Put in most specific terms General Musharraf felt that a solution should be based on the UN Resolution, the Security Council Resolution on Plebiscite. Elaborating his perception on the Kashmir issue he stated that the situation in Kashmir is characterised by a freedom struggle. "Realistically speaking, the dynamics of the Kashmir situation is that a freedom struggle started by Kashmiris from all parts of the world." He felt that India should take note of this reality in dealing with the issue both with Kashmiris and Pakistan.

In recent months neither India nor Pakistan have referred to the solution visualised at Shimla in 1972, that is, the conversion of the Line of Control into an international frontier with needed adjustments, a solution which may get the support of the international community, if somehow India and Pakistan could agree on that. The people of Jammu and Kashmir may accept this solution if it is combined with enhancement of autonomy and guarantees of access and normal relations with Pakistan.

Vajpayee and Musharraf come to this summit burdened with history and static negotiating stances. They are subject to further limitation of the complexities of contradictory suggestions for a solution and public opinion on both sides governed by emotional and psychological impulses born of 50 years of an adversary relationship. Both of them can be sure of one thing that their initiating a personal dialogue will project a tentative image of India and Pakistan being capable of a rational and practical interaction with each other. An imperative of this summit is that it should generate the process of continuous discussion. Though there may be no breakthrough, there should be no abrupt termination of the dialogue because it did not lead to concrete results. The summit at the profoundest level provides an opportunity for India and Pakistan to decide whether future of the peoples of the two countries should be held hostage to the Kashmir issue.

8

ANTI-INDIAN PAK MOVES ON HUMAN RIGHTS—POST-GENEVA PROSPECTS

The very evening of the day on which the Indo-Pak Foreign Secretary level talks concluded on 3rd January, 1994, the Pakistani Foreign Office announced that Pakistan will continue to agitate the Kashmir issue in terms of human rights violations, and other advocacies in various international fora.

The then Prime Minister of Pakistan Mrs. Benazir Bhutto announced a few days later that Pakistan would move a resolution against India in the UN Human Rights Commission meeting in Geneva in February and that she would make a personal appearance at the Commission meeting in Geneva to argue the Pakistani case. In the event she went to Geneva; Pakistan tabled a resolution. It was the most controversial issue at the HRC meeting on which participant delegations cogitated throughout the HRC session. To get their resolution passed somehow the Pak delegation submitted successive drafts diluting the more intrusive or assertive clauses. In the end they withdrew the resolution on the advice, according to them of Iran and to some extent of China.

In the very short term the Pakistani diplomatic effort failed despite their worldwide lobbying efforts and canvassing at Geneva.

In a sense, for India, "it was a famous victory". We fielded a delegation led by political figures representing opposing spectra of political parties of India. It was also a multi-ethnic, multi-religious delegation. We also had two Kashmiris, a prominent Muslim Farooq Abdullah and a prominent Hindu T.N. Kaul on the delegation. We backed up the political component of the delegation with a trans-continental, trans-regional array of senior Indian diplomats with contacts in Geneva and New York. We ensured participation in the effort, outside the conference, by Indian NGOs and external publicity experts. To cap this our Minister of External Affairs went to Iran to convey our concern to Iranian leaders and to persuade them to influence Pakistan to relent. Iran respondeed positively and delivered. The contact of Dinesh Singh with the Chinese Foreign Minister in Tehran also contributed to our success at Geneva. There is every reason to be satisfied with the outcome. Self-congratulation, a sense of relief and a feeling of achievement are natural. The media hype in India following the HRC session was also to be expected.

But what justification is there for the type of exultation, anticipatory confidence for the future, as reflected in briefings and statements and media commentaries that followed? Is it not more relevant, absolutely necessary to reflect on, what is likely to happen next, where do we proceed from the success at Geneva. What are the challenges and crises that Pakistan will engineer against us? The skirmish, an intense, hotly contested one, but it was only a skirmish that was over, to our satisfaction, no doubt. The battle, however, goes on. It will continue for some time to come. Taking note of Pakistani statements made by Benazir Bhutto downwards post-Geneva, we should not have a moment doubt about this prospect. We have to respond to this continuing diplomatic and media offensive by Pakistan both in the bilateral and multilateral context.

Taking stock of the achievement at Geneva, and its ramifications is necessary for fashioning, structuring our response.

First the achievements, we showed our capacity for a cohesive, structured, strategically insightful foreign policy response to a challenge which we faced; the composition of our delegation, its leadership, and its advocacies conveyed a firm and clear national consensus in India, on issues related to Kashmir, to the international community and the UN agencies. We managed to persuade important friends of Pakistan (Iran and China) to persuade her to move back temporarily from confrontation in multilateral fora, against India. Our arguments were sufficiently convincing to the majority of the fifty-three members of the Human Rights Commission to incline them to abstain on the Pakistani resolution. We successfully prevented motivated politicisation of human rights norms, norms which are of increasing international concern. We can claim that we prevented the procedural internationalisation of the Kashmir issue through the UN Human Rights Commission. In domestic political terms the Government got credit for diplomatic adroitness in dealing with a sensitive national issue.

Secondly, the downside of the proceedings, we have to acknowledge that Pakistan has succeeded in focussing international attention on the Kashmir issue, and need for some international pressure or action on the issue, after a gap of nearly three decades. It is to be noted that no delegation at Geneva expressed the view that Pakistan should not make such moves at the HRC or UN in future.

By giving so much attention and putting in so much effort to counter the Pak resolution in a UN forum, we have indirectly indicated our apprehensions about UN's acquiring some legitimacy in dealing with an issue which on all counts is an internal matter of India. It was concern about the cosmetic impact of such a resolution succeeding at the HRC, on domestic public opinion that resulted in our hyper activity at Geneva, an approach somewhat at variance with our Prime Minister's intellectual conviction and confidence that (a) an adversary relationship with Pakistan is something India has to live with as far as Pakistan continues its present attitude and approach on Indo-Pak relations, (b) we should not be nervous about Pakistan's shenanigans in various multilateral fora, and (c) that India has the self-assurance and capacity to resist any multilateral or extraneous bilateral moves to interfere in the internal affairs of India. Though we are loath to admit it, the Iranian representatives' intervention during the end of the discussions on the Pak resolution and Pakistani statements explaining the reasons for the withdrawal of the resolution, indicated that Iran has expectations of playing some sort of a role in future deliberations on Kashmir, both in the Indo-Pak and multilateral context. It would be relevant to know, to the extent possible, subject of course to considerations of confidentiality in inter-State relations, as to what were the decisive considerations emerging from the Velayati-Dinesh Singh discussions, which resulted in Iran's assuming such an active role in Geneva to prevent the Pak resolution being moved. Given Iran's religious and ideological inclinations, and its policies on the Kashmir issue which one accepts, is finely nuanced to allay Indian concerns regarding India's territorial integrity, it is difficult to believe that Iran does not anticipate some role for itself, even if we may not have specifically acquiesce in such a role for Iran in the last high-level political contact. True, the US delegation in its statements at the Human Rights Commission meeting did not refer to Kashmir and related issues. But the United States Government remained neutral and distant about Indian concerns, about Pak interference in Kashmir and the violation of human rights by militants. United States remained committed to a patronisingly Dutch avancular stance towards India on human rights issues despite India's commitment to democracy and India's overall human rights record.

An analysis of the motivations of China and Iran at Geneva is relevant. It would be wrong to believe that China and Iran were supportive of India only due to the diplomatic and political interaction with them in the short three or four weeks preceeding the Geneva meeting. China has been the target of country specific Human Rights resolutions at various UN fora, particularly since 1988-89. Iran has faced the same predicament since the Iranian resolution. India took a deliberate decision early in 1993 not to support any country specific resolutions on human rights issues in any multilateral forum. This benefited Iran and China. The self-interest of both countries resulted in their opposing country specific resolutions. They did not wish any precedent to be created in any UN agency in this regard. Iran has the additional motivation to play a mediatory role in Indo-Pak resolutions in terms of her regional aspirations and for her own stability and security. Our then Prime Minister's visit to China and Iran in September 1993 just before the commencement of the UN General Assembly session provided an opportunity for India to convey her views and concerns at the highest political levels in these countries. The personal rapport between Narshimha Rao and Li Peng and Rafsanjani had the additional positive fall out at Geneva. We should not have any illusions about Chinese and Iranian support at Geneva nor should we expect any trilateral "Iran-China-India axis or strategic equation" an idea projected on the basis of the Dinesh Singh-Qian Qe Chen discussions at Tehran. China has no such intention. Their approach and decisions were based essentially on their own concerns in the sphere of human rights and their respective national interests.

With Great Power consensus on giving the UN an incrementally intervensionist role on matters of international concern, be it non-proliferation, peace-keeping, environment management or human rights, India should remain forewarned about an activist UN role instigated by Pakistan. We must also be prepared for the controversy on Kashmir being projected through the prisms of human rights, self-determination, non-proliferation, interim disarmament measures and what not.

There are, therefore, no grounds for excessive exultation or smug satisfaction. Pakistani leaders across the entire political spectrum have confirmed their unending efforts on campaign against India in their pronouncements since their debacle at Geneva. Our task therefore is to reflect on realistic political prospects, evolve measured policies, keeping always in mind Jawaharlal Nehru's admonition on foreign relations that publicity is never a substitute for policy. Be firm in our resolve to safeguard our interests, to pursue the objective of a dialogue with Pakistan and over and above all not to be over-enthusiastic or desperate about things.

9

INDO-BANGLADESH RELATIONS—NEED FOR BETTER HANDLING

When Bangladesh's Foreign Secretary Farooq Sobhan visited Delhi in August, 1996, it signified the revival of meaningful contacts between India and Bangladesh after a gap of nearly four years. The visit had taken place in the background of new governments coming into power both in Bangladesh and in India. The Indian government deputed Foreign Secretary Salman Haider to Dhaka and Farooq Sobhan's paying a return visit within six weeks of Haider's visit to Dhaka indicated the desire on the part of both governments to put Indo-Bangladesh relations back on the track after the distances and derailments which had occurred between the two countries since 1993.

The elections in Bangladesh held in June, 1996 brought about a transformation in Bangladeshi politics after nearly 21 years. The Awami League which spearheaded the movement for autonomy in East Pakistan and then led the freedom struggle leading to the creation of Bangladesh came back to power after a long gap of time. The politics and patterns of governance of Bangladesh have had a chequered history ever since its coming into existence. Begum Khaleda Zia-ur-Rahman revived democratic governance in Bangladesh, in 1990. She and her party nevertheless represented the post-Awami League dynamics in Bangladesh's politics from 1990 to middle of 1996.

Mujibur Rahman's daughter Sheikh Hasina, who inherited the Awami League tradition and its leadership came back to power after a prolonged struggle. The fact that her party had to get the support of President Ershad's party and other political parties including sections of the Muslim orthodoxy reflects two trends. First, that the Awami League, though re-emerging as a major influence in Bangladeshi politics, has not re-acquired its pre-eminent position in the interplay of political forces in the country. Secondly, Begum Khaleda Zia's BNP and President Ershad's Jatiya Party coming into parliament in sufficient numbers indicates that these political parties, despite being created by military leaders, have acquired democratic credibility and political legitimacy. The point to be noted is that the socio-political dynamics of both the society and the power structure of Bangladesh have changed profoundly compared to the period between 1956 and 1975. The characteristics of this change, as one perceives them, are: the ethos and the ideology of the movement for autonomy and the liberation struggle are no longer relevant to Bangladeshi politics, Secondly, there is a re-emergence of Islam as a factor considered necessary to consolidate Bangladesh's separate national identity. The increasing influence of the Jamaat and other religious groups confirms this assessment. Even the Awami League which considered secularism as a significant element in its political platform has moved back from its commitment to this principle.

Thirdly, the armed forces are actively involved in party politics of the country. Fourth is the emergence of a sizeable merchantile and consumerist middle class (I use the adjectives 'mercantile and consumerist' advisedly, as the entrepreneurial, professional and industrial segment of Bangladesh's middle class is a minority in this group) as an influential factor in Bangladesh politics with strong linkages with South East Asia and the West and even with Pakistan.

The fifth characteristic is the disappearance of the left of centre and leftist parties from Bangladesh's political scene. They have been marginalised. The sixth characteristic is the general consensus in Bangladesh about the country's consolidation and survival being dependent on Bangladesh being a part of the Pan-Islamic movement. These trends in Bangladesh's politics would inevitably impact on Bangladesh's foreign policy generally and on its policies towards India in particular. We should accept these realities and the first point to be remembered by us in structuring our relations with the new government in Bangladesh is that we should not presume or expect that because the Awami League has come back to power, its attitude towards India would be that of reviving the close emotive reactions towards India in the immediate aftermath of the liberation war of Bangladesh. This is not going to happen. If we express such expectations or predicate our policies on such an expectation, it would be unrealistic and counter-productive; it would also impose embarrassment and unnecessary burdens on the new Awami League government. Our fundamental orientation should be to interact with all political parties in Bangladesh as representing the current aspirations and trends in public opinion of the people of Bangladesh. This is essential to create an atmosphere of credibility and trust between India and Bangladesh. An issue-specific analysis of the problems that India and Bangladesh have to tackle would be pertinent. The most important issue is that of deciding the manner in which both countries will share the waters of the Gangetic basin. Bangladesh's requirements of augmented flows below the Farakka during the dry season between January and May is genuine and legitimate. The point at issue is the amount of water required for Bangladesh. The last two rounds of Foreign Secretary level talks, in Dhaka and more recently in Delhi, seem to have made some tangible progress. First, there must be an agreement between both countries that the decision on the issue has to be basically "political" aimed at establishing a positive equilibrium in relations between the two countries. A purely technical approach will only prolong the controversy. The Bangladesh Foreign Secretary Farooq Sobhan said at a press conference in Delhi in August, 1996 that there is an evolving consensus between the two governments that the agreement on sharing of water resources will have to be a permanent one instead of the current practice of short-term arrangements. On all counts, depending on the size of the water flows available above Farakka, India should be able to guarantee to Bangladesh between 21 and 26 thousand cusecs of water during the lean season. That this should be possible despite some technical difficulties was indicated by general information available after the bilateral talks that both sides are likely to consider the long-term augmentation of water flows into Bangladesh by exploiting the resources not only of the Ganges, but all rivers and their tributaries draining the territories of India and Bangladesh in that region. The second issue is the imbalance in the trade between India and Bangladesh. This has resulted in the political and economic frustration in this important neighbour of ours. While we are moving towards liberalisation of trade arrangements under the SAARC, India should take initiatives in the bilateral framework also. Even if India removes all tariff and non-tariff barriers against Bangladesh's exports to India, it is not going to have any major adverse impact on our exports or our economy. While it will not harm us, we will be making a significant contribution to Bangladesh's economy, which in turn will have a positive political impact.

All the political leaders of Bangladesh have expressed their desire not to renew the Indo-Bangladesh Treaty of Peace, friendship and cooperation signed in March, 1972 between Mujibur Rahman and Indira Gandhi. Foreign Secretary Sobhan stated in Delhi that while the treaty might have been necessary and might have met bilateral requirements when it was signed, the objectives of the treaty have already been achieved and it is no longer relevant. Instead of allowing continued controversy on the subject, we should agree with Bangladesh immediately not to renew the treaty. Some new declaration or joint statement defining the new terms of reference of political relations between India and Bangladesh could replace the treaty. These new terms of reference, while safeguarding India's interests, should be clearly responsive to Bangladesh's concerns.

There are still some outstanding territorial issues between the two countries despite the handing over of *Berubari* and the allocation of the *Teen Bigha corridor* to Bangladesh. There are still some enclaves to be exchanged. There are also the unresolved problems related to the Indo-Bangladesh maritime boundary and the New Moor Island. Our Central Government, in consultation with the West Bengal Government, should be able to settle these issues amicably with Bangladesh. The territorial controversies with Bangladesh have no major strategic or security implications for us, though they evoke political emotions. These have to be overcome in the larger interests of regional stability. There was welcome news at the end of Farooq Sobhan's discussions in Delhi that Bangladesh authorities are agreeable to receive back *Chakma* refugees. This should not only remove a controversy in Indo-Bangladesh relations, but would also remove misunderstandings between India, Bangladesh and Myanmar. Both India and Bangladesh desire transit facilities through each other's territories for trade. India wants the transit facilities to reach our eastern and north-eastern states more expeditiously. Bangladesh desires transit facilities to Nepal and Bhutan to augment its exports. Both sides have reservations about granting these facilities not primarily due to economic considerations. The reservations are based on political considerations and security perceptions.

There is the seemingly intractable problem of large-scale illegal migration from Bangladesh into India. Bangladesh flatly denying that such illegal migrations have taken place does not help matters. It is time that the new government in Bangladesh takes a fresh and more objective view of this extremely difficult issue and negotiate a practical solution with India. The problem goes beyond politics. The complexity of the issue is because of the intense demographic pressure on land both in Bangladesh and in the Indian States surrounding that country.

In overall political terms, Bangladesh has some general apprehensions about India. In an interview given to an Indian magazine, Foreign Secretary Sobhan expressed the view that India does not focus its attention on Bangladesh. It considers itself a large power which should interact more intensely with the important centres of power in international politics. This criticism is not quite valid because Bangladesh always looms large in our foreign policy radar screen, as an important and populous neighbour which is geo-strategically even more important than Pakistan for us because of its location intervening between the North Eastern portions of India and the rest of India and its sharing an international frontier with us and Myanmar. If Bangladesh has any threat perceptions about India, we should give very specific assurances to Bangladesh about India respecting Bangladesh's territorial integrity and unity and about India conducting its relations with that country on the basis of sovereign equality. Being sensitively responsive to political concerns and limitations of Bangladesh should be the governing consideration rather than insistence on point to point reciprocity in the details of our interaction with them.

Indo-Bangladesh Treaty of Friendship of 1972—Political Cogitations in Bangladesh

The leaders of the ruling party as well as the Opposition in Bangladesh, Begum Khaleda Zia and Sheikh Hasina, since the summer of 1993 have generated controversies about the Indo-Bangladesh Treaty of Peace, Friendship and Cooperation signed between Sheikh Mujibur Rahman and Mrs. Indira Gandhi on the 19th of March, 1972. While Sheikh Hasina has been putting forth the argument that the treaty has become irrelevant due to changed circumstances and passage of time, Begum Khaleda Zia has been talking about abrogating the treaty "to free Bangladesh from the shackles of Indian domination" and "the limitations on Bangladesh's sovereignty which the treaty imposes due to the lack of foresight of the late Prime Minister Sheikh Mujibur Rahman".

Both Begum Zia and Sheikh Hasina have affirmed that the treaty would be an important political issue during the next elections in Bangladesh. Ex-President Ershad's party and the Islam-pasand political groups of Bangladesh are also attributing negative Indian motivations in getting this treaty signed in exercises of retrospective analysis. It is time to clear the cobwebs and put the record straight about the background in which the treaty was signed.

Though Bangladesh was liberated on the surrender of Pakistani forces at Dhaka on the 16th of December,1971 some Pakistani forces had escaped to the Chittagong Hill Tracts and Cox's Bazar and were continuing anti-Bangladesh military operations from there. Almost till the end, Bangladesh faced hostility from Pakistan, China and the United States. This hostility against Bangladesh was intense during the first half of 1972. The capture of 93,000

Pakistani prisoners of war and the uncertainty about the course that political events would take due to Bangladesh's original intention of holding war crimes trials against Pakistani officers compounded the tension. Considering his country vulnerable, Sheikh Mujib made suggestion to Mrs. Indira Gandhi as early as January, 1972 that the Indian armed forces should continue to remain in Bangladesh upto the end of 1972 to neutralize anti-Bangladesh forces which remained operative. Mrs. Gandhi's response was that Indian forces will have no moral or political justification to remain in Bangladesh after his release and his assuming charge as the Prime Minister of Bangladesh. She said she would like to withdraw the Indian forces as early as possible.

Sheikh Mujib came on an official visit to Calcutta in February, 1972. During his discussions with Mrs. Gandhi who had gone to Calcutta for his visit, he conveyed a desire to institutionalize political and security cooperation between India and Bangladesh by means of a treaty or agreement. He said that he would like to sign the agreement in Calcutta itself. Mr. P.N. Haksar, then Principal Secretary to the Prime Minister, correctly pointed out that India should not rush into signing any political or security agreement with Bangladesh and specially on Indian territory, so soon after the liberation of Bangladesh. Pakistan and China as well as the international community would indulge in the motivated criticism that India had pressurised Bangladesh to sign the agreement regardless of what the facts of the matter were. Mrs. Gandhi considered this anticipation valid and told Mujib that while India would stand by Bangladesh in every respect, treaties etc. could wait. It was in Calcutta that Mujib extended a formal invitation to Mrs. Gandhi for an official visit to Bangladesh in March 1972. The dates agreed to were between 17th and 19th March,1972.

Mrs. Gandhi, after her return to Delhi, and consulting her senior Cabinet colleagues, conveyed a message to our army headquarters as well as to our High Commissioner in Dhaka that she was quite clear that all Indian troops should be withdrawn from Bangladesh before she lands in Dhaka, except for portions of a brigade operating against the remnants of the Pakistani forces in the Chittagong hill tracts. Initially Sheikh Mujib was not happy about this decision, but he agreed. He took the salute of Indian Army contingents in Dhaka at a farewell parade on the 12th of March, 1972. All Indian troops were withdrawn back into Indian territory by the 15th of March. Mrs. Gandhi reached Dhaka on the 17th March forenoon. During his one to one discussions with Mrs. Gandhi, Sheikh Mujib again suggested some sort of an institutional agreement on political and defence cooperation. The final decision to sign the treaty was taken on the 18th of March, 1972 while Sheikh Mujib and Mrs. Gandhi alongwith their aides went on a boat cruise between Dhaka and Narayanganj. The exchanges which led to the signing of the agreement had a human and spontaneous political background. Soon after the cruise boat reached the docks at Dhaka, Sheikh Mujib asked Mrs. Gandhi as to what could be the document that could be signed at the end of the visit. The late Mr. P.N. Dhar said there could be a joint press statement. Mujib asked: "What is better than a statement?" Mr. Dhar replied that this could be a joint communique. Mujib then asked what would be more impactful politically than a communique and Mr. Dhar said that it could be a joint declaration by the two Prime Ministers. Mujib continued the discussion asking what would be better than even a joint declaration. Then Foreign Secretary T.N. Kaul said "a treaty of peace, friendship and cooperation. Mujib turned to Mrs. Gandhi and said that he would like to have both a joint declaration and a treaty of peace, friendship and cooperation.

Mrs. Gandhi asked Sheikh Mujib whether he was really keen on both the documents. Mujib replied in the affirmative. Bangladesh Foreign Secretary Inayat Karim and Indian Foreign Secretary T.N. Kaul were directed to start preparing a draft treaty on the boat itself. The task of drafting the joint declaration was entrusted to me and the then Director-General for South and South Asia Division of the Bangladesh Foreign Office Mr. H.M.S. Kibria. Both the documents were then submitted to the Prime Ministers after being vetted by more senior officials and signed on the same day.

Border Conflict : A New Twist in Indo-Bangladesh Relations

The military confrontation between the Border Security Force of India and the Bangladesh Army and Bangladesh Rifles between the 15th and 19th of April, 2001 gives a critical twist to Indo-Bangladesh relations. While reading about the progress of the conflict over three days, one was reminded of a remark by Major General Rao Farman Ali, the politico-military advisor to General Niazi during the 1971 Liberation War of Bangladesh. Farman Ali while being escorted along with other senior prisoners of war to the Indian Air Force Plane turned to his escorting officer and said: "These chaps whom you have liberated, will turn against you. Don't be sure of any long-term friendship with Bengalis. Their antagonism towards you will revive again. Remember they were the greater advocates of the creation of Pakistan".

On DG BDR Fazlur Rehman's statements after the BDR-Bangladesh army operations in the Pyrdiwah, one ruminated whether Rao Farman Ali was prophetic. The crisis in its immediate dimensions seem to have simmered down by the morning of 20th of April. The question remains whether this is the end of the story. What are the implications and prospects of this violent event. This is the second time that such a large-scale military confrontation have taken place between Indian and Bangladeshi security forces in the last 29 years. This latest conflict resulted in large-scale Indian casualties (15 dead, two missing) in a single skirmish. It would be pertinent to recall the background of territorial misunderstandings and then to assess the reasons why this unexpected (from Indian point of view) military confrontation took place. One has to go back to the partition of India to understand the origins of this confrontation.

While demarcating the boundaries between the Indian and Pakistani dominions, the boundary of East Bengal (which was designated as East Pakistan) on the one hand and West Bengal and Assam on the other, was delineated in a manner where some pockets of territories were allocated to East Pakistan or to the Indian states but with populations which had economic and religious affinities in contradiction of the territorial allocations. India came into possession of border areas with Muslim populations with linkages with East Pakistan and East Pakistan came into possession of areas where Hindus lived with linkages with Indian states. The whole phenomenon being described as territories in adverse possession or enclaved, the future status of which was to be resolved by discussions between India and Pakistan. India and Bangladesh inherited this problem. The biggest dispute was about the enclave of *Berubari* which had to go to Bangladesh but access to which had to be through Indian territory. This problem was resolved through painstaking negotiations in 1992 with India providing Bangladesh access to *Berubari* through the *Tin Bigha* corridor. But there are still about 111 such small enclaves in adverse possession of India or Bangladesh, the official jurisdiction on which have not yet been negotiated and settled. More specifically the enclaves on the Assam-Meghalaya -Bangladesh border involves 755 acres of land out of which 520 acress of land is with India and Bangladesh holds 235 acres of land. Minor border skirmishes have occurred off and on the Bangladesh-India border for more than two decades now. But this latest conflict was a regular operation launched by between five or six battalions of Bangladesh army and Bangladesh Rifles. Discussions regarding the settlement of these border enclaves been prolonged despite their being a general political agreement to resolve the problem through dialogue because of the constitutional and legal stipulations regarding the delineation of territory by one country to the other as well as demographic factor of economic and religious linkages of people living in these enclaves on both sides of the border. Another critical facet of the existence of these enclaves is that they form the conduit for smuggling from India into Bangladesh and for illegal migration from Bangladesh into India. As this issue has remained unresolved, it is exploited by those segments of Bangladeshi political and establishment groups which carry a deep-seated suspicions and antagonisms against India. It has also to be acknowledge that after Sheikh Mujibur Rahman's demise both the military and democratic regimes have off and on taken an anti-Indian stance for domestic political gains. It is in this context that one has to analyse the events between the 15th and 19th of April, 2001.

That the Bangladeshi military operation was pre-planned and carefully implemented is obvious because the military incident was not rooted in a sudden and accidental flare up. Nearly five battalions of the 19th Division of the Bangladesh Army with additional personnel from the Bangladesh Rifles launched the attack against the Indian position beyond midnight at 1 a.m. on April 16th. The Bangladeshi forces moved in with heavy infantry weapons and mortars in armoured vehicles from their base in Mymansingh. Apart from evicting the Indian Border Security Forces personnel, the Bangladeshi armed forces, according to preliminary reports acted against the civilian population too. This resulted in most of the villagers (about three thousand in Number) deserting their homes and moving into safer zones in the surrounding countryside.

In his initial statement, the Chief of the Bangladesh Rifles Major General Fazlur Rehman justified the operation of his forces and claimed that he had retrieved the territory which rightly belong to Bangladesh. The persona of Fazlur Rehman must also be taken note of. He belongs to those groups of Bangladesh military officers who are not committed to Bangladesh liberation from Pakistan. He has linkages with the extremist Islamic political parties. He also acquired somewhat assertive and high profile military reputation in Bangladesh because he had prevented Myanmar authorities from building a dam over a river on the Bangladesh-Myanmar border and from strenthening their posts some months ago. He was sure that neither Prime Minister Hasina nor any other political leader could afford to be critical of the action taken by him if he succeeded. He had also expected critical political reaction from India which would give more substance and strength to his overall anti-Indian political orientations. This did not happen. The Government of India's reaction was measured and sober, at the highest political level. Foreign and Defence Minister Jaswant Singh advised the restoration of *status duo ante* and a resolution of problems by dialogue.

The Government of India refrained from making any anti-Bangladesh or assertive statements in contrast to Major General Fazlur Rehman's assertions. There was some criticism in India that our government was underplaying the dangers arising out of this conflict and was not reacting with strength enough. This was not the case. BSF troops from 112th and 74th Battalion of the force moved into the Mancachar area in Dhubri District of Assam in sufficient strength, Senior Indian Officers in the operational area contacted BDR officials suggesting that they withdraw from Indian positions and areas which they had occupied, as otherwise Indian forces would have to launch a limited operations to meet this objective. Parallel to this, Bangladesh High Commissioner in New Delhi and Indian High Commissioner in Bangladesh, were involved in high level diplomatic discussions to defuse the situation. Ultimately good sense prevailed and the policy or restraint worked. India was back in possession of the areas taken over by Bangladesh by the 20th of April and that too without any action. There are reports that Major General Fazlur Rehman spoke to the Direcetor General of the Indian Border Security Force Gurbachan Jagat and conveyed his regrets about the incident. It is significant that India deliberately did not ask for any formal apology and regret to avoid embarrassing the Bangladesh government or senior political leadership of that country. There are, however, reports that the official discussions on the question of compensation for the losses incurred by India, being considered.

One can only speculate about the reasons for this unnecessary and avoidable military incident. The territory involved is very small. Neither the area is economically very important. Therefore, the reasons could be first, Fazlur Rehman's own personal agenda rooted in his political attitudes and sense of importance. Secondly, this being an election year in Bangladesh. The incident could have been engineered by him either on the instigation of Begum Zia's party to embarrass Prime Minister Hasina or some advisers or Prime Minister Hasina could have endorsed the misadventure to prove her credibility about being firm with India during an election year. It is significant that neither Hasina nor Begum Zia-ur-Rehman made any public statement on the incident till the 20th of April. Fazlur Rehman undertaking this adventure autonomously need not be ruled out. His anticipation being that after he had achieved the limited objective, he could then link up with political elements of his voice to influence the Bangladeshi elections. That Bangladesh authorities have been indirectly involved in giving support to Indian secessionist elements from the North East should also be borne in mind which has serious security implications for the North East as well as for the Indo-Bhutan and India-Nepal border.

What then is to be done to manage our important and critical relations with Bangladesh? First, our policy should be underpinned by a deep sense of awareness that Bangladesh is an important neighbour of strategic and political importance to India. Secondly, as an immediate measure, Jaswant Singh should visit Dhaka for high level discussions to clear the atmosphere and bring it back to normalcy, to the extent possible. He should meet not only Sheikh Hasina but Begum Khaleda Zia also. Third, our security forces should be deployed at higher levels of intensity and with greater alertness. Most importantly, India should take the initiative to sort out the issue related to all the enclaves which are a matter of controversy with Bangladesh. We should be as generous as we can to relinquish the enclaves to Bangladesh unless any of them affect our territorial security. This should be done expeditiously because the broader mutuality of interests in the political and economic spheres between India and Bangladesh should take precedence over such problems of small pockets of territory.

10

SINO-INDIAN RELATIONS—AN OVERVIEW

Despite the improvement in India's relations with China since Prime Minister Rajiv Gandhi's visit to China between December 19 and 23, 1988, long-term prospects, questions and speculations persist.

Can the *Celestial Kingdom* and *Mera Bharat Mahan* forge a durable, positive and stable bilateral relationship devoid of under-currents of competition and incipient suspicions? Would China countenance a powerful India on its southern flank? Can India accept a powerful China strategically dominating South East Asia in the Indian Ocean region? These are macro-level question marks on Sino-Indian relations, leaving aside the boundary dispute and other specific issues where there is a difference of opinion between the two countries. In the short term, Sino-Indian relations have shown a qualitative improvement since Mr. Rajiv Gandhi's discussions with Mr. Deng Xiao Ping in Beijing in December, 1988. This trend received a purposive impetus during Chinese Prime Minister Li Peng's visit to India between December 11 and 16, 1991. The leadership of the two countries agreed that the difficult boundary question needs to be tackled with patience over a period of time. It was accepted that in the interim, peace and tranquility should be maintained all along the border. The politically significant consensus was that the boundary question need not be a hurdle against general expansion and improvement of India-China relations.

Consequently, varied contacts at different levels took place. After a gap of nearly three decades Sino-Indian relations were again becoming multi-faceted. Former President Mr. R. Venkataraman visited China in May, 1992. Prime Minister Rao visited China in September, 1993. There has been a stream of visitors moving between the two countries from the political leadership, academic, media, administration, and the scientifie their community.

Significant among these were the visits by former Defence Minister Pawar to China in July, 1992 and of the then Speaker of the Lok Sabha Shivraj Patil leading a delegation of our Members of Parliament early in 1993. From the Chinese side Mr. Li Ruihuan, Chairman of the Chinese Peoples Consultative Committee and a member of the Politburo came to India in November-December, 1993, so did a Vice President of the Chinese Republic, Mr. Liao Hansheng, who came to inaugurate and be present during the Cultural Festival of China held in India late in 1992/ early 1993.

Sino-Indian Agreement on the Maintenance of Peace and Tranquility along the Line of Control in the Indo-China border areas signed in Beijing in September 1993 signified two points: (i) the willingness of the two Governments to ensure an atmosphere of reasonableness and peace in dealing with a tense issue, (ii) that neither Government shies away from the boundary controversy albeit there is a realistic consensus that resolving the boundary dispute will take time. The crucial policy decision of both Governments is that the boundary issue will not be allowed to prevent growth in bilateral relations. This decision is getting translated into action. Agreements for cooperation have been signed between India and China in the spheres of science and technology, environmental management, media and information, space-related technologies and culture.

Apart from the Joint Working Group and its more recently established Expert Group dealing with the boundary question and related matters, there is a Sino-Indian Joint Group on trade, economic, scientific and technological cooperation, which has been meeting regularly to find ways and means to increase trade and other forms of economic exchanges. India is the process of negotiating further agreements with China on establishment of bilateral banking arrangements, shipping links, and avoidance of double taxation. Discussions have been held for establishing cooperation in diverse and new areas like traditional medicines, agriculture, civil aviation, and non-conventional sources of energy. The Joint Group on Economic Cooperation is also examining possibilities of India and China cooperating with each other in joint bidding for project exports and joint ventures in the management and construction fields.

The commodity structure of bilateral trade covers a wide range from agricultural products, industrial raw materials, to sea food, textiles and machine tools. China is keen to develop joint venture iron ore mines in India to ensure supply of iron ore for the Chinese steel industry. There are many Sino-Indian joint ventures already in operation in India. These joint ventures cover the iron ore, pharmaceuticals, ball bearings and specialised glass manufacturing categories. Projects for cooperation in the fields of agriculture, lasers, bio-engineering, and chemistry have also been initiated with a plan of action. These developments portend a friendly and mutually beneficial relationship with China.

Why should this have happened? Leaving aside the larger context of the changed global situation and equations between the Great Powers, there are also some other factors which have contributed to the transformed Chinese attitude towards us. First, Mr. Deng Xiao Ping's world view and regional perspective is more practical, rational and less assertive than that of the previous Chinese leadership. Secondly, the modernization of Chinese economy and the restructuring of internal political arrangements necessitate China having a peaceful and stable environment in its neighbourhood. Thirdly, despite the apparent cohesion of the polity and the party system of China, China has to manage domestic uncertainties at least for the coming decade. Chinese leadership will have to restructure itself and refashion the command and control mechanisms of Chinese politics. The impact of economic modernization of China is not even or balanced within the vast expanse of the Chinese Republic. Economic imbalances between different parts of China are unavoidable in this process. Chinese leadership itself acknowledges problems of distributive justice, social equilibrium and of maintaining political stability, which has to be tackled. Though the Tien-An-Men crisis was met, it was only symptomatic of the fissiparous tendencies.

There are ethno-religious and sub-regional centrifugal forces affecting the Chinese polity from provinces like Sinkiang, Tibet, and so on. While managing these internal trends, China is also engaged in adjusting to the changing world at large, fashioning new relations with Great Powers and the important economic powers. This latter exercise is also not devoid of difficulties and controversies. Overall Chinese approach seems to be to temporise, be practical and to prevent tension with States around it. The approach to India is a part of this process.

India is in a similar predicament. India is also in the process of economic transition, facing requirements of meeting problems generated by this transition. Though our political system is entirely different from that of China, our nation-building effort is going through the processes of restructuring of party systems, refashioning of methods of political consolidation, where institutions, leadership structures, new regional equations between different parts of India are taking place. We are also engaged in the exercise of adjusting economic relations with countries in the region and the world at large. The objective of national re-consolidation through the changes that we are making requires a peaceful, tension-free stable and secure environment around us, a good working relationship with China is *sine quà non* for this purpose.

Emerging positive trends in Sino-Indian relations should be tempered by an awareness of limitations that are there. Though, boundary question remains a hurdle, it has been put in proper perspective in the context of overall relations. China's status as a great political power and a military superpower necessarily affects India's security and regional perceptions. China's views on issues like non-proliferationa and arms control, its relations with Pakistan, and its role in the UN, are all matters on which some distances are endemic to our relations with that country.

In this background, those who over-zealously visualise possibilities of any grand strategic equation between India and China to counter the West or other important centres of power, are suffering from a contrived illusion. Neither the Government of China nor the Government of India have any such thoughts or intentions nor is there any such prospect in the foreseeable future on the other hand, there is a convergence of interests and views on a number of issues which make for cooperative and positive relations.

Both India and China share the perception that the post cold war world has made the situation for developing countries more difficult politically and economically. Both countries have similar reactions to the "tutorial" stance of the western countries on issues like human rights, environment, and political conditionalities governing economic cooperation. Both countries share an imperative concern for maintaining peace and avoiding tensions in the Asian region. Both countries have reservations, about the wish of industrially advanced countries to exercise control on transfer of technologies, trade and investment. Both countries share concerns about ethno-religious, sub-regional and communal forces disrupting existing State structures and the territorial integrity of plural, multi-ethnic, multi-religious nations. These considerations and shared attitudes provide the basis for the constructive and practical lines on which Sino-Indian relations are developing and are sought to be developed.

Premier Li Peng in an interview in September, 1991 before he came to New Delhi said about the logic for Sino-Indian relations "India and China, two great nations, should exchange views on the establishment of new international order, so as to reach a common understanding (on matters of importance). The five principles of peaceful co-existence initiated by China and India should be the norm governing the international order. This is a task that we share. China and India have more and more similar points on major international issues... , the Chinese and the Indian peoples who have created splendid civilisations are seeking areas of greater accomplishments as we move into the 21st century."

Submitting his work report to the National People's Congress on March 15, 1993, Premier Li Peng asserted "improvement and development of Sino-Indian relations will not only conform to the interests of the two peoples, but will also have a positive impact on peace and stability in Asia and in the world as a whole."

These are terms of reference shared by India and form the basis of our policies towards China in recent times.

Sino-Indian Relations: An Appraisal of Trends and Prospects

There has been much activity concerning Sino-Indian relations in the recent past. There has been joint seminars, discussions over maintaining peace on the line of actual control (LAC) but the outcome of these activities has been rather slow. This, however, is not a cause for despair. Indian stance has been predicated on the 'inevitability of slowness or gradualness in making progress in the discussions.' China, too, accepts this predication as it is an established fact that in international relations the most different negotiations are concerned with territorial disputes and boundary settlements.

While accepting the complexity and prospects of delay in resolving the important issues of the Sino-Indian boundary, we must also realise that a prolonged drift in discussions, even if engineered deliberately by both sides, is not a meaningful negotiation. These discussions will lose credibility in both Indian and Chinese public opinion if they do not show some tangible results in the interim—in terms of mutually acknowledged and accepted delineation of the line of actual control, and the implementation of confidence building measures, conceptually envisaged in the Sino-Indian agreement on maintaining peace and tranquility on the Line of Actual Control (LAC). In immediate future of a year or two the Sino-Indian shared approach that the boundary question should be tackled separately in a slower time frame, while other aspects of bilateral relations should be expanded and consolidated, remains in operation. The exchange of visits and discussions, the holding of cultural festivals in each other's countries, the endeavour to increase bilateral trade and augment scientific and technological cooperation, reflect this shared approach. The expectation being that multifaceted and contentful relations will generate mutual trust and educate public opinion in both countries, which will enable the resolution of the complex boundary question. The question has been shelved for practical purposes, but it has to be tackled. It cannot be wished away.

We in India, therefore, must analyse and understand the Chinese approach towards us and the reasons governing that approach. The governing objective of China's recent foreign and defence policies is to ensure an atmosphere of peace and stability in its neighbourhood so that China can carry on its programme of modernisation and economic restructuring without disruptions born of bad relations with neighbours or critical international developments. China's programme of Perestroika is subject to two categories of pressures. Firstly, the ethno-religious fissiparous tendencies emerging in some parts of China and, secondly, the problems of regional imbalances in economic prosperity, affecting different parts of China differently. China needs a stable peaceful relationship with its important neighbours to counter these pressures and meet this overarching objective. The unipolarity of the world with the US as its military and technological magnetic centre is as worrysome to China, as it is to other developing countries. China would be interested in encouraging and consolidating other centres of power to counter this situation. But the practicality of the Chinese psyche does not aim at alliances or formal strategic equations for this purpose. The Chinese approach seems to be to generate a framework, understanding and cooperation based on fashioning a common approach in relation to major issues affecting international relations. This understanding and cooperation are to be built on substantive patterns of bilateral relations, economic, technological and cultural. While China remains a great and nuclear weapon power, it is perhaps a more inward looking China that we are dealing with.

As far as the boundary question goes, we must take note of the fact that China has settled its boundaries with most of its neighbours except with India, Bhutan, and the maritime boundary with Vietnam. Secondly, there is some validity in the argument that the Sino-Indian boundary which became the focus of controversy was based on actions and decisions taken during the colonial period affecting both China and India, and therefore this boundary conceptually need not be treated as unalterable. The first priority should be to implement the mandate of the agreement on peace and tranquility on the line of actual control. A beginning should be made by both sides to disentangling themselves from close confrontation, moving on to removing differences on the location of the line of actual control and putting the military confidence building measures into place. It is time now for the Joint Working Group to give thought to principles on which the boundary should be demarcated and settled.

Both India and China have strategic concerns about different sectors of the Sino-Indian border. So the first principle could be mutual respect for these concerns. The other principles to govern the demarcation could be historical and traditional data, geophysical features accepted by international law and practice for determining boundaries, the boundary to be demarcated on the basis of updated cartographic principles and technology. The Joint Working Group should move gradually towards examining such principles. The approach should be to give up old attitudes and to examine respective claims with historical objectivity and realism. Public opinion in both countries should be made aware of this requirement and educated to look at this matter in a balanced perspective in the larger interest of peace and development in our region.

The frequency, the number and nature of bilateral visits and exchanges confirm shared interests and concerns in and about the evolving international situation. On issues related to international trade and development, human rights, environment, transfer of technology and nurturing technological and security self-reliance, there is a convergence of views and interests between China and India.

So apart from the emotive and cultural factors supportive of Sino-Indian rapprochement, there are substantive factors contributing to the process. These should be encouraged, but India should remain aware of China's status as a great power endowed with nuclear weapons. It, therefore, has its own agenda on non-proliferation, disarmament, missile development, regional arrangements, regional peace and stability as well as the new world order. India's aim should be to establish a practical, generally friendly relationship with China without illusions or excessive expectations.

Sino-Indian Relations— Realities Versus Desirabilities

Chinese Foreign Minister Tang Jiaxuan was in Delhi from the 21st to the 24th of July, 2000. Apart from substantive discussions with Foreign Minister Jaswant Singh, he called on Prime Minister Atal Behari Vajpayee, Leader of the Opposition, Mrs. Sonia Gandhi and did an infrequent thing which the Chinese Foreign Ministers normally do not, do. He gave a news conference. His coming to India following the visit of our President, our Foreign Minister and our Minister for Commerce and Industry to China, over the last ten months, signals the fact that the Sino-Indian relations are on a high and getting back on rails after substantive disruption in the normalisation process which occurred between July and November 1998 in the aftermath of India's nuclear tests and related political pronouncements. At the formal level, the linear continuity of the normalisation process which began with Rajiv Gandhi's visit to Beijing in 1988, stands revived. What one should analyse and speculate on, however, is the prospects of Sino-Indian relations in terms of emerging realities not only in the bilateral context, but in terms of China's economic policies, China's security concerns, and Chinese military capacities and patterns of China's defence cooperation with other countries in our region.

Deliberations of the Apex Bodies of the Chinese Communist Party and its economic planning groups since 1995, indicate the following objectives for the fulfilment of which coordinated action is underway in China:

(a) Acceleration of internal economic development in China, focussing on strengthening the infrastructure, ensuring technological progress and food production;

(b) Modernising Chinese defence capacities, maintaining the strength and operational effectiveness of China's defence forces to meet the evolving global and regional strategic environment and challenges arising therefrom;

(c) Being alert and responsive to any threat to China's internal cohesion and domestic stability;

(d) Augmenting and consolidating energy security as well as technological and financial inputs for economic modernisation of China;

(e) The creation of new strategic and political equations with the important power centres of the world, particularly, the United States, the Russian Federation and the European Union in the post-Cold War context dealing with Japan,

Australia and the ASEAN in the context of China's more immediate security and economic concerns;

(f) Structuring relations with Central Asian and South Asian countries to ensure a stable political and steategic environment so that China can focus on its broader and higher priority objectives undisturbed (This is in particular relations with India, Chinese problems in Tibet and China's concerns about religious and cultural centrifugal forces which can affect western provinces of China).

China's power structure acknowledges that China would face problems of imbalances in development and levels of prosperity between different parts of China by the year 2025. This would include problems of migration from less developed parts of China to more prosperous parts of China, China also faces the prospects of large-scale unemployment. Concerns about energy security has led China to undertake investment and cooperation arrangements in the energy resources sphere with countries of Central Asia, countries in the Gulf and even in distant regions like South America. The most critical political and strategic dimension of this exercise is China's territorial claims in the South China Sea, the Spratley Islands, and so on which has introduced tension in China's relations with important ASEAN countries like Indonesia, Malaysia Philippines and Vietnam.

In terms of internal and external security concerns, China's expectations and aspirations regarding Taiwan remain not only challenged but these challenges stand somewhat augmented with the new Government in Taiwan which at the substantial level is more committed to Taiwan's independence. Political and strategic controversies related to Taiwan and other security considerations have made Japan and the United States move towards deploying

Theatre Missile Defence which is perceived by the Chinese as a substantive strategic threat to its security.

Apart from diplomatic and political initiatives taken by China, to oppose this prospect, China has taken an initiative for expansion and modernisation of its armed forces by domestic efforts as well as large-scale cooperation with the Russian Federation. Between years 2000 and 2004, China is planning to obtain arms and defence technologies of the value of 20 billion dollars from the Russian Federation. This includes armour, aeroplanes, submarines, Uranium centrifuges, and the creation of joint production facilities of defence equipment in China.

Moving down from this macro-level strategic and security exercise, China has created and nurtured defence and security cooperation arrangements with two of India's proximate neighbours, Pakistan and Myanmar, to meet its regional strategic objectives. This is significant in the context of India's adversary relationship with Pakistan and somewhat distant relationship with the military Government of Yangon. Given India's concerns and commitments about democracy, China's defence cooperation with Pakistan and Chinese military presence in the Bay of Bengal and in the northern portions of the Indian Ocean based on defence cooperation with Myanmar is a matter of legitimate security concern to India. It is in this broad strategic context that one should take note of the question of Chinese policies and realities on the ground affecting Sino-Indian relations. China remains concerned and doubtful about India's policies on Tibet. This concern is heightened by the incremental support that the Dalai Lama is getting from the international community. Despite the interim and indirect signals given by China between 1991 and 1994 about China recognising Sikkim's integration with India, China is unwilling to formally acknowledge

Sikkim as being a part of India. Despite dozen or more sessions of the Joint Working Group, held since 1989, the Chinese are in no hurry to address the substantive question of the demarcation of the Sino-Indian boundary. The original impetus given and policy orientations initiated by Deng Xiaoping, Rajiv Gandhi, Li Peng and Narasimha Rao seem to have lost momentum. Fact of the matter is that the Chinese seemed reluctant to take even the interim steps necessary to move towards a solution of the boundary question, namely, to delineate the Line of Actual Control in the seven segments where there is a difference of opinion between India and China about the LAC. The experts'Sub Group, dealing with this issue has not been able to make any substantive progress since 1993. This predicament particularly contradicts the expectations on the basis of which the Sino-Indian Agreement on the Maintenance of Peace and Tranquility on the Line of Actual Control was signed in September, 1993 as also the expectations on which 1996, Confidence Building Measures proposals were agreed upon. While there have been no major tensions or military incidents on the Line of Actual Control for over the last 7 years, there are reports that China is steadily improving road communications and logistical facilities all along their side of the Line of Actual Control "as perceived by them". They have also quantitatively increased patrolling in those areas of the Line of Actual Control on which India has claims and where there is a difference of opinion on where the Line lies. The frequency of such patrols is on the increase, which can become the basis for the Chinese claiming jurisdiction in these areas as they did in the period preceding the Sino-Indian conflict of 1962. The Chinese power structure should also take note of certain broader strategic perception in certain segments of Indian establishment that while China desires a normal relationship with India, they seem insistant about having this normalisation on their terms. There is also an Indian-view that China's relations with Pakistan and Myanmar could be an exercise or creating a Chinese Cordon Sanitaire around India.

The results of Foreign Minister Tang's visit to New Delhi, have to be assessed in this background. The most important decision taken by Tang and Jaswant Singh as announced is that the Joint Working Group should accelerate the process of setting the differences of opinion on the Line of Actual Control. It was also agreed to underpin this process by making institutional arrangements for more regular exchanges on issues related to security, including a military relationship. It is expected that the exchanges of military delegations and discussions on security and strategic issues would commence from this autumn onwards as a result of Tang's visit. If a balance sheet is drawn up about the current state of Sino-Indian relations, it could be this.

- the Sino-Indian Border is relatively peaceful and stable despite the lack of agreements on the Lines of Control and the boundary question.

- some of the operational confidence building measures have been put in place since 1993, but the CBMs agreed upon in 1993 and 1996, can be fully implemented only after problems affecting the Line of Actual Control are settled. There is a gradual expansion of economic and cultural cooperation. The high tension created after India's nuclear tests has abated.

- differences of Opinion on the Line of actual control still remain unresolved. Now there would hopefully be a forward movement.

- China has no inclination to resolve the boundary question. China remains opposed to India's nuclear weaponisation and missile programmes. Chinese Defence Cooperation, particularly with Pakistan remains a major security concern of India to which there has been no satisfactory Chinese response.

- establishing a long-term, stable cooperative relationship with China remains a complicated task which will take time and patience. High level visits like that of Tang and Jaswant Singh's visit to Beijing could contribute to the process. The success of this exercise will also depend on India remaining alert about the realities of Chinese intentions and policies of becoming economically, technologically and militarily strong, to cope with China.

-a measured and practical approach towards China is more desirable option than agitation or jingoistic confrontation with this neighbour of ours.

11

SINO-INDIAN RELATIONS: SLOW DOWN IN MOMENTUM

The signing of the Sino-Indian Agreement on maintenance of Peace and Tranquility on the Line of Actual Control in Beijing on the 7th September, 1993 was the climax of a process of rapprochment which commenced with Mr. Rajiv Gandhi's visit to Beijing in December, 1988. Rajiv Gandhi and Deng Xioping had particularly agreed on a framework for normalising Sino-Indian Relations, the main elements of which were first, that the boundary dispute being a complex one, we will take time to be resolved to mutual satisfaction. Two, since this is so, India and China should gradually build up relations in other spheres of activities for mutual benefit. The initiation and growth of such interaction would create necessary atmosphere of mutual trust and confidence to ultimately tackle the boundary dispute. For the long term period, India and China should agree to reduce tensions on the Sino-Indian border and on the Line of Actual Control. Three, for this latter purpose a joint working group of senior officials from both sides was constituted which will finalise concrete measures to reduce tension and maintain tranquility.

High level visits between senior government figures followed from July, 1991 onwards, including a visit by Premier Li Peng to India in December, 1991 and visits by our President and Prime Minister to China in May, 1992 and September, 1993 respectively.

Chinese and Indian cultural festivals have been held in each other's countries successfully. Cooperation has gained in content in spheres ranging from civil service and financial management to civil aviation and related technologies. While there is certain parallelism of interests between China and India on issues like international stipulations on human rights and management of environment, there are also points of differences on disarmament, vital issue of the boundary, etc. While there was certain measure of momentum and growth in Sino-Indian relations till about the autumn of 1994, one gets the impression that neither India nor China seem interested in focussing attention on bilateral relations and moving forward to resolve boundary question.

It may be recalled that after the signing of the agreement on maintenance of peace and tranquility an experts group was formed under the jurisdiction of Joint Working Group to work out delineation of Line of Actual Control in those sectors where the situation is not clear on the ground. The Experts Working Group was also to work out areas to end close confrontation between Indian and Chinese forward posts facing each other in Arunachal Pradesh. There has been frequent meetings of the Joint Working Group and the Experts Group in 1994 and 1995. Unless the main issues related to ending close confronatation due to the proximity of the Chinese and Indian border posts and unless the uncertain sectors on the line of actual control are defined by mutual agreement two important objectives envisaged in the peace and tranquility agreement cannot be met. First, that a reducing level of military personnel by both countries on the Sino-Indian border and second, moving forward to discuss substance of the boundary dispute.

Though the Sino-Indian relations should be the main focus of our attention and general trends in these relations should be available to Parliament and Public, this has not been the case. One only hopes that the Standing Committee of our Parliament on External Affairs remains interested and fully informed in these aspects of Sino-Indian relations.

Sino- Indian trade has been increasing total volume of trade between India and China in the year 1994 recorded an increase of more than 32.4 per cent, over the volume of trade in 1993. While from 1990 to 1993 Balance of Trade was generally in India's favour, the trend has been reversed with China having a favourable balance of trade. China has a number of joint ventures in India, most of them based on buy back arrangements. These joint ventures are in the spheres of Iron, metallurgy, spare parts for civilian aircraft, etc. Indian companies have also begun to establish joint ventures in China. Companies like Ranbaxy and Hero Motors pioneered the trend by entering into arrangements to manufacture their products with Chinese collaboration in China.

While these trends of interaction is increasing gradually, the overall pattern seems to be that of very slow process. It will be relevent to analyse Indian figures in Chinese scheme of things and China as visualized by us at this stage of our foreign relations.

The indication regarding Chinese assessment of India for the immediate and long-term was there in an article on India's Politics and Society which appeared in the newspaper of the Chinese Army, *The Liberation Army Daily* during one of its 1992 issues. The article gave the assessment that though India is a large country with large population with sufficient raw material, technology and human resource capacity, India's society was not disciplined enough to fully exploit these advantages to become a influential power in the region or in the world. The article also assesses Indian Republic as a soft state enmeshed in too many controversies with its neighbours. The final assessment was that while China should maintain stable relations with India, it should concentrate more on Japan, and the ASEAN region in Asia and US and Russia, the super powers who can affect China's well-being. As far as India's assessment of China goes, it is realistically acknowledged that China is a super power with nuclear weapons capacity. While India is willing to work out a fair and just solution to the boundary dispute, India also realises that China may not be in a great hurry to resolve the substance of this issue because China is satisfied with the present situation on the ground. While India acknowledges Tibet as autonomous part of Chinese Republic, it is of the view that China should be more responsive to the religious and political aspirations of the people of Tibet. This view is not just generic but has been conveyed at political level by India to China. What is interesting is that Chinese response was not negative or polemical though they expressed concern about possibility of India being used as a base for dis-affection against the Chinese by the Tibetans.

India is also carefully monitoring Chinese policies and activities in the Asia Pacific Region. China's keenness to open up another border trade point into India through *Nathu La* is indicative of China's continuing interest in enhancing its political influence in the eastern part of India and on border states of Nepal and Bhutan. The desire of the Chinese to open up trade routes from *Gyantse-Gartok* to *Kalimpong* via *Nathu La* has political and security implications both for India and Bhutan which should be considered with much more care and abundant caution.

We must take note of the fact that apart from claims to Spratly Islands of Vietnam, the Chinese are now laying claims to certain islands north of Indonesia and Philippines. China has steadily increased its activities and influence in Myanmar. These are politico-strategic developments which have to taken into account while formulating our China policy.

Chinese active interest in participating in ASEAN and the APEC and the role that China has played as an intermediary between North Korea on the one hand and Japan and US on the other during the North Korean nuclear contratemps are perceived by India as part of their strategic plans of Chinese foreign policy. China's large scale import of arms from Russia, is also a factor affecting the security environment of our region.

China's interest in normal stabilised relations with India is limited to ensuring that developments in the sub-continent or in Tibet do not affect China's stability and Security. China does not desire to get us involved too closely in the regional activites and it was proved by India not being invited to an international conference held in Beijing on the subject: "China and its Neighbours, Economic Relations in the region of rapid growth." It is interesting that Pakistan was represented at that conference by its Finance Minister Makhdoon Shahabuddin. It should be added that while China has taken equi-distant and impartial posture between India and Pakistan on the Kashmir issue the range and content of China's economic and defence relationship with Pakistan is greater than what they have with India and this trend will remain constant.

Given this general ambience our policy has been that of maintaining relations on an even keel. Competition or confrontation are not elements of our policy towards China and they should not be. But at the same time after having remedied the situation of mutual isolation and distances, we must let our bilateral relations drift. There is considerable scope for increasing our cooperation in the spheres of trade, technology, culture and investments. We must take initiatives and motivate the Chinese to increase interaction in these spheres. At the same time a greater political push to the work of joint working group and its experts panel should complete their tasks envisaged in the agreement on Peace and Tranquility to further the cause of normalisation of our relations. We must remain alert to strategic challenges and strategic opportunities that may emerge in China's policies in the Asian region as well as in relation to important powers of the world. We must not be reticent in countering the strategic challenges where they affect our interests in any manner. And we must not be inhibited in utilising the opportunities to further these interests according to our needs.

China in Indian Eyes—Current Perceptions

China is one of the two most important neighbours India has the other being Pakistan. It is about time India examined how China should figure in our scheme of things in the context of its concerns and its external orientations. What kind of China are we likely to deal with? How is China going to behave in relation to the great powers, in relation to South East Asia, in the Asia Pacific region? What are our value judgements about China's political predicament, its economic interests and its perceptions about its own role in Asia and the world at large?

The dates for President Jiang's visit now stands finalised. He is expected to be in New Delhi for about two days from November the 20th. There has been a revival of Sino-Indian interaction in preparation for this visit since the second half. The experts group dealing with maintenance of peace and tranquility on the line of actual control had a meeting in Beijing in September 1996 : The Sino-Indian Joint working Group met in Beijing on the 14th of October, 1996. Both these meetings took place after a comparatively long gap of one year, instead of meeting once in six months, as is the norm. The reason for Sino-Indian interaction being in a state of drift was because of the domestic political preoccupations of both China and India. Both countries faced domestic political difficulties on which their respective leaderships were concentrating their attention. The revival of these bilateral meetings resulted in the much needed the galvanising impulse. Sino-Indian relations naturally depend on our perceptions about China and our attitude towards issues constituting important ingredients in Sino-Indian relations. First, the existentialist characteristics of China which we should perceive. China is territorially and demographically the largest nation-state on the Asian land mass and the Asia Pacific region. Secondly, it has potentialities of becoming the most important economic power in this region. Third, it is a dominant strategic entity endowed with nuclear and conventional military capacities. Fourth, despite its denying any claims for regional dominance, China has always considered itself the most important politico-cultural entity in Asia. The evolving Chinese domestic, political and foreign policy ethos merit evaluation. The over-arching Chinese predicament is that of its going through profound processes of transition. There are many facets of this transition. There is going to be a change in the highest levels of the power structure of China with the inevitability of Deng Xiaoping's fading away from the scene. Jiang had emphasized the need to have China's "spiritual civilisation as the fundamental terms of reference for national consolidation and reconstruction", as opposed to interim compulsions of "material civilisation". The first of these jargons refers to maintaining the commanding priority of Chinese Communist political doctrines and philosophy. The second jargon "materialist civilisation" refers to the economic and political trends generated by the economic modernisation and reforms programmes in China. The plenum's final communique declared that the party should be "resolute in tightening the grip on both civilisational trends, while maintaining the supremacy of the spiritual civilisation from the start to the end." The communique went on to say "At no time can we sacrifice the spiritual values in the name of momentary economic development." This declaration is expressive both of the concerns and the intentions of the Chinese power structure. The concern that economic liberalisation may generate impulses of political liberalism and democracy which needs to be checked; the indication that the leadership of the Chinese Communist Party will firmly oppose trends towards political liberation and democracy to the extent possible. Economic modernisation and reforms have been asymmetrical in geographic terms in China. Despite the image of discipline, integration and unity of the power structure which China projects, the relationship between the armed forces and the younger generation of political leaders is going through a critical phase. The older leadership which has moved away from centre stage had the advantage of being participants in the military struggles which led to Mao Tse-tung's victory over the Kuomintang. The younger generation of leaders of the party and the armed forces are not endowed with the shared experience. They have grown in compratively compartmentalized activities requiring mutual understanding of each other's role and adjustments in power equations at the apex political level. Lastly, China is adjusting its political and strategic stances aimed at new equations which it wishes to establish as a more open and outward looking society. The ramifications of this predicament in China's foreign policy are that it desires a peaceful and stable environment in its neighbourhood and in the Asia Pacific region, so that China can fully concentrate on its domestic developmental and political stabilization objectives. Secondly, China remains firm in reacquiring its territorial identity as conceived by it. Having integrated Hong Kong China aims at Taiwan, Macao and the territorial seas to be integrated into metropolitan Chinese territory. China is firm on nurturing its great power status in economic and military terms. China perceives for it a central role in Asian developments in the 21st century. It wishes this to be acknowledged in the foreign policies of all Asian countries even if this expectation is not articulated in so many words. It is a powerful China in transition that we are dealing with. China's inherent capacities and its foreign policy stances necessarily make it an important factor in our foreign policy planning. Though Sino-Indian relations have taken a positive turn and relations are improving gradually Indian public opinion perceives China as a strategic competitor and a potential adverse politico-military particularly because of the ongoing defence cooperation between China and Pakistan which includes the sensitive spheres of missile development and nuclear activities. India would also be concerned if China's relations with the South East Asian Countries assume security or military dimensions of an operational nature. Therefore, there is no Indian desire for the revival of any emotional closeness of the type with China which we presumed in the late 1940s and early 1950s. This is as it should be. India and China, however, have parallel interests as developing Asian countries in creating inter-regional equilibrium with the powerful Western countries in a manner so that the latter do not intrude into our political management of our own societies or impinge on our freedom of options in determining our economic policies. China is figuring and should figure in our scheme of things as an important factor affecting our stability; Our objective should be to structure a realistic and practical relationship with China, a relationship which will address the boundary usual devoid of emotionalism of the past and discarding the inaccurate historical and cartographic arguments which led to the boundary crisis between 1956 and 1962. Our relations should be mature and balanced enough for both sides to be able to candidly articulate concerns about each other's policies and attitudes on specific usuals like Tibet, Sino-Pak defence Cooperation, and to see how they can be overcome. We should be able to caution China about the negative implications of its arms supplies to and nuclear cooperation with Pakistan. The Chinese should be able to voice their concerns about Tibet without getting impatient or offended about it. Both sides must now lay the foundations of a stable relationship despite the undercurrents of politico-strategic rivalry in the larger interest of both the countries.

President Narayanan in China—An Assessment

President Narayanan was initially invited to visit Beijing in 1999, while China comemmorated the 50th anniversary of the establishment of the People's Republic of China. Narayanan could not visit Beijing in 1999 due to various political reasons, most important of which was the Government of India desiring to make a comprehensive assessment of Sino-Indian relations so that there was no embarrassment or inhibitions on both sides following the complications which arose in Sino-Indian relations after India's nuclear tests of 1998 and the tentative thaw which followed Foreign Minister Jaswant Singh's visit to Beijing in the second half of 1999. I was told during my visit to Beijing in October 1999 that the Chinese were looking forward to the visit of President Narayanan for two reasons; First, India was the first among the countries who gave recognition to the People's Republic of China when it was established. Secondly, President Narayanan is held in special esteem by the Chinese due to the tact and political sensitivity with which he discharged his role as India's Ambassador to Beijing when Mrs. Indira Gandhi restored diplomatic relations with China to ambassadorial level.

This was a presidential visit to China after a gap of 8 years. President Venkataraman had visited Beijing in May 1992. The political conext in which the visit took place is also significant. While there is no delusion about China's critical stance on India's nuclear weaponisation, its stridency had abated because of non-ratification of the CTBT by the USA, the US stand on Theatre Missile Defence in the Western Pacific, and most importantly USA's announcements at the Review Conference on Non-Proliferation in New York about its inclination to dilute the Anti-Ballistic Missile Treaty. There was tangible, though gradual normalisation in interaction between India and China after Foreign Minister Jaswant Singh's discussions with his Chinese counter-part Tang Jiaxuan. The Indo-Chinese Joint Working Group on the boundary question and related issues had met, a general agreement had been reached for having an institutionalised security dialogue with China and there were indications that Sino-Indian economic relations should be brought back on track after the hiccups of 1998 and early 1999. Though our President does not exercise executive responsibilities (he is head of State and not Head of Government), the Chinese were conscious of his personal background which they knew would be impactful on India's foreign policy. Apart from his foreign service background of three decades and more, President Narayanan had specialised knowledge about China because he dealt with China and East Asia in the mid-60s, as a Director in the Ministry of External Affairs. Apart from being Ambassador to China, his comprehension of political and strategic issues affecting Sino-Indian relations and China's foreign policy, was rooted in his having served in South East Asia as Ambassador and also having been Ambassador to the USA, when Sino-US relations commenced their positive orientations.

President's weeklong visit to China was in every sense more than a ceremonial visit. The programme drawn up for the President reflected this dimension. Narayanan had discussions with President Jiang Zemin, Prime Minister Zhu Rong ji and also with former Prime Minister Li Peng, who, with Narasimha Rao brought about qualitative changes in Sino-Indian relations between 1991 and 1995. Our President was invited to speak to the Faculty and students of Beijing University, perhaps the first time that an Indian President addressed the University. Most significantly, instead of being taken to visit places of cultural and historical interest outside Beijing, he was invited to visit Kunming in Southern China, capital of the Yunan Province, an area abutting our North Eastern States with which prospects of economic and commercial relations are being examined by think-tanks and policy planners, both in China and India. Reports indicate that our President had wide-ranging and substantive discussions with the Chinese leadership on issues affecting bilateral relations, regional security and economic problems as well as international issues like terrorism, human rights, UN reforms and problems related to international regimes affecting trade, transfer of technologies and developmental processes. There is a certain parallelism and convergence of interests between India and China on this latter category of issues.

Having said this, one has to acknowledge that both sides assiduously avoided any detailed discussions on issues about which there are basic differences between China and India. The Chinese did not hold forth on India's nuclear weaponisation and avoided polemics on the isssue. Measured reticence was practised on issues related to India's concerns about the formal Chinese stance on Sikkim and

China's concerns about Tibet rooted in the activities of Dalai Lama's followers in India. While China shared India's anxieties about international terrorism and the need to counter it, the Chinese policy stance on Kashmir and their defence and nuclear cooperation with Pakistan remained unchanged. Discussions regarding the most fundamental issue affecting Sino-Indian relations, namely, the boundary question remained anodyn. The general conclusion reached was that the Joint Working Group should continue its efforts to expeditiously resolve the pending issues related to the implementation of the 1993 agreement on maintaining peace and tranquility on the Line of Actual Control, that further progress should be made in implementing Confidence Building Measures, to enhance mutual and equal security between the two countries, and the resolution of substantive issues related to the demarcation of the boundary between the two countries, will be a gradual process, and that it should not stand in the way of expansion and consolidation of Sino-Indian relations on a broad front.

President Narayanan's strong conviction about the international community cooperating to counter unipolar trends in international relations were shared by the Chinese leadership.

What then were the concrete results of this important visit, to China? The Indian Presidential visit signifies the end of a critical phase in Sino-Indian relations which commenced after India's nuclear weapons tests in 1998. The visit has resulted in a high level first hand assessment being made by the leaderships of the two countries about each other's perceptions and policy orientations. The visit resulted in an agreement to bring Sino-Indian relations fully back on track on those areas where there is agreement and mutual parallelism or complementarity. It was agreed that the differences of opinion on some very basic issues while being acknowledged, should not stand in the way of moving forward in other areas where relations can be expanded. It is clear that China is not inclined to address the Sino-Indian boundary issue expediciously. Nor is there any likelihood of China diluting its defence and defence supplies cooperation arrangements with Pakistan, despite its concerns about cross-border terrorism and the spread of Islamic centrifugal forces in certain areas of China. These realities should underpin our China policies despite the generally positive impact of the Presidential visit. The over-arching reality which we should keep in mind is the asymmetry between India and China. The larger military and economic strength of China compared to that of India, should caution India that Sino-Indian relations are not entirely based on mutual complementarities, but that they should aim at generating stabilising atmosphere to remedy the above imbalances and to temper those dimensions of China's policies which should be of political and strategic concern to India.

President Narayanan's visit served the purpose of giving an impetus to a progressive normalisation of relations and of countering potentialities of tension and conflict in the context of Sino-Indian differences on a number of vital issues mentioned above. If the President's meetings with the Chinese leadership served the purpose of creating an incremental environment of trust, it augers well for Sino-Indian relations.

India-China Security Talks— A Contextual Analysis

Indian and Chinese delegations met in Beijing from the 6th to the 8th of March, 2000 for a security dialogue which was agreed upon during Minister for External Affairs, Mr. Jaswant Singh's visit to Beijing in July, 1999. This bilateral official interaction on security matters is the very first between the two countries. There have been high level exchanges on global issues, the international strategic environment and on regional developments between China and India since early 1950s from Pandit Nehru's times. There was an interregnum between 1962 and 1976, but from 1979 onwards when the present Prime Minister Atal Behari Vajpayee went to Beijing, such high level exchanges stood revived. Such contacts continued during the tenures of office of Mrs. Indira Gandhi, Rajiv Gandhi and Narasimha Rao, and Mr. I.K. Gujral. However, the discussions held at official level between the 6th and 8th of March 2000 are unique because instead of a broad survey, officials dealing with security and strategic matters were engaged in issues-specific and region-specific discussions on security matters and their shared assessments and prognosis on the developing strategic and security environment, at the operational and technical levels.

The Indian delegation was led by the Joint Secretary Incharge of Arms Control and Disarmament, in the Ministry of External Affairs, Rakesh Sood. The Chinese delegation was led by the Director General of the Asian Department of the Chinese Ministry of Foreign Affairs Zhang Jiuhan. The decision that such security dialogue should take place originated in the exchanges between Prime Minister Narasimha Rao and Prime Minister Li Peng in September 1991 and September 1993. The Sino-Indian agreement on Maintenance of Peace and Tranquility signed in September 1993, has a specific provision that both countries shall endeavour to further the cause of mutual and equal security. Further informal exchange of views on security matters continued in the meetings of the Sino-Indian Joint Working Group on the Boundary question and particularly during President Jiant Zemin's visit to Delhi in November, 1996.

India's nuclear weapon tests of 1998 and the statements by the Indian Defence Minister and Prime Minister that one of the reasons for India's acquiring nuclear weapons, is perceived Chinese threat, created a crisis in Sino-Indian relations and the consequence was that the political and security dialogue which was being held at informal functional level, was discontinued. To resume the security dialogue separately from the Joint working Group under a specific institutional arrangement was one of the most significant results of Foreign Minister Jaswant Singh's discussions with his Chinese Counter-part Tang Xijuan. The importance and implications of Sino-Indian dialogue held in Beijing between the 6th and 8th of March needs to be assessed in the more immediate context as well as in the broader orientations of China's strategic thinking. The ingredients of the immediate context are that this is the first security dialogue after India's nuclear and missile weaponisation and that it was held despite Chinese strong criticism of India's nuclear weapons and missiles acquisition policies. The dialogue was held despite India's objections to China's defence cooperation linkages and defence assistance programmes with Pakistan. And despite China's continuing commitment to continue its relationship with Pakistan.

The talks were held in the context of Sino-Indian boundary despite still remaining unresolved and China's territorial claims vis-a-vis India, and in the South China Sea and some adjacent areas. China is critical of US-Japan security arrangements and emerging additional dimensions of it like the proposal for theatre missile defence to be provided by the US to Japan. Taiwan remains a high point of tension between China on the one hand and Japan, the US and Taiwan on the other. There are undercurrents of apprehension about China's future assertiveness among South East Asian countries and some thought is being given to evolve counter-vailing strategic equations between important countries in the regions of South Asia, and South East Asia.

Keeping in mind its objections to the US moves to set up a national missile defence system for itself and regional theatre missile defence for East Asia, and in the context of tensions related to Taiwan, China increased its defence expenditure 12.7 per cent more than the previous year's defence budget, on the very day when Sino-Indian dialogue commenced, on the 6th of March. Chinese Finance Minister Xiang Huaicheng announced that China's defence expenditure would be of the order of 120.5 Billion Yuan, equivalent to US dollars 14.5 billion. China would be spending about 1.40 per cent of its GDP and 8.2 per cent of its budgetary expenditure to maintain its armed forces numbering 2.5 million personnel. There are also reports of additional amounts being allocated by China to acquire high tech weapons of all categories and to improve its nuclear and missile arsenal. Most of these sophisticated defence supplies are being obtained from the Russian Federation, in the context of both Russia and China having agreed to strategic partnership to ensure regional stability since Jiang Zemin's visit to Moscow in 1998. In the context of USA's over-arching military and political impact on international relations, China is also engaged in structuring strategic and security equations with important powers of the world.

It is necessary to assess the significance and prospects of this Sino-Indian dialogue. Beijing's attitude towards South Asian and South East Asian countries which are of particular relevance to us, without doubt are based on China's current perceptions about likely developments in regional politics and power equations. These views and doubts are inevitably influenced by China's own military and technological capacities. China has undergone profound transformation over the two and half decades. It has undertaken an extensive economic modernisation and reforms successfully. China's strategic and external policies are subject to the following objectives and motivations:

At present China wishes to concentrate primarily on domestic political consolidation and economic development. The focus is inwards. It is China's assessment that an atmosphere of stability and peace around China is essential to meet its priority objectives of internal stability and economic development. China, therefore, desires a practical and cooperative working relationship with all its neighbours and other important power centres of the world like, the USA, Russia, West Europe and Japan. This approach of cooperation is subject to the rider that China shall not compromise in any manner about its territorial, strategic and security interests. There is a deep but unarticulated conviction in China that its destiny is that of becoming a world power with super power status. It will, therefore continue to build its technological and defence capacities with a view to countering external challenges from other technologically advanced countries. An additional objective is to prevent any of the existing nuclear powers from dominating the world scene and also prevent, if possible, the emergence of additional nuclear powers in its neighbourhood.

It is in this background that we assess the significance and the prospects of Sino-Indian security dialogue and its institutional continuance. The asymmetry between the larger military and economic strength of China compared to India should caution India that the security and strategic dialogue is based not on complementarities but aimed at generating a stabilising atmosphere to remedy the above imbalance. The dialogue is also aimed at counter potentialities of tension and conflict in the context of differences of opinion on the boundary question between the two countries. The dialogue is also aimed at creating an incremental environment of trust which could lead to the resolution of the boundary question. The bilateral exchange of views could also serve the purpose of removing misunderstandings about India's nuclear and missile weaponisation and structuring a political and strategic understanding on non-proliferation and arms control issues. The dialogue would also serve the purpose of evolving an understanding between India and China on issues affecting South and South East Asian security in general, and perhaps in reducing tensions between India and Pakistan. A stable relationship of security and understanding between China and India will temper Pakistani adventurism and extremism despite Sino-Pakistan defence cooperation.

All these are not only desirable but objectives of immediate relevance. The security discussions between India and China is on all counts a positive political and strategic development in our region.

The Karmapa Crisis in Sino-Indian Relations

The 14-year old Ugyen Trinley Dorji, the 17th Gyla Karmapa, the head of the Karmapa or Kagyu Sect of Mahayana Buddhism, has been the centre of public attention and controversy in the early part of year 2000 His escape from Tibet into India has generated complexities in the Tibetan community in India, in the power politics of the Rumtek Monastery, the headquarters of his sect in Sikkim, in India and at the macro-level created an issue of tension between India and China. Resolving problems created by his escape to India also involves Indian policy stances on human rights, on the question of relations between the state and religion and attitude towards politics in the Tibetan community in India.

Mentioning some factual background about the Karmapa Sect, and events attending the selection of this

17th Karmapa, would be relevant to understand the issues involved. The Kagyu sect of Buddhism is one of the most influential sects, not only in Tibet, but the sect commands widespread following in Sikkim, Bhutan and the North Eastern States, especially in Arunachal Pradesh, and to a limited extent in Ladakh. The reigning Karmapa has always been the third ranking most important and religious and temporal figure in Buddhist politics in Tibet and its adjacent regions, ranking after Dalai Lama and Panchan Lama.

The selection and the detemination of reincarnation of every new Karmapa is determined by the same procedure which is followed on the selection of the Panchan Lama and the Dalai Lama. In some respects after the decline of the influence of the Dalai Lama in Tibet, the temporal influence and physical resources of the Karmapa sect, have been the most noticeable. The sect and its Monasteries are rich and influential. Consequently, there has been continuing struggle between different factions of Monks belonging to the Sect, particularly those manning the Rumtek and other main Monasteries, over the physical resources and on reigning Karmapa. This situation has been compounded by the Chinese Government's incremental desire to control the religious power structure in Tibet, which is a part of Chinese exercise in progressive integration of Tibet with Metropolitan China. The origins of the current controversy about the escape of the 17th Karmapa from Tibet into India, are rooted in this combination of factors. The specific background of the appointment of the 17th Karmapa is even more relevant to the points at issue now. Rival candidates for the position of the Karmapa were sponsored between 1989 and 1991, one by a section of the Monks of the Rumtek and other by the Chinese. The Rumtek Monastery faction tried to pressurise the Government of India through Sikkimese Government to ensure the installation of its candidate and prevent the arrival of the

Chinese nominee. The Dalai Lama has a crucial role in the nomination of the Head of this sect because confirmation of his position depends on Dalai Lama's approval. I recall the initial manoeuverings regarding appointment of Karmapa from my days as Foreign Secretary. The Government of India took the principled position that it is not for any particular group or Monks from Rumtek Monestery or the Chinese Government to decide as to who should be Karmapa. The confirmation of the reincarnation of the 16th Karmapa was to be based on clearly defined and traditional tests plus the rituals. The authenticity and legitimacy has to be finally confirmed by the Dalai Lama. Whomsoever the Dalai Lama confirms in the position, would have the legitimacy. The Government of India will not get involved. This policy stance was also predicated on the logical assumption that His Holiness the Dalai Lama's decision would be accepted by the followers of the Sect as well as by the Tibetan Community in general. The difficulties about the nomination of the Karmapa was ultimately resolved in the mid-90s by the Dalai Lama accepting the nomination and selection made by the Chinese Government. The Chinese authorities, however, did not allow the Karmapa (Ugyen Trinley Dorji) to come to Rumtek monastery and occupy the religious throne, at the Headquarters of his sect. The logic of this measure was obvious. The Chinese authorities desired the centre of power of this sect to be located within Tibet itself under their political and territorial jurisdiction. This has been the part of their general policy not only to exercise control over temporal and political affairs of Tibet, but also over religious affairs with a view to gradually metamorphosis the autonomous identiy of Tibet.

The 17th Karmapa's arrival in India on the 5th of January, 2000, has created a situation for India which India could have done without. His arrival has revived rival candidatures for his position. Two more have emerged at Rumtek and the Chinese have hilariously discovered another incarnation of 16th Karmapa while the first incarnation, the 14-year old Dorji is still alive. His arrival has generated dissensions as well as political and theological controversies within Tibetan community. The internal contradictions within the Tibetan community and the religious establishment, need not be a major concern of the Government of India in terms of ripple effects, as it does not generate additional tensions between India and China. This latter reservation remains relevant because, one of the understandings which the Dalai Lama gave to India, when he came and settled down in India, was that he and his followers will refrain from political activities, particularly of the category which may impinge on Sino-Indian relations. This understanding has not been fully adhered to in recent years. What is more relevant at the Governmental level is the manner in which we should deal with the Chinese reaction to the 17th Karmapa's escape into India. Chinese spokesmen have cautioned India from giving political refuge or asylum to the Karmapa. They have implied that India giving asylum to Karmapa would be a contradiction of the Principles of Peaceful Co-existence and that it can affect Sino-Indian relations negatively.

Our response to the Chinese message has been undulatory and somewhat defensive. This is not necessary. Two of the principles of peaceful co-existence are mutual respect and respect for sovereignty and territorial integrity of each other. Non-interference in each other's internal affairs is the third Principle relevant in this context. It would be partinent to tell government of China that their cautionary note to us referring to the Five Principles of peaceful co-existence, applies to the Government of China also. There is a mutuality about the application of these Principles, which is sacrosanct. It should be pointed out to the Chinese Government that the 17th Karmapa who was their nominee, voluntarily left Tibet due to reasons with which India has nothing to do. Nor did India play any role in his escape from China into India. India has assiduously refrained from interferring in the internal affairs of China, especially related to developments in Tibet. We have remained constant in our policy of recognising Tibet as Autonomous Region of China. The Karmapa's coming to India is a matter between him and the Chinese authorities. The granting or not granting refugee and political asylum to him, when he is in Indian territory is a matter of sovereign discretion of the Government of India, which does not constitute any challenge to China's jurisdiction over Tibet or India interferring in Chinese affairs. China giving any other interpretation or making demands on the basis of such interpretations is not logical, politically or in terms of international law. In fact, China should respect India's sovereignty and territorial jurisdiction in the matter of granting asylum. It should also be emphasised to the Chinese that India attaches importance to its relations with China and desires normal and expanding contacts, and that Sino-Indian bilateral relations have much larger and diverse dimensions that the case of an individual Buddhist leader coming away from China because of problems he might have had with the Chinese authorities. Sustaining of normal bilateral relations and improving them would depend on India and China focussing on the larger issues of resolving the boundary question, expanding economic, cultural, scientific and technological cooperation and structuring an environment of security and stability by mutual consultations. It should be clearly indicated that India will not be subjected to pressure on issues which fall within its sovereign jurisdiction. Whether, we in our own judgement, give political asylum or not, to the Karmapa, is a different matter. And the conditions under which such asylum may be given, will be consistent with our policies on Tibet. The over-riding principles among the Principles of the *Panch Shila,* to be adhered to in this case is equality and mutual respect. Unilateral demands have no place in Sino-Indian relations.

Li Peng's Visit to India - A Step Forward in Sino-Indian Relations

Li Peng, Chairman of the Standing Committee of the National People's Congress of China (the Chinese Parliament) visited India in the first half of January, 2001 accompanied by a large delegation of Chinese officials, businessmen and political aides. His visit has breathed a fresh life into the Sino-Indian relations. The significances of the visit has to be assessed in terms of his personal contributions for Sino-Indian relations over the last decade, his current stature in the Chinese political system and the regional environment in which he undertook this visit to India. Li Peng has a certain external image of having been the architect of the suppression of the Tiananmen Democratic Movement in 1989. But singling out him as the sole leader responsible for the decision would be unfair to him. It was a collective decision by the orthodox and authoritarian segment of the leadership of the Communist Party led by Deng Xiaoping. The twin motives which Li Peng manifested at that point of time were, to focus on China's economic modernisation and reforms and to ensure the necessary political stability within the Chinese State. It must be remembered that Li Peng and the senior leadership of China had trends towards disintegration of the Soviet Union very much on their minds to face the upsurge of democratic impulses questioning the authorities in China. In moral terms, Li Peng comes out as a negative and authoritarian personna, but in terms of Realpolitik, Deng Xiaoping and Li Peng ensured the continuation of China's journey towards the path of modernisation and world power status. What is of greater significance is the role that LI Peng played in Sino-Indian relations during his tenure as Prime Minister of China till 1996-1997 and thereafter. It need to be remember that it was during his Premiership that high level visits between India and China came to be revived after Rajiv Gandhi's path-breaking visit to Beijing in December 1988. Li Peng's visit to Delhi and discussions with the then Prime Minister Narasimha Rao translated the decisions taken during Rajiv Gandhi's meetings with Deng Xiaoping into operational policies. Substantial negotiations were undertaken by Sino-Indian Joint Working Group on the Boundary question which led to the signing of the Sino-Indian Agreement on the Maintenance of Peace and Tranquility on the Line of Actual Control in September 1993.

President Ventakaraman had visited Beijing in May 1992, followed by Prime Minister Narasimha Rao's visit in September 1993. Present Prime Minister Zhou Rongji. Chinese President Jiang Zemin and the Chinese Chief of the Army Staff visited India in the second half of last decade. It would not be an exaggeration to point out that Li Peng's assessments about India and his advice had their influence at the back of these interactions. The substantive orientations in Sino-Indian Relations signified in these contacts were the following:

Both India and China decided to move away from the negative historical memories affecting their relations from 1960 to the 1990s. This, however, did not mean that China or India decided to by-pass critical perceptions about each other or to reduce the importance of resolving specific critical issues, like the boundary dispute. In fact, a conscious decision was taken that since the boundary dispute is not likely to be resolved quickly, India and China should create and expand relations in other spheres where there is mutual complementarity and mutual benefit. The prognostication being that the normalisation and expansion of bilateral relations would lead to necessary atmosphere of mutual trust, confidence and an inclination towards compromise which might create the atmosphere to resolve the boundary question. That this complementarity in each other's needs in certain economic and technological spheres, bilateral relations stand acknowledged and a decision is to enhance cooparation in these fields. There are also certain multilateral issues like Management of environment, stipulation of external standards of human rights. WTO trading arrangements, on which there is a parallelism in Indian and Chinese approaches. Though there are fundamental differences between India and China on the issue of non-proliferation of nuclear weapons and related issues. China has adopted a realistic approach towards India on this matter, after the initial critical reactions due to India's mentioning China as a specific factor leading to its nuclear weaponisation. China's defence supplies and defence cooperation relationship with Pakistan and its supplying materials and technology for the nuclear weaponisation and missile weapons capacities of Pakistan has been a worrying factor to India which has been conveyed to China.

Li Peng's visit to India was obviously permeated by awareness of these trends and mutual interaction. Significant characteristics of the Politico-strategic environment in which he visited India should be taken note of. The critical and hostile fall out of India's nuclear weaponisation has been overcome to some extent by the exchanges between President Narayanan and External Affairs Minister Jaswant Singh and their Chinese counterparts over the last two years. China's security concerns are focussed on the implications of US's moving forward on programmes of Theatre Missile Defence in the Western Pacific and development of National Missile Defence. The renewal of US-Japanese security arrangements is another security concern of China. China also faces centrifugal and fissiparous movements in Xinjiang and in

Tibet. Though China has a great record of economic achievements, it is still likely to face problems like unemployment, uncontrollable migration movements from rural to urban areas and the problem of food security. The Chinese took note of India's nuclear weaponisation and missile capabilities as a factor affecting its security environment to some extent. India's overcoming its political, economic and strategic isolation resulting from India's nuclear tests of 1998, the qualitative improvement in India's relations with the US and West Europe, India's incremental acceptability in the ASEAN Community, and its participation in the ASEAN Security Forum (ARF), are factors, which have impinged on China's India policies. Similarity in China's and Indian concerns about terrorism and narco-terrorism about separatist and secessionist movements, are also factors affecting India and China's attitude towards each other. It is also pertinent to mention that Li Peng has been a consistent advocate of the normalisation of Sino-Indian relations.

What then are the concrete results of Li Peng's visit to India. Li Peng repeatedly articulated the objective that China wants a better relationship with India and that China is willing to have exchanges at high political levels with India on a continuous basis to resolve differences and to enhance cooperation, During his exchanges with the Indian leaders he acknowledged that resolving the boundary dispute is an important issue that needs to be tackled. It was agreed between the two sides that the Joint Working Group on the Boundary Question has not made sufficient progress in resolving the residual problems affecting the delineation of the Line of Actual Control which is a pre-requisite to move on to resolving the boundary question. Li Peng conveyed to Prime Minister Vajpayee that China would like to complete work related to the Line of Actual Control expeditiously so that the provisions of the 1993 Agreement can be fully implemented after which the substantive issue of the Boundary can be taken up by the Joint Working Group. Li Peng indicated the Chinese willingness to get Sino-Indian relations back on track by affirming that while the importance of the boundary issue could not be denied, China and India should focus on expanding economic and technological cooperation. Li Peng's being in India for nine days and visiting Hyderabad and Bangalore underlines China's interest not only in expanding economic relations but specifically expanding technological cooperation in the sphere of Information Technology.

Given this outcome, Li Peng's visit can be considered one more important step in the direction of normalisation of relations between China and India since the contretemps of Pokhran tests of 1998. There are however a number of important Indian concerns to which a more contentful and positive response from China is necessary if out bilateral relations are to reach the requisite levels of mutual trust and cooperation. There has to be substantial move forward for delineating the Line of Actual Control and the Chinese side should agree to initiate substantial discussions on the boundary question. While India does not expect China to scale down its close relations with Pakistan, China should carefully re-consider the implications of its defence supplies and defence technological cooperation with Pakistan which causes serious implications for India's security. While China has taken a neutral stand on the Kashmir issue compared to its previous pro-Pakistani stance, it needs to be more forthright in acknowledging the parallel threats that India and China face in terms of cross-border terrorism, religious extremism and separatist movements. China must consider being more active in furthering the processes of cooperative security in the South Asian and the South East Asian regions, bilaterally as well as through multi-lateral mechanisms, like the ARF.

While Li Peng's visit has furthered the processes of normalisation of Sino-Indian relations, India must be conscious of two factors in its China policies. First, that China still remains an uncertain competitive factor in regional strategic equations, second that there are still a number of issues to be resolved and a long way to go before Sino-Indian relatins are fully normalised.

Sino-Indian Relation— The Current State through the Prism of Track-II Discussions

There was some cogitation in the media regarding reports that Chinese Prime Minister Zhou Rongji will not visit India during his forthcoming visits to Bangladesh, Nepal amd Pakistan, and perhaps to Sri Lanka, Analysts suffering from the fever of over-interpretation alleged that this means that China is downgrading the importance of India and re-affirming the importance of Sino-Pakistan relations. It is relevent here to examine the present state of Sino-Indian relations and to bring to public attention the interaction between China and India at different levels.

The current state of India's relations with China and its prospects have to be assessed in this context. First and foremost, following Jaswant Singh's contacts with his counterpart Tang Xiejuan and President Narayanan's visit to Beijing in 1999, there has been tangible forward movement in the discussion and the work of the Sino-Indian Joint Working Group on the boundary question. Its experts sub-group after a delay of nearly seven years since 1993 has now agreed on initiating an exchange of maps to ascertain and if possible finalise the delineation of the Line of Actual Control between India and China which would be the geo-physical basis for implementing confidence building measures between the two countries conceptualised in the Sino-Indian Agreement of 1993, which were translated into specific confidence building measures in the Sino-Indian Agreement of 1996 during President Jiang

Zemin's visit to India in November that year. An important nuance in this decision is the fact that instead of just exchanging maps and discussing differences of opinion on specific sectors of the Line of Actual Control where Indian and Chinese views differ, about the delineation. The agreement is that discussions on delineation should cover the entire Line of Control from North-West to the East. The approach to delineation is to be integrated and comprehensive which to my mind is a constructive step forward. The second significant development is the agreement reached between Mr. Jaswant Singh and Tang Xiejuan to expand the bilateral exchanges on political matters to bilateral security dialogue, which will cover not only bilateral security concerns but also the regional and global conerns and their strategic ramifications. This would naturally include issues related to nuclear weapons and other weapons of mass destruction, related to management of proliferation of such weapons and their delivery systems, the role of regional groupings, interactions between India and China in the ARF (ASEAN Regional Security Forum), the impact of power equations between the greater powers on the regional security environment of Asia and so on.

It is in this context that the second seniormost figure in the Chinese political heirarchy Li Peng recently paid a nine-day visit to India accompanied by a large delegation of Chinese businessmen and economic experts, in February, 2001. His visit and his discussions underlined the Chinese interest in expanding economic and technological cooperation with India in selective and focussed manner in areas of special interest to China and naturally of special interest to India, Li Peng's long visit and his going to the southern states of India where economic and technological activities are getting incremental international acknowledgement, indicated the areas of particular interest to China. There was criticism in certain quarters that Li Peng's discussions in Delhi did not touch upon two vital issues of the boundary question and China's defence, nuclear and missile collaboration with Pakistan, the issues which cause particular concern to India. This criticism is factually valid but its relevance has to be assessed in terms of possibilities of any practical compromise emerging on these issues given the Indian and Chinese policy orientations rooted in their respective structure of geo-strategic and security interests.

Since Rajiv Gandhi's visit in December, 1988, there is governmental acknowledgement from both sides that these particular issues will require patience and the graduality of approach, as these issues will take time to get resolved. The alternative approach would be both polemical and confrontationist which neither India nor China consider necessary or desirable. What is important is that these issues are not wished away.

Parallel to inter-governmental exchanges, a pattern of Track II non-governmental institutional exchanges was initiated in 1997 which have continued except during the second half of 1998 and first half of 1999 as a critical fall out of India's nuclear tests in May 1998. This international exchange has been between the Centre for Policy Research, Institute of Chinese Studies, Delhi University of India and the following Chinese think-tanks: Chang Ruisheng, Senior Advisor, Chinese Institute of International Studies, Beijing, China Institute of Contemporary International Relations, Institute of Asia Pacific Studied, Chinese Academy of Social Sciences, Institute for South Asian Studies, Yunan Academy of Social Sciences and Asia Development Centre of the People's Republic of China.

So far four rounds of discussions have taken place between Indian and Chinese experts belonging to these organisations. Two of them were held in New Delhi and two in China (Deijing and Kunming). The fourth and last round was held in New Delhi between the 22nd and 24th of March, 2001. It is the discussions in this fourth round which indicates to prospects of Sino-Indian relations in the foreseeable future. Ambassador Chang Ruisheng, Senior Advisor Chinese Institute of International Studies, was the leader of Chinese team (He has been the leader since the first round since 1997). I led the Indian team, Indian experts belonged to the Institute of Defence Studies and Analyses, senior strategic analysts from major Indian newspapers, representatives of the Institute of Chinese Studies and Economic experts, both from the media and Indian economic research institutes. The structured discussions spread over two days had a comprehensive agenda covering global, regional and bilateral issues impacting on Sino-Indian relations. It is significant that the views expressed by both sides were not subject to the caution and inhibitions of the policy stances of the Chinese and Indian Governments. The views expressed were of course within the framework of the overall policy orientations of the two countries on all the issues but the presentations and exchanges were frank and more detailed and direct in the analytioal dimensions of the discussions. It is worthwhile recalling specific conclusions and general anticipations arrived at during this round of discussions. On prospects of cooperation, there was agreement that Sino-Indian bilateral economic cooperation, may not have total complementarity but in certain spheres of technological, administrative and trade, such complementarity exists and there is potential for growth. There was broad agreement that given the Chinese focus on economic development of its southern areas abutting India and Myanmar, possibilities of cooperation between India, China, Myanmar and Bangladesh, has positive possibilities. In the discussions there were also indications that there could be cooperation and linking developmental processes between the Mekong, Brahmaputra and the Eastern Gangetic River basins.

The controversial dimensions of Chinese goods driving out Indian goods from Indian market itself, specially in the context of China entering into WTO was discussed at length. The Chinese side did not reject the negative implications perceived by India and suggested: frist non-governmental and then governmental expert level discussions to meet these points of concern. Parallelism in interest and general approaches of India and China on issues related to human rights, environmental management and economic development was accepted. It could be the basis of bilateral cooperation. At the same time differences of opinion on democratisation of the UN, UN reforms, expansion of the Security Council and non-proliferation issues were frankly accepted in view of the framework and the differing interests of India and China, Importantly, the Chinese side stated that while its formal policy stance on nuclear non-proliferation will remain what it is, the Chinese intention is to deal with India's nuclear and missile weaponisation on the basis of existing realities and facts. The Chinese approach would not be punitive or confrontationist. India should structure its responses to China, on the basis of this Chinese realism. Elaborating on this point the Chinese side gave the assessment that this realism is going to be an incremental international phenomenon which would be reflected in the policies of the major powers. The Chinese side specially emphasised that its major security concerns were related to Taiwan and the plans of the USA to evolve and deploy National Missile Defence and Theatre Missile Defence projects. It was added that while China will monitor India's nuclear doctrine and deployment plans, China does not expect any critical confrontation with India as far as the current processes of normalisation is sustained.

On the question of Chinese nuclear missile and general defence cooperation with Pakistan, the Chinese side emphasised that this relationship is based on their assessment of China's security and strategic interests. They accepted the validity of Indian concerns in these matters which were clearly and firmly conveyed to them. The chinese response was that there are both economic and security reasons for Sino-Pak defence relationship and that India and China should consider measures of managing this critical phenomenon in a realistic manner. The Chinese side stated that this defence cooperation with Pakistan does not mean that China will take a pro-Pakistan stance on issues of bilateral controveray between India and Pakistan, Chinese approach is detached and impartial, On the question of China recognising Sikkim's Integration with India, the Chinese side clarified that China's approach is realistic and it accepts the factual position. It was suggested by them instead of demanding formal declarations on the subject, India and China should sign a border trade agreement between Tibbet and India in which goods will pass through Sikkim the procedural formalities involved in this frading arrangement will automatically acknowledge India's jurisdiction over Sikkim, a suggestion which is worth examining.

As far as the boundary question goes, both sides agreed that progress made in the delineation of the Line of Actual Control was constructive development. The Indian side suggested a long-term proposal for discussing the boundary question in due course on the basis of the following general principles : 1. Move away from colonial period of terms of reference: 2. Determination of boundary on the basis of recognised principles of international law governing boundary demaraction in high mountainous terrain: 3. Use of most modern cartgraphic methods to delineate the boundary: 4. Minimal change in jurisdictional phenomenon on pupulation: 5. Subject to point 4, mutual give and take of territory.

It was also generally accepted that the main points of Sino-Indian cooperation could be the following: 1. Managing development, distribute justice of civil societies, migration, etc. 2. Managing security environment in Asia, domestic and external strategic environment: 3. Globalisation: 4. Emerging trends in multi-lateralism and 5. Bilateral relations.

In overall terms this exercise in Track II could be a mainingful, supplementary and supportive input to ongoing inter-government exchanges between India and China. As far as Prime Minister Zhou Rongjl's omitting from his south Asian itinerary is converned, the Chinese side to my mind offered a rational explanation. Li Peng had visited India only recently. A second visit by a senior Chinese leader in April would not result in any substantive results beyond what Li Peng discussed in Delhi and other parts of India. Such visits should have substantive results. It was indicated that Zhou Rongji's visit is on cards perhaps late this year on early next year. I agree, we need not predicate the state of Sino-Indian relations on the basis of high level state visits. What is of greater importance is to sustain dialogue on substantive issues on a continuous basis.

12

THE SRI LANKAN CRISIS—DILEMMAS OF INDIA

The recent crisis faced by Sri Lankan has been described by the president of Sri Lanka Chandrika Kumaratunga as the gravest threat faced by her country since its achievement of Independence. Appeals have been made to the Government of India by the various segments of Sri Lankan society to get involved in Sri Lankan affairs yet again, to prevent a military debacle for the Sri Lankan forces and for reviving some kind of negotiations between the LTTE and the Sri Lankan Government. Speculation on the trajectory which the Sri Lankan crisis will take in the coming times should necessarily be preceded by recounting of the ground realities as they have evolved. Since the capture of the Elephant Pass the LTTE has swept across the Jaffna Peninsula in a more or less victorious manner despite the use of air power and armour by the Sri Lankan forces. LTTE has been able to sustain this successful campaign primarilv because of the passionate commitment of its cadres to their political and ideological objective of creating an independent Tamil State in Sri Lanka. Added to this are the factors of the resilience of the LTTE cadres. Their tactical and strategic competence, their not being short of resources and weapons, and their having captured large amounts of weapons from the Sri Lankan forces.

The LTTE is in control of most of the Jaffna Peninsula. Srilankan Forces are in control of the Palaley Air Base and Kakasenthurai Port. Reports from Sri Lanka indicate patterns of incremental desertions affecting the morale of Srilankan Army. Their morale is low and they seem to be exhausted by the long campaign of attrition to which the LTTE has subjected them over the last five years. It should also be remembered that while sustaining their campaign in the Jaffna Peninsula, the LTTE continued to confirm its capacity to undertake major violence in other parts of Sri Lanka from Trincomalee to Colombo, including a near successful bomb attack to kill President Kumaratunga. The over-arching ground reality is of the LTTE being militarily and politically strong while the Sri Lankan Government appears to be on the defensive.

The question arises as to why the LTTE has launched its current campaign while only recently it had agreed to resume dialogue with the Sri Lankan Government through Norwegian mediation. The answer based on experience of the last decade of more, is that the LTTE wanted to lull the Srilankan Government and the armed forces into a mood of military relaxation anticipating negotiations, while they themselves regroupded marshalling their resources and decided to achieve significant military victories to negotiate from a position of strength whenever negotiations took place. They appear to have succeeded in meeting this objective. History has come full circle in an ironic framework with the very segments of Sri Lankan political circles which refused to respond to Tamil aspirations despite several commitments given over the years and which demanded the abrupt departure of the Indian Peace Keeping Force, claiming that they are in touch with their LTTE compatriots and that the Indian role was not relevant. The Buddhist monks, the then representatives of the former ruling UNP, and even sections of Sri Lankan armed forces are now asking for India's re-involvement. Given India's reticences in this regard, they even advocate an Indian role in support of the Norwegian facilitating effort. The Government of India's response so far has been measured, reticent and cautious, as it should be in the context of our experiences in Sri Lanka between 1978 and 1990. India has ruled out any military intervention in Sri Lanka of the type which was undertaken in July 1987. India has indicated a willingness to extend humanitarian assistance to the people of Jaffna and to the Srilankan armed forces bottled up in the Peninsula subject to a formal request being received from the Government of Sri Lanka, and subject to certain logical pre-conditions which should necessarily precede India extending any humanitarian assistance. Though no formal request was received, informal suggestions asking for such assistance have been converyed both through governmental and non-governmental channels, from Sri Lankan. Though India has not spelt out details of humanitarian assistance, the form which such assistance is likely to assume, its large-scale supply of food and essential medicines to the people of Jaffna, and India assisting in the evacuation of Sri Lankan forces from Jaffna to Colombo by sea. Intense consultations took place in the Indian Cabinet Committee on National Security and in the Strategic Policy Group of the National Security Council which includes the three Service Chiefs, the Chiefs of our intelligence Agencies, and Secretaries to the Ministry of Defence, external Affairs and Home. There have also been reports of the Eastern Naval Command of India being put on alert for possible evacuation operations.

The Government of India has also been in touch with the representatives of the Norwegian Government and US Government apart from continuous communication with Sri Lankan authorities to help resolve the critical military situation. It is obvious that undertaking any evacuation of

Srilankan forces and the distribution of essential supplies to the Jaffna Peninsula, should be preceded by an effective ceasefire, not an andulatory ceasefire with violence erupting in between. A more important question is about the prospects of resumption of negotiations, if the immediate military confrontation ends. Will the LTTE be amenable to a ceasefire when it is on the ascendent. Secondly, a pull back of Sri Lankan forces from Jaffna will enable LTTE to consolidate its hold over the Jaffna Peninsula. The likelihood is that the LTTE would focus its attention on Eastern regions of Sri Lanka—Trincomalee, Batticoloa and Amparai which the LTTE considers part of traditional homelands of Tamils of Sri Lanka.

Any negotiations for resolving the Sri Lankan crisis and any involvement by India in the process, should be subject to the following considerations. It must be remembered that Prabhakaran and the LTTE have a passionate and deep ideological commitment to create a Tamil *Eelam* in Sri Lanka. The military and political successes and survival which the LTTE has achieved would have made these commitments stronger. The Tamil demands of 1987 would be pitched higher this time. Conversely, the military conflict and reverses suffered by the Srilankan armed forces would have hardened Sinhalese attitudes about coming to any compromises with the Tamils. Despite LTTE's authoritarian and violent culture. Srilankan Tamils in general support the LTTE. Whether this support is based on fear or voluntary endorsement of the LTTE is not relevant. What is relevent is that the support exists. The Tamil diaspora living in different countries which supports the LTTE has a vested interest, perhaps in continuing the conflict situation in Sri Lanka because political uncertainties in Sri Lanka enables them to stay abroad in comfort, with privileges of political asylum and refugee status.

The Muslim population of Sri Lanka, though Tamil speaking, claims a separate ethno-religious identity. They would have their own compartmentalised demands which they would want to be an integral part of any settlement package. Though LTTE is a banned organisation in India, it maintains its connections in Tamil Nadu. Tamil public opinion in India and Tamil Nadu politics is bound to influence Indian policies towards Sri Lanka in proportion to the intensity of critical predicament which Tamil population in Sri Lanka may face, even after and even if the present crisis is overcome. India in the context of its own geo-political predicaments has declared its commitment to the unity and territorial integrity of Sri Lanka, indicating that solutions to the ethnic conflict should be in this framework. Adjusting the commitment of this square to the circle of LTTE's demand for *Eelam* is going to be a difficult task. It is also pertinent to note that during the present crisis, there has been no demand or request from the LTTE to the Government of India to mediate or interfere in Sri Lankan affairs. In this context, Norwegians have indeed taken a very difficult mission. Our government has taken a measured and practical policy stance in which we are politically supportive of any constructive effort to meet Sri Lanka's problems.

The nature and content of India's involvement in Sri Lanka however, cannot be predicted with any certainty. Prime Minister Vajpayee is therefore right in keeping Indian options open when he stated thus, that India is prepared to cope with any eventuality in Sri Lanka by appropriate means.

Elections in Sri Lanka

General elecions in Sri Lanka were held in the beginning of October, 2000. President Chandrika Kumaratunga is due to face Presidential election in the current year, i.e., 2001.

Her People's Alliance could not secure an absolute majority in the elections held in the first half of October. She managed to form a government of her party on the basis of an uneasy alliance with the Islamic Party of Sri Lanka with respresentatives of Tamil Parties in Parliament and with some support from the JVP.

India's foreign policy focus over the last one year has been on relations with the US, China, Russia and Japan. But it is time to pay attention to our immediate neighbourhood, (leaving aside Pakistan which continuously intrudes into our foreign policy radar screen). Political developments in Sri Lanka subjected to the continuing complications of the ethnic conflict, remain a matter of interest and concern to India as the fall out of events in Sri Lanka impacts of India's stability, security, even territorial unity.

Elections in Sri Lanka, therefore, merit our attention. Before coming to any value judgements about the elections and their results, or implications, it is necessary to examine the military, the political and economic situation in Sri Lanka which constitutes the back-drop of the elections. Militarily, the civil war situation is continuing in Sri Lanka. The Kumaratunga Government, however, has retrieved its military position somewhat after the major debacles which Sri Lankan forces suffered in the summer of this year 2000 with LTTE's capture of the Elephant Pass and its being poised to capture the entire Jaffna Peninsula. Sri Lanka was on the brink of territorial fragmentation earlier this year. But timely politico-military initiatives by Sri Lankan Government underpinned by military and defence assistance from a number of countries, particularly, the United States of America, Israel, Britain and Pakistan stemmed the LTTE's run off military and territorial successes. India also played a low-key but contributive role in assisting Sri Lanka counter the LTTE's offensive. The present situation is that of a military stand off between the

LTTE and the Sri Lankan security forces, with the Sri Lankan security forces showing an incremental capacity to resist the LTTE. President Kumaratunga had to take some radical and drastic decisions about changing the command structure of the armed forces which might not have made her popular with her military establishment. She nevertheless showed courage and determination to retrieve Sri Lanka from a situation where the Government was on the brink of a military defeat.

Sri Lanka has succeded in countering the LTTE's military onslaught despite the internal crises which the Sri Lankan armed forces faced in terms of low morale shortage of adequate military equipment for a brief period and the recurring phenomenon of desertions from its ranks. It is to be noted that the Sri Lankan security forces have managed to restore their credibility to some extent, despite these difficulties.

The political predicament of Sri Lanka, is even more involuted and complex. The ethnic conflict remains the focus of party politics, the processes of Governance and economic management. Kumaratunga's initial efforts to find a solution by direct negotiations with the LTTE failed despite purposive efforts by her. Her attempts to structure a constitutional package responsive to basic Tamil demands in consultation with other Tamil groups who have been part of the mainstream democratic processes of Sri Lanka have also not fully succeeded. The Tamil groups feel that the constitutional proposals put forward by Kumaratunga since 1995 are not satisfactory enough. This view found expression when the constitutional proposals were referred to a select committee of the Parliament which has representatives from the Sinhala majority and from the Tamil Muslim Minority. Complicating matters further was the reluctance of the main opposition party, the UNP, to move towards a rational national consensus on these proposals. The situation was compounded further by the security establishment and senior officers of the armed forces not being very enthusiastic about offering a compromise to the Tamils, given the LTTE's continuing violence and assaults against not just the Sri Lankan military but Slinhalese civilians. The most disappointing and difficult predicament that President Kumaratunga faced was that of the Buddhist clergy opposing any compromise responsive to the Tamil minority which were sought to be concretised in the proposals for constitutional reforms which President Kumaratunga formulated.

Despite all these difficulties, President Kumaratunga managed to put together a set of constitutional proposals the more substantive Tamil demands, except one, namely the merger of the northern and eastern Provinces of Sri Lanka and this integrated Province being formally declared a Tamil Homeland. In some respects, the proposals put forward by her government were an advance on the proposals which President Jayawardene planned to implement towards the end of his tenure before Premadasa succeeded him and scuttled the whole process. Despite these difficulties, the Kumaratunga Government was in the process of submitting these constitutional proposals to the Parliament for approval though there were uncertainties about the proposals being endorsed by the requisite majority in the Parliament. She had managed to persuade UNP and its leader Ranil Wickramasinghe to rise above partisan considerations and agree to a visionary solution which might have been a major step towards resolving the long drawn out ethnic conflict. The proposals not only took note of Tamil demands but the more recent demands and aspirations of Sri Lankan Muslim Community. The UNP and Buddhist clergy however prevented the proposals being submitted to the Parliament for a vote before the Parliament was resolved prior to the recent elections. This must have been a matter of disappointment to President Kumaratunga who remains committed to a peaceful solution to the ethnic conflict despite the general atmosphere of violence which she faced and despite having been subjected to a nearly successful assassination attempt on her last December 1999.

The economic situation in Sri lanka remains stable despite enormous resources that Sri Lanka has to devote to its defence budget and the political uncertainties affecting the northern and Eastern Provinces due to the continuing violence in those regions.

Sri Lanka's Central, western and southern Provinces continue to maintain standards of economic performance in the spheres of tourism, agriculture, the plantations sector and manufacturing sector, like textiles. This is reflective of the patience and resilience of the people of Sri Lanka despite the violence which they have suffered over the last seventeen years. It is in this context that the elections took place. It is worthwhile taking note of some basic facts related to these elections. There were 42 political parties in the election fray, putting up 5048 candidates. The main parties are: the People's Alliance led by President Kumaratunga and the United Nations Party led by Mr. Ranil Wickeramasinghe. The People's alliance within it has representatives of the Sri Lankan Muslim League also. Leaving aside the LTTE proper, a number of Tamil groups also fighting the elections. Significantly it is reported that the EPRLF participating in these elections after a considerable gap of time. Even more important is the fact that the leftist political Party, the JVP (Janata Vimukthi Peramuna) is participating in the elections. Most recent reports indicate that there a large-scale turn has been out of voters for both the legislative and Presidential elections, reflective of the abiding and deep commitment to democracy of the people of Sri Lanka. There have been critical developments before the elections commenced. The most prominent leader of the Muslims in Sri Lanka Ashraf was killed in a helicopter crash while flying over the eastern province of Batticoloa. His successor escaped an assassination attempt. The senior leadership of the moderate Tamil Party, the TULF, has been decimated over the last three years by the assassinations carried out by the LTTE. The Tamil parties participating in the elections, have undertaken the exercise under continuing threats from the LTTE. This is an act of courage under extreme pressure. The election campaign has been bitter and controversial, influenced by the enthnic divide, questioning the middle ground and rational approach advocated by Kumaratunga. One also expects that there are segments in the senior leadership of the UNP which are inclined towards a political and constitutional compromise on the ethnic issue. But electoral politics prevents this view getting effective public expression. It is a pity that the Buddhist clergy continues to play an obstructionist Sinhalese ethno-centric role in influencing public opinion. This create not just a complicated but a profoundly contradictory predicament in the processes of governance of Sri Lanka.

Another influencing impating on political prospects in Sri Lanka originates in India. The LTTE still has extensive contacts in Tamil Nadu. A number of political groups though they are not mainstream political parties have held public rallies and meetings demanding the creation of *Eelam* and recognition by India of such a Tamil State. This phenomenon vitiates the political processes in Sri Lanka. It is difficult to counter, given the democratic norms about political activities obtaining in India, whatever the results of the general and Presidential elections in Sri Lanka, the new Government of Sri Lanka would continue to face intractable complexities. These can be overcome only if a national consensus emerges in Sri Lanka to be substantive responsive to the aspirations of its Tamil citizens. This is the only method by which the Tamil population of Sri Lanka can be liberated from the confrontationist and complex motivations of Tamil militant groups led by the LTTE.

India should assist whichever Sri Lankan Government comes into power, to go down this path of accommodation and compromise with the Tamils. This assistance has to be diplomatic and political. There should be no direct participation, mediation or involvement by India in the Sri Lankan political processes.

Danger Signals from Sri Lanka

Sri Lanka is in serious crisis again. The LTTE in a major military offensive expelled the Sri Lankan Army from the Elephant Pass and Iyakachchi, the main points in land approaches from rest of Sri Lanka to Jaffna Peninsula. Before one analyses the implications of the current crisis, it would be pertinent to briefly refer to the background in which Sri Lanka's territorial unity stands threatened again, perhaps more seriously than event before.

First and foremost, the Sinhala only policy and the Buddhist religion being given the supreme position in the Sri Lankan constitution in 1958 initiated a process of systematic and drastic discrimination against the Tamil population of Sri Lanka which constitutes nearly fifteen per cent of the population of that country. Secondly, since Sri Lanka's independence in 1948, right upto the late 1980s, a number of agreements were signed between Sinhalese leaders and the Sri Lankan Government and the leaders of the Sri Lankan Tamils to ensure justice, equal treatment and opportunities for the Tamils. Each and everyone of these agreements were scuttled and betrayed despite the solemn assurances given to the Tamils. Thirdly, the attempts at genuine mediation and finding a solution made by India between 1983 and 1990 was sabotaged primarily by members of the Sri Lankan Government. This included Sri Lankan Government hobnobbing with the LTTE while requesting the Indian troops to contain them. All the negotiations between the Sri Lankan Government and the

LTTE between 1990 and 1999, remain cosmetic efforts without a purposive move forward. Hence the LTTE's military offensive which has resulted in nearly 20,000 Government troops being dislodged, nearly 140 Sri Lankan soldiers being killed, and 600 Sri Lankan soldiers being injured in the last week of April, 2000.

According to conventional wisdom, these developments can be considered as anti-climatic because the expectation was that of the Sri Lankan Government and the LTTE representatives commencing negotiations somewhere in Europe through Norwegian mediation. An amount of background information and historical memory should however, have made all concerned anticipate a significant military initiative from the LTTE before the negotiations commenced. First of all, instead of agreeing to commence the dialogue immediately, both the Kumaratunga Government and the LTTE stipulated parallel pre-conditions. The Sri Lankan Government demanded the complete cessation of LTTE's operations, whereas the LTTE demanded the cessation of the Sri Lankan military offensive and the withdrawal of Sri Lankan forces sought of the Elephant Pass. Given the political and military orientations of both sides, it was obvious that these demands would not be met. There might have been some calculated, tactical lull in the fighting engineered by the LTTE in preparation for the massive assault which resulted in their capturing of the Elephant Pass, displacing the Sri Lankan army North and South of the Pass and bottling up the Government forces in Jaffna town. The military objective now of the LTTE is to consolidate to dominate its domination of the Jaffna Peninsula and the political objective to enter the negotiations sponsored by the Norwegians, from a position of strength and credibility based on territorial control of the Tamil areas of Sri Lanka. While the LTTE is incrementally dominating the Peninsula, it is also effective in questioning the Government's jurisdiction in Trincomalee, Baticoloa and Amperai. The developments since the second fortnight of April were a culmination of the critical predicament faced by the Sri Lankan Government. President Chandrika Kumaratunga was subjected to a suicide bomb attack in December 1999. LTTE's military pressure in Jaffna increased to a level between January and March where President Kumaratunga ordered her three service Chiefs to locate themselves in Jaffna to personally command the operations against the LTTE. But this initiative did not serve the purpose of boosting the morale and determination of the Sri Lankan forces for which it was envisaged. The fall of Elephant Pass and Iyakachchi to the LTTE, means that the LTTE is now in control of the main land route from rest of Sri Lanka to the Jaffna Peninsula. Parallel to this the LTTE's capacity to disrupt the land and sea communicatins as well as the administration in the Eastern Provinces of Sri Lanka, remains unabated.

The emerging situation in Sri Lanka, therefore, is that of a brief military stand off between the LTTE and Sri Lankan Government. Sri Lankan authorities have sent four thousand additional troops into Jaffna Peninsula. It has obtained aircraft, patrol boats and ships from Israel, and multi-barrel rocket firing mobile artillery and other sophisticated infantry weapons from Pakistan on an emergency basis. The assertive military posture seems to have been blunted for the time being. In the meanwhile, the LTTE, has again shown its capacity to perpetrate violence in the Sinhalese areas of Sri Lanka by killing nearly thirty people, including the Minister of Industries of Sri Lanka, C.V. Gooneratne, and his wife at Ratmalana, near Colombo.

Given the military stand off and the LTTE's violent posture, the Norwegian initiative will go into a limbo in the short time. President Kumaratunga has undertaken consultations with the opposition parties and more importantly with the Buddhist monks about the stances to be adopted by the Government in the negotiations being launched by Norway. These consultations have not been encouraging. The main opposition party, the UNP is critical of the fact that the Kumaratunga Government did not have any detailed discussions with the Opposition Parties before formally accepting the Norwegian initiative. The two main Buddhist religious leaders of Sri Lanka, the *Mahanayakas* of the *Asgariya* and *Malwatte* orders of Monks indicated to President Kumaratunga that they have reservations about the Norwegian initiative in the context of developments over the last one year. While the LTTE has indicated a willingness to participate in negotiations through Norwegian mediation, their objective remains to see that all their fundamental demands are fully met by the Sri Lankan Government. If negotiations do not achieve this purpose, the LTTE may dissociate itself from the process. More so now when they seem to have the upper hand.

Apart from the critical military situation that the Sri Lankan Government faces, its ramification in terms of internal politics of Sri Lanka, creates additional problems for the stability of the country. Future prospects, therefore, have to be assessed not only in the above context, but also in terms of the overall politico-military situation. The Sri Lankan armed forces have been under continuous military pressure for the last five years, which they have not been able to cope with despite some interim military successes. There are reports of desertions and low morale, in contrast to the LTTE's cadre's commitment and battle-hardened determination regarding their cause. Apart from land operations, the LTTE has acquired weapons capable of shooting down aircraft. They are also becoming incrementally effective in operations at sea against the Sri

Lankan Navy. Despite their being a secessionist organisation, they do not seem to be short of finances or arms. They seem to have grown in strength and organisational capacities specially from 1993-94 onwards. A critical dimension affecting India in this whole situation is the fact that despite being an organisation banned by the Government of India, the LTTE retains its extensive political and logistical connections in Tamil Nadu and along the coast, including the ports of Rameshwaram and Vedaranyam. The most recent reports in the audio-visual media indicate that areas in Tamil Nadu still serve as bases for supplies and logistical support to the LTTE. LTTE's political links with some political parties and groups in Tamil Nadu remain strong, indicating that segments of public in Tamil Nadu remain supportive of the LTTE. The access and support which the LTTE enjoys in Tamil Nadu could not have been achieved without support of sections of administration and security forces.

Sri Lanka—The Agony Continues

A suicide squad of the LTTE drove an explosive-laden truck through the main gates of the Central Bank building in Colombo on January '96 and exploded it, causing the largest damage to life and property at a civilian target since the ethnic conflict commenced in Sri Lanka. When Jaffna fell to Sri Lankan forces in December '95. Prabhakaran had asserted that he would continue the struggle from the east of Sri Lanka. Even earlier, when the battle for Jaffna was on. Prabhakaran was asked about his movement's future in the context of the military pressure on him, his reply was "He who dares wins". He has been true to his word, though the consequences for the people of Sri Lanka are abysmally tragic. The operational military and security predicament of the Sri Lankan Government since the fall of Jaffna became clearly problematic. The results of moves made by the LTTE since November '95 were: firstly, that the major segment of the LTTE's political and military leadership and a fair number of its trained cadres have successfully moved out of Jaffna and regrouped themselves in the Vavunia and Batticaloa regions; secondly, that though militarily defeated in Jaffna, the determination and commitment of LTTE cadres to continue the conflict and take it to Sinhalese heartlands remained undiminished; thirdly, that despite the disruption caused by moving out of Jaffna, LTTE's sources of military supplies remained generally intact; fourth, that its organizational efficiency and operational daring was affected by the military defeat in Jaffna and that it can still generate effective violence against the government not only in the north and east of the country, but at the capital, Colombo, itself. LTTE blew up the main oil storage tanks in Colombo itself and destroyed the Central Bank building which was literally a stone's throw away from the official residence of the President, from the Foreign Office, from the Naval Headquarters, from the Defence Ministry and the main port facilities of Colombo.

Reports from both foreign Tamil, and Sri Lankan sources indicated that the LTTE has adopted a shrewd strategic option in relocating itself in the Vavunia jungles and the Batticaloa region. An operational axis between these two points in North-Central and Eastern Sri Lanka, if it becomes totally effective, can disrupt communications links between Colombo and Trincomalee and also affect the security of the important religious centre of Anuradhapura. If the LTTE manages to revive its activities further west in areas around Talaimannar, they can pose a potential threat to Elephant Pass and to the victorious Sri Lankan military garrison in Jaffna. Two other factors contributing to the fighting capacities of the LTTE were discernible, namely, support from expatriate Sri Lankan Tamil populations in different parts of South East Asia, Australia and Europe did not appear to be diminishing. Secondly, the Sri Lankan Tamil youth in Batticaloa, frustrated by economic pressure, high rates of unemployment and the impact of Muslim communal politics in the region (encouraged since the days of the UNP Government) could provide a fertile cadre recruiting ground for the LTTE.

President Chandrika Kumaratunga, therefore, faced difficult and violent situations despite the genuine efforts which she had made to find a political solution to the ethnic conflict in her country. Basic elements in her conflict resolution approach have been: first, to be responsive to the maximum extent possible to Tamil demands subject to two considerations—that she has to carry the Sinhalese majority, the Buddhist clergy and the armed forces with her in structuring a compromise package with the Tamils; second, she took the transformed political reality of the Muslim population in Sri Lanka assuming a separate identity and demanding delegation of powers similar to those for the Tamils. Third, while showing a willingness to deal peacefully with the LTTE, she felt that the long-term well-being of the Tamil people could not be ensured by dealing with the LTTE alone as the sole representative organization of Sri Lankan Tamils. Fourth, she has made it clear that her concern is the well-being of the Tamil population of Sri Lanka and not meeting specific LTTE demands of a military or narrower political nature. Fifth, while willing to refashion the Constitution of Sri Lanka to be responsive to the plural multi-ethnic nature of Sri Lankan polity, she was rightly, not ready to compromise on Sri Lanka's territorial unity and integrity. And lastly, she did not rule out the military option if the LTTE persists in its military operations.

President Kumaratunga had certainly garnered better international support and sympathy for her policies, aimed at resolving the ethnic strife compared to the UNP Governments of Jayawardene, Premadasa and Wijayatunga. The support was not just political, but also material. Western democracies, Israel, Pakistan and some of the Asia Pacific countries had provided military assistance to the Sri Lankan Government. India has been politically supportive of the Kumaratunga proposals and had also taken action to prevent India being a source of supplies and bases for the LTTE.

She, in turn, had managed the fall-out from the military conflict more effectively. So far there has been no massive exodus of Tamil refugees from Sri Lanka to India and other parts of the world. Though excesses of the security forces were inevitable in an operation of the type which was undertaken in Jaffna, the overall impression among human rights NGOs and the international community was that her government had been mindful about its responsibilities towards its Tamil civilian citizens to the extent feasible. She had repeatedly appealed to her Tamil citizens and other Tamil political parties and groups in Sri Lanka to negotiate a durable solution with her and to wean away the LTTE from violence. The reaction of the Tamil population and the Tamil political parties and groups has been cautious and reticent, partially due to fear partially due to their deep-rooted uncertainties about Sinhalese governments fulfilling their promises to Sri Lankan Tamils and partially because her proposals of August, 1995 for meeting Tamil requirements have some inadequacies.

Tamil reactions to the bomb blast at the Central Bank in Colombo on 30th January '96 have been mixed. The EPRLF had condemned to the terrorist act. Other Tamil political groups were either silent or their reaction had been muted. The leadership of Tamils of Indian origin inhabiting the Central Highlands, though opposed to LTTE's violence because of its impact on their own economic well-being, have not been too vocal in criticizing the LTTE, because of their apprehension of Tamil militancy spreading to their areas also. Establishing her credibility and effectiveness with the non-LTTE Tamil political parties, and the Tamil population in general remained an objective which the Kumaratunga government had to achieve. Meeting this objective is the most important factor on which her success in resolving the ethnic issue would depend.

LTTE's continuing the conflict after the fall of Jaffna complicated President Kumaratunga's task. The successful military operations in Jaffna, and LTTE's continuing attacks on Sinhalese generated pressure on the Sri Lankan President from the Sri Lankan army and the Sinhalese majority led by the Buddhist clergy to limit herself to the military option.

13

THE TRAGEDIES OF SRI LANKA : UNCERTAIN PROSPECTS

It would be impossible to recall the number of political figures eliminated in Sri Lanka by violence by one group or the other since 1977-78. The last twenty years have seen the pristine democratic image of Sri Lanka sullied and eroded by religious, ethnic, ideological and communal violence. It would also be a lengthy exercise to go back to the origins of the tragedies of Sri Lanka and make an assessment of uncertainties about the country's future prospects. Suffice it to say that when political leaders resort to short-sighted populism with shades of demogogy to remain in power, the inevitable and sorry price paid is the erosion of democracy.

Had not S.W.R.D. Bandaranaike resented Dudley Senanayake succeeding his father as Prime Minister in the mid-fifties of twentieth century, he would not have set a civilized people like the people of Sri Lanka, regardless of their being Sinhalese, Tamils or Muslims, on the path of ethnic, religious and linguistic animosities, by adopting the Sinhala-only policy as an instrument to gain power. He rode the tiger of ethnic communalism and paid the price for it in his own tragic assassination. The attitudes, policies and trends which he set in motion then have resulted in the whirlwind that is being reaped by the power structure and the people of Sri Lanka today.

Any attempt at rational speculation about future prospects in Sri Lanka must take note of the violent elimination of certain political groups and leaders by organizations opposed to them. The first was the elimination of the entire EPRLF leadership in Madras (Chennai) between 1989 and 1990. The Eelam People's Revolutionary Liberation Front was trying to get Tamils back into the mainstream of Sri Lankan politics within the framework of the Indo-Sri Lanka agreement. The Sri Lankan Governments of Jayawardane and later Premadasa nullified their efforts. The LTTE eliminated them, the senior figure being Padmanabha. Similarly, the LTTE eliminated Amrithalingam and two other top leaders of the Tamil United Liberation Front around the same period.

The assassinations of Premadasa and Lalith Athulathmudali and that of Gamini Dissanayake followed. One has doubts about the LTTE being accused of these assassinations. The LTTE should not be the catch-all accused for all assassinations in Sri Lanka. The political culture of Sri Lanka in the 1980s and 1990s has assassinations as a permeating characteristic. The brutalisation of Sri Lankan politics (as it has happened in India too) does not leave the monopoly of killings to the LTTE alone.

The net result of these murders has been: first, the removal of moderate democratic political leaders from the Tamil political spectrum; secondly, this has resulted in the removal of prominent Sinhalese political leaders who with their first hand knowledge of the ethnic crisis might have veered around to resolving the problem in a rational and practical manner; thirdly, the assassination of Dissanayake is a setback to attempts being made by Prime Minister Chandrika Kumaratunga to initiate a dialogue with the

LTTE and other Tamil groups to find a practical solution to the long-festering ethnic crisis; fourthly, Gamini Dissanayake's assassination reflects the undesirable phenomenon that extremist elements remain dominant in the power structure of both Sinhalese and Tamil politics.

Gamini Dissanayake was one of the main architects of the Indo-Sri Lankan agreement from the Sri Lankan side, though he had strong Sinhalese affiliations and orientations. He believed that Sri Lanka's continuity as a plural society and Sri Lanka's having stable relations with India depended on coming to terms with Tamil militancy and meeting legitimate Tamil aspirations. This was the reason of his active participation in structuring the terms of the Indo-Sri Lanka agreement. The agreement was responsive to all Tamil aspirations. It provided for a merger of the northern and eastern provinces of Sri Lanka though subject to a referendum after the proposed interim government had managed the affairs of the merged province for a certain period of time. It recognized this merged province as a Tamil homeland. It provided for devolution of constitutional, political, financial, administrative and economic powers to all the provinces constituting the Sri Lankan Republic. It provided for Tamils being given equal status with Sinhalese in the Sri Lankan polity as far as Tamils are concerned. It provided a framework for removing discrimination and disabilities against the Tamils. The agreement did not get fully implemented mainly because the Sri Lankan Government after signing the agreement did not implement its provisions with sincerity in given timeframes. The UNP had domestic political compulsions on which one would not sit in judgement. But the stark fact is that there were delays and bitterness in implementing the provisions of the agreement. The inevitable consequence was Tamil disillusionment and reversal to violence. Mr. Premadasa was against the agreement from the very beginning regardless of his protestations about Gandhian approach to politics. His objectives were first to neutralise the JVP and the LTTE and retaining the basic features of Sinhala dominance of Sri Lankan politics. So he first requested the IPKF to be moved out, which we did, transcending political interests of both Sri Lanka and India, but abiding by our commitment to international law. Secondly, his involuted attempts at negotiating with the LTTE failed.

After Premadasa's assassination, President Wijetunga generally took a militaristic and assertive stand against the Tamils. This resulted in extremist Sinhalese elements and the Sri Lankan army becoming important and increasingly influential factors in Sri Lankan politics. It stands to reason that they would have a vested interest in prolonging a conflict situation with the Tamils.

Prime Minister Chandrika Kumaratunga attempted a fresh beginning by organizing discussions with the LTTE. Long before she became active in Sri Lankan politics in the early nineties, even in mid-eighties, she and her late husband had attempted contacts with various Tamil groups to curb the violence afflicting Sri Lanka and to find practical solutions. But Dissanayake's assassination put a limit to her capacity for initiatives in this direction in the immediate future. The previous ruling party, the United National Party, had fielded the widow of Mr. Dissanayake—as their candidate for the Presidential elections. The predicament in dealing with Tamil issue merits being spelt out. The first constituent element of the predicament is, of course, the fall out of Gamini Dissanayake's assassination and LTTE being the main suspect. No government in Sri Lanka can be seen restarting negotiations with the LTTE in the short-term unless it is very bold and does not care for Sinhaless public opinion.

Even if this hurdle is overcome, the governments of Sri Lanka, whoever constitutes them, and the Sinhalese majority should remain fully aware that unless the genuine and legitimate aspirations of Sri Lankan Tamils are met in a spirit of accommodation and mutual respect, no amount of talking would solve the problem. The problem has become more complicated with the emergence of Muslim consciousness in Sri Lankan society. The Sri Lankan Muslim population, the majority of which is concentrated in East, Central and South Eastern Sri Lanka, both due to internal impulses and external encouragement, has started emphasizing its separate entity, though most of the Muslims are Tamilspeaking. This relatively new factor militates against the Tamil demands for a merger of the Northern and Eastern provinces and its being politically and constitutionally acknowledged as a Tamil homeland. This is one of the most significant of the demands of the Tamils. Apart from dealing with this knotty problem, Sinhalese negotiators would have to seriously and sincerely deal with questions of devolution of powers across the political and economic spectrum. They would have to find formulae to give Tamil equal and appropriate status as a language of the Republic. They would also have to remove the discriminatory practices and arrangements against Tamils which have crept into the political system of Sri Lanka. This would perhaps involve further decentralisation and proportional representation for Tamils on a guaranteed basis in the armed forces, the police and all branches of administration. Given the background of Sri Lankan politics over the last three decades and the repeated backing away by the Sinhalese majority from confirmed agreements covering these subjects with Tamil leaders, one should expect Sinhalese reservations about practical accommodation with the Tamils on these complex issues. The role of the Buddhist clergy in encouraging or preventing such accommodation should not be under-estimated. But if Sri Lanka is to sustain itself as a plural democratic society and is to preserve its territorial integrity, a dialogue with the Tamils and appropriate practical compromises are imperative. India having tried to actively mediate and even to implement compromises during the 1980s should not again get involved in Sri Lankan politics in any manner. The goodwill, effort and concern of the late Shri Rajiv Gandhi for the people of Sri Lanka and for South Asian stability have been misinterpreted and criticised in recent years. We should encourage the dialogue, howsoever difficult it may be, as a friendly neighbour interested in the stability and welfare of the people of Sri Lanka. We must resist any attempt by any of the protogonists in Sri Lankan politics to reinveigle us into the Sri Lankan situation. Once has been more than enough:

Sri Lanka— On the Brink of a Break Up?

The ongoing crisis in Sri Lanka is becoming serious. My focus has been on ground realities and on the Indian reactions so far. It is equally relevant to examine the context of Sri Lanka's tragedy after the withdrawal of the IPKF and what the Sri Lankan Government's substantive as opposed to formal expectations are from India. The period between 1989 and 1994 when the UNP Government led by President Premadasa was in power was characterised by both President Premadasa and the LTTE leadership playing a cat and mouse game with each other. Premadasa's scheme was to pretend to do a deal with the LTTE on the basis of removing the Indian military pressure on them. Once the Indian army moved out of Sri Lanka, Premadasa had hoped to militarily overcome the LTTE. Premadasa's ploy succeeded partially when the IPKF pulled back from Sri Lanka in 1990. The LTTE had however, seen through his plans and successfully resisted the Sri Lankan military campaign against them. Negotiations for a political solution during the period 1994 proved abortive because Premadasa's objective was to dilute even the concessions which were promised to Tamils in the 13th Amendment to the Sri Lankan Constitution. The LTTE on the other hand, got more committed to its separatist aspirations. The LTTE brought this Chapter of interaction with the Sinhalese to an end by assassinating Premadasa in May 1993.

The Government of Chandrika Kumaratunga had the advantage of not being a part of political negotiations and military conflicts from 1987 onwards. It could start on a clean slate. President Kumaratunga undertook a serious exercise for negotiations from the end of 1994, almost till the end of 1998. The proposals which she put forward for resolving the ethnic problem between 1995 and 1998, reflected a greater sincerity and seriousness about devolving power to the Tamil areas of Sri Lanka and decentralising administrative and financial authority. Her proposals, however, had a major shortcoming in pulling back from the previous commitment of the merger of the Northern and Eastern Provinces of Sri Lanka into a Tamil homeland, and creating a Tamil Government in that region. She could not avoid this modification of the earlier package because of the demands of the Sinhala and Muslim population of Eastern Provinces of Trincomalee, Batticoloa and Amperai; that they did not wish to be merged into a generic Tamil territorial entity.

Even these fresh proposals of 1995, went off into a spin because the Buddhist clergy and the opposition UNP Party refused to accept them. These proposals went into a drift by being referred to a Parliamentary Select Committee and other Consultation patterns which Chandrika Kumaratunga initiated to create a Sinhalese consensus on the proposals. By the middle of 1998, this process had gone into a limbo and the LTTE relaunched full-scale and widespread military operations against Sri Lankan forces. The Sinhalese establishment perhaps felt confident that the LTTE would be persuaded to political compromise: because the Sri Lankan Government had re-gained control over Jaffna and it managed the tense law and order situation in the Eastern Provinces. The Sri Lankan armed forces felt between 1995 and 1997 that they are gaining an upper hand in the ongoing battle of attrition against the LTTE. This anticipation has proved to be incorrect with the LTTE perpetrating major terrorist attacks in Colombo as well as in the Eastern Provinces and its conducting a fairly successful military campaign in Northern Sri Lanka and particularly in the Jaffna Peninsula. The Sri Lankan Government has no option but to take a firm stand against the LTTE in Jaffna despite the incremental successes of the LTTE. It is, however, clear that the Srilankan Government is on the defensive. The offer of Chief Ministership to Prabhakaran did not get a positive response from Prabhakaran who had categorically rejected a similar offer from President Jayawardene in 1987, when he was in a much weaker political and military situation.

There was the view that India should not commit the mistake of the IPKF which it did in 1987, getting embroiled in the internal affairs of another country. There was the view that given our security concerns regarding Pakistan and China and related defence expenditure, India should not take on additional regional security responsibilities. Then there was the view if India is committed to the unity and territorial integrity of Sri Lanka, India should not back peddle from giving full political and military support to the Sri Lankan Government. There was even the view that India should not hesitate to undertake military operations against the LTTE, if the opportunity arises to avenge the assassination of the Rajiv Gandhi and its killing a large number of Indian soldiers, who had gone there to safeguard

Tamil aspirations. There was also the view that the break up of Sri Lanka with the creation of an independent Tamil state there need not be a matter of concern to India.

Sri Lankan reactions to the prospects of any possible Indian re-intervention in Sri Lankan affairs are equally complex.

Sri Lankan Foreign Minister Kadirgamar has declared that the UN getting involved in Sri Lankan affairs, without Sri Lankan consent, would be a serious interference which would not be tolerated. Former Sri Lankan Ambassador to the United Nations Stanley Kalpage, has expressed the view that no organisation or country has the right to meddle in the internal affairs of another country. There have formal objections in Sri Lanka to the resolution passed by the EU Parliament in Brussels, suggesting that the Sri Lankan ethnic crisis be brought to the notice of the United Nations for appropriate action.

Most importantly, whatever compulsions there are for the Sri Lankan Government asking for India's military support, the reality and substantive prospects are that the segments of the Sri Lankan Government and Sinhalese majority would be critical of any Indian intervention rooted in their deep-rooted suspicions about India's emotional involvement with Tamils and India's alleged hegemonistic intentions. They would like Indian military support only as a short-term convenience, not for a solution of the ethnic problem. The Government of India's policies have been practical, measured and conscious about the limitations under which all parties concerned are functioning. We are politically supportive of the unity and integrity of Sri Lanka but according to both the LTTE and the Sri Lankan Government they wish to decide the issue between themselves by alternating military and political interaction. We should leave it at that. India should become operationally active only if the fall out of the Sri Lankan conflict tangibly and directly affects India's territorial integrity and security interests.

Ethnic Conflict in Sri Lanka— Current Predicament

Sri Lanka today is amidst chaos following the continuing ethnic conflict between Tamil and Sinhales. To understand how the seeds of this were sown a little bit of recalling the socio-political developments leading to the present ethnic conflict in Sri Lanka and some facts would be relevant.

Brief History of Socio-Political Developments

The first point to remember is that historically the trends of migration from India have led to the current demographic composition of India. One is talking about atleast three to four centuries before Christ. The first trend of migration was from East, Central coastal India stretching from Orissa to amost Bengal. These are today's Sinhalese in Sri Lanka. The second trend of migration was from Tamil Nadu and Tamil-speaking people of what is now Kerala. There were also migrations of descendents of Arabs and Malays. These constitute the Tamils of Sri Lanka today.

In more contemporary times since the third decade of 19th century more Tamils were taken to Central Highlands of Sri Lanka as Indentured labour. Today of the total population of Sri Lankans, about 15 per cent people are Tamils while the remaining majority is Sinhalese.

Language and religion contributed to the separate identity of the majority and minority communities in Sri Lanka. Buddhism came to Sri Lanka during the time of Emperor Ashok in the Maurya Period of Indian history. This is the religion of majority. The Sinhalese language is derived originally from Pali with further Philological contributions from Bengali, Portuguese and Oriya languages. Its script is of Brahmi style. The Tamil speaking people are either Hindu or Muslim. Their language is derived from ancient Tamil dialects.

Sri Lankan history right up to the advent of western colonial powers like Portuguese, Dutch and the English in that order is replete with trends of invasions from Southern India into Sri Lanka and Sinhala attacking the southern tip of Indian Peninsula and part of Tamil Nadu. The western colonial powers played the Tamils against Sinhalese and Sinhalese against Tamils to gain domination over the island. The British were most successful in this exercise when they took over Sri Lanka late in the 18th Century. They played the divide and rule tactic to the hilt of which Tamils were major beneficiaries, socially, administratively and economically. So at the time of Sri Lankan independence after the Second World War the seeds of Tamil-Sinhala antagonism were already sown during the British Colonial period.

With the advent of a democratic form of Government based on universal adult franchise, Sinhala majority naturally moved to redress the imbalances of previous Tamil influence in the polity and economy of the country.

But by the late fifties this attempt on redressing the imbalances of Sinhalese got converted into process of discrimination and later persecution of Tamils. Attempts were made by senior Sri Lankan Tamil leaders like Poonam Balun, Chelvanayakam and Thiruchelvan with Sinhalese leaders like Senanayake, Kotlawala and Bandarnaike to ensure that the Tamils get proportionate and fair share in the power structure administration and economy of Sri Lanka. But after coming to agreement, the Sinhalese leaders invariably backed out of these agreements.

This is the background in which Tamil militancy emerged from the mid-seventies in the island. Matters came to a head when Tamil militants killed Sri Lankan soldiers in Jaffna in July, 1983 which led to massive anti-Tamil riots in the Sinhalese areas. Nearly two lakh Tamils fled to India as refugees.

India got involved in Sri Lankan situation in 1983 and remained involved till the withdrawal of Indian Peace Keeping Force (IPKF) from the Island early in 1990. This is the over-simplified version of broad trends in Sri Lankan history and contemporary politics. The facts related to Indo-Sri Lankan agreements, the entry of IPKF into Sri Lanka and then its withdrawal are well known.

The new Government under President Chandrika Kumaratunga came to power in 1994 and immediately made peace overtures to the LTTE. The LTTE after some initial response did not consider the Sri Lankan Government's peace initiative enough and resumed hostilities. The Tamils of Sri Lanka are divided into three groups, the original Tamil migrants in the North and East of Sri Lanka, Tamil workers and Tamils known as Tamils of Indian origin who were in Central Highlands of the country and thirdly, Tamil Speaking Muslims who now claim separate socio-cultural identity.

Then, there are many Tamil militants and political parties; the LTTE is the most disciplined, dominent and effective Tamil Group who claim to represent Tamil interests. And they are in no mood for half-way compromises. Their main demand is of a separate Tamil country in Sri Lanka, 'EELAM'. In the interim phase they may be agreeable to complete autonomy, devolution of power, etc. though what Sri Lankan Government can give in response does not seem to be sufficient. President Chandrika Kumaratunga's attempt at making peace is now in disarray.

Hostile LTTE and Dilemma of Sri Lankan Government

Everybody interested in the strategic dilemmas of Sri Lankan should keep in mind that unless the Sri Lankan government meets the Tamil demands for autonomy and self government and a fair share in the power structure of Sri Lanka, the ethnic conflict might eventually break up into two countries which would be an unfortunate development from every point of view. It must be emphasized that compared to the Presidents and governments which have governed Sri Lanka over the last four decades, the present President of Sri Lanka has her heart in the right place and have both vision and the courage to work for an amicable solution of the ethnic problem with her Tamil patriots including the LTTE.

When Kumaratunga came to power she tried assiduously to come to terms with LTTE. The LTTE however felt that all the initial and preliminary concessions that she had given to facilitate discussion on substantive political issues have not been enough. The consequences have been the renewal of hostilities between the LTTE and the Sri Lankan Government.

At the height of LTTE hostalities President Kumaratunga asked a number of friendly countries for defence supplies and cooperation but she did not ask for anything strategically significant from India except that the Indian Navy to take preventive action in the Palk Straits against LTTE acquiring weapons and supplies from Tamil Nadu where they still have sufficient connections. Newspaper reports indicate that Indian Navy did undertake some such operations. Mr. Prabhakaran warned the Sri Lankan Government and the world at large that LTTE has taken on Sri Lankan Army successfully. That it has taught IPKF a lesson and LTTE is capable of teaching similar lesson to US forces if President Chandrika Kumaratunga invites any such force to help her in confronting the LTTE.

14

INDO-NEPALESE RELATIONS—SIGNIFICANCE OF G.P. KOIRALA'S VISIT

Nepalese Prime Minister G.P. Koirala's recent visit to Delhi has come after a gap of nearly four years, his last visit being in 1996. The visit is timely as Indo-Nepalese relations seem to be in the doldrums with undercurrents of anxieties and suspicions. Relations between India and Nepal have been a Kafkaesque phenomenon of attachments flavoured with emotional hostilities and complexes. The commonalities at the profoundest level of religion, language and culture generate impulses of apprehensions and disappointments on the part of Nepal towards India. Conversely, there is emotional and political frustrations in India about Nepal not being an uninhibited partner and supporter of India despite the factors which bind the peoples of India and Nepal together. It is a curious irony that Indo-Nepal interactions have always been animated by a deep responsiveness in India towards the well-being and aspirations of the people of Nepal. But after each successive stage of political transformations in Nepal in which India helped, relations between India and the successive power structures of Nepal have been subject to tensions and distances. India helped the Monarchy in Nepal free itself from the feudal and Oligarchic hold of the *Ranas*. But for nearly two decades after that, relations between the

Monarchy and the Government of India, remained adversarial.

India again supported the revival of democracy in Nepal in the early 1990s, but the successive elected Governments of Nepal have had problematic relations with the Government of India. The purpose here is not to dilate on the history of Indo-Nepalese relations, but to refer to the current dilemmas affecting bilateral relations and contrasting them with the benefits of uninhibited cooperation in certain spheres, if it could be achieved.

The problems affecting Indo-Nepalese relations could be conceptually categorised as follows:

(a) Re-structuring of the macro-level political terms of reference of bilateral relations;

(b) Fashioning a relationship in the context of Nepalese perceptions about the regional balance of influence which would serve Nepalese interests;

(c) Resolving territorial disputes and anxieties taking into account Nepal's views on its territorial identity and India's strategic concerns;

(d) Coming to equitable and fair arrangements about the utilisation of the water resources of river basins shared by the two countries;

(e) Resolving issues affecting the internal security of both Nepal and India arisen out of militant terrorism, secessionist separatist movements and problems of migration from Bhutan;

(f) Final practical solutions for Nepal's economic and commercial anxieties rooted in its being a land-locked country.

As far as re-structuring of terms of reference at macro-level bilateral political relations are concerned, there have been incremental demands from Nepal to revise the Indo-

Nepalese Treaty of Peace and Friendship of July 1950 and some of the guiding principles about bilateral trade, contained in the Treaty of Trade, Commerce and Transit, signed in the same year. Both these agreements while diluting assertive role envisaged in the previous agreements between Nepal and the British Government of India, still provide for a special relationship between Nepal and India. Though the agreements between the Government of free India and Nepal have been beneficial to the people of Nepal, it has to be acknowledged that Nepalese feel that the 1950 Indo-Nepalese Agreement somehow militate against their national identity and freedom of options. Now that fifty years have passed since the signing of the agreement and the world has changed in terms of global and regional politico-strategic equations, India should be responsive to Nepal's sensitivities on the subject. There should be no objection to re-negotiating the Treaty of Peace and Friendship of July, 1950. Nepal perhaps wishes to modify or amend articles 2 and 5 of the Treaty. Article 2 of the 1950 Treaty stipulates: "The two Governments hereby undertake to inform each other of any serious friction or misunderstanding with any neighbouring state likely to cause any breach in the friendly relations subsisting between the two Governments (of India and Nepal). Article 5 stipulates : "The Government of Nepal shall be free to import from and through the territory of India, arms, ammunition or warlike material and equipment necessary for the security of Nepal. The procedure for giving effect to this arrangement shall be worked out by the two Governments." Nepal feels that these Clauses restrict its sovereign discretion in conducting its foreign relations and fashioning its defence and security policies. The fact of the matter is that Nepal has not been inhibited in exercising its sovereign discretion in these matters. The only negative dimension of the situation has been that India has been worried and concerned about Nepal's security and defence cooperation and certain dimensions of its economic cooperation with China, off and on, over the last fifty years. In my view, India should not be averse to re-negotiating the 1950 Treaty in the context of contemporary geo-strategic environment. A certain chemistry and symbiosis in security, political and defence relationships which exist between Nepal and India would stand diluted and to that extent India has to backtrack from some aspects of this special relationship, to balance off this dilution. Nepal should be willing to accept this in the context of its keenness to revise the 1950 Treaty. We should be willing to initiate discussions for the revision of the 1950 Treaty. A logical consequence of this process, if it is agreed upon, would be for India to stop being over-anxious about Nepal's relations with China. The less anxiety we express, the less would the Nepalese feel that they can play the China card against India, and India card against China. But this does not mean that India should not be alert about any extensive Chinese politico-strategic presence in Nepal. Our approach should be to acknowledge Nepal's right to exercise its options, but at the same time convey categorical and clear message to Nepal that India would have to take remedial action to redress plans of any excessive involvement of China inside Nepal, and that India would to whatever is necessary for its security in the way of strategic, foreign policy and defence planning. The activities of the Intelligence Agencies of Pakistan and secessionist groups from our North East in Nepal, have become a matter of increasing concern to India. What is more important is that these activities can affect the internal cohesion and security of Nepal itself more seriously. Though at the formal governmental level the Nepalese side has given repeated assurances over the last decade on cooperation with India in this matter and about taking effective internal steps, the situation leaves much to be desired. India should not be assertively demanding in these matters but our case should be categorical and backed up with factual details. The Nepalese tendency to question Indian anxieties and describing it as unwarranted criticism, is also wrong. There is a substantive mutuality of interests in Nepal and India working together to deal with this particular problem. This cooperation is important to ensure the broader objective of sub-continental security and stability.

As far as the residual problems relating to trade and transit go, we must be a accommodating as possible, to meet Nepal's requirements in terms of additional transit routes and port facilities. In this era of global liberalisation, free flow of goods and of modernisation, the old anxieties which may have affected India in commerce and trade matters are not relevant at the most substantial levels. We must be helpful to Nepal in achieving its full international, economic and trade potential.

As far as *Kalapani* goes, both India and Nepal should avoid static negotiating positions which seems to have been the case so far. Some via media should be found by which India could acknowledge Nepal's *de jure* jurisdiction over the area while Nepal showing sensitivities to Indian security concerns else a *de facto* Indian presence in the area, till the pending issues relating to Sino-Indian boundary get finally resolved. Cooperation in utilising river water resources shared by India and Nepal, have potentialities of benefiting both countries economically and in developmental matters. But they have not taken off so far primarily because of Nepal's inhibitions and secondly because India has been adopting a strictly technical and commercial negotiating stance in finalising these objectives and then transforming them into reality. The agreements signed on the *Tanakpur* Hydro-electric Project and later the *Mahakali* Project still remain on paper. If these resources are fully exploited the prospects are of energy requirements of Nepal, Bihar and UP, even Northern Bengal, being met over a period of time with 85,000 megawatts of energy becoming available. Both technical anxieties on thc part of India and political anxieties on the part of Nepal have stymied the prospects of such cooperation.

It is time that a creative and innovative approach underpins policies of both countries in this important sphere of cooperation for mutual benefit. Though smaller than India's larger neighbours, Bangladesh and Pakistan, good relations with Nepal are of high strategic importance to India. Our endeavour should be to encourage consolidation of this relationship despite the complexities and pressures impinging on them in the foreseeable future. Our approach should be to convey assurances to Nepal about India's desire to have a stable partnership with that country on the basis of equality and mutual respect and for mutual benefit.

One of the points related to Nepalese migration from Bhutan to Nepal, though a bilateral matter between the two countries merits our assistance in resolving the problem. India's National Security Adviser, Brajesh Mishra, has visited Nepal earlier this summer. Prime Minister Koirala's visit to New Delhi raises the discussions to the highest political level. It is reasonable to anticipate that all these problems must have been discussed between Vajpayee and Koirala. One earnestly hopes that the discussions were animated by a spirit of reasoning together and give and take.

India and Nepal-Dilemmas of Asymetrical Co-existence

The latest round of Indo-Nepalese foreign office consultations, was concluded in the first weekend of February, 2001. Nepalese Foreign Secretary Narain Shamsher Thapa, led a four-member delegation to exchange views with our Foreign Secretary Lalit Man Singh. This is a part of the annual exercise in bilateral consultations which India has with all important countries. Relations with Nepal being a matter of high priority in India's regional policies, would be labouring a truism. The importance of the latest round of bilateral talks, therefore need hardly to be overemphasised. Of late, Indo-Nepal relations have been in doldrums with some negative undercurrents, particularly during the last 18 months or so. The outcome of the recent round of talks has to be assessed in the context of trends and developments of the recent past.

Nepalese relations with India are particularly subject to the impulses and pressures of domestic politics in Nepal, more so than Nepal's relations with other countries of the SAARC region or with its other important neighbour, China. The roots of this phenomenon can be traced back to the Indian involvement in restoring the authority of the monarchy and democracy in Nepal in the early 1950s in which India was significantly influential, ending the feudal authoritarian rule of the Ranas.Whatever the legitimacy or merits of India's involvement in the domestic politics of Nepal at that time, Nepalese political circles and public opinion acquired an apprehensive under-current about potentialities of India to interfere in Nepal's domestic affairs at the deepest emotional and psychological levels. The shared cultural, religious and to some extent linguistic identities between India and Nepal underpinned by India's largeness compared to Nepal, compounded this apprehension and still constitutes an important ingredient of Nepalese mindset about India.

Close connections between Indian political parties and the political parties of Nepal during the long period of monarchical Panchayat rule in Nepal, especially influenced the elite segments of the power structure of Nepal, almost till the beginning of the last decade, the 1990s. One expected that restoration of democracy in Nepal in the early 1990s and monarchy assuming a constitutional role, would bring about some stability in Indo-Nepalese relations. This did not happen because political parties of Nepal had to cope with broadly shared apprehensions about potential Indian influence or domination in Nepal's public opinion as India and Indian policies have been used as an instrumentality to gain power by different political parties at different times. The result has been the undercurrents of appehension and concern affecting Indo-Napalese relations, despite geographical proximity, convergence of interests and shared ethno-religious and cultural identities.

Nepal having being sand-witched between China and India, has placed it in a difficult predicament which India should appreciate. The 1962 Sino-Indian war enhanced the criticality of this predicament because India's Nepal policies were affected by Indian apprehensions about China in terms of potentialities of expansion of Chinese strategic and political influence in the border states of Nepal and Bhutan. India became more concerned about possibilities of closer Nepalese political, particularly, defence cooperation with China. This was logical from India's point of view. Conversely, for a period of nearly two and half decades, from the beginning of 1960s, Nepal's foreign policy did not show any inhibition about playing the China card in the structuring of its relations with India. To some extent Nepal's close relations with the military regime of Pakistan added to Indian concern, Nepal being landlocked, its only easy access to sea and trade routes being through India, constitute a dependency on India which the Nepalese could not avoid, but do not relish very much. India due to its own security concerns and certain aspects of its own economic interests, could not afford to be fully responsive to Nepal's demands and aspirations regarding this aspect of bilateral relations.

This is the basic matrix in which Indo-Nepalese relations are evolving. More recent developments during the last decade have not helped the situation. The return of the

Bhattarai and Koirala Governments in the 1990s generated expectations about a qualitative improvement in Indo-Nepalese relations. The Narashimha Rao and Gujral Governments' interaction with the democratic regimes in Nepal and resulting initial policy decisions were the basis of this expectation. But the Nepalese government was subject to continuous pressure from other political parties about succumbing to Indian influence and pressure. The consequence was not only these policy decisions not being implemented but the emergence of new issues, complicating Indo-Nepalese relations. The agreements on the utilisation of water resources and for hydro-electric projects like the Tanakpur and Mahakali projects have not taken off the ground. Nepal still chafes at India not granting additional transit routes to Nepal through Indian territory, to Bangladesh. A major issue affecting India-Nepal relations over the last decade has been Nepal's demand that the Indo-Nepalese Treaty of 1950 should either be replaced by a new treaty of it should be extensively modified to remedy the Nepalese perception of the 1950 treaty diminishing Nepal's sovereignty particularly in the sphere of Nepal's freedom of options to fashion its defence cooperation and security policies. The Government of Bhutan expelling a large number of Nepalese from its territory, questioning the Bhutanese national identity resulted in large number of Nepalese from Bhutan taking refuge in Nepal. Nepal wanted India to intervene with the government of Bhutan to take back these Nepalese. While India made a general suggestion to the Government of Bhutan to reconsider its decision fairly and objectively, its policy stance was that it was a bilateral issue between Bhutan and Nepal which they should sort out themselves. Nepal was not pleased with the detached attitude that India took on the issue. The more recent decisions of the Government of Bhutan and Nepal creating a joint investigative or fact-finding mechanism to deal with this question is a welcome development which hopefully will change Nepalese views about India on this issue.

Nepal's desire to re-claim the *Kalapani* area demanding Indian pull out has introduced a territorial dispute in Indo-Nepalese relations. As if this was not enough, the increase in anti-Indian operations by the Inter-Services Intelligence Agency of Pakistan from Nepal and Nepal being used as a spring-board for subversive activities in Jammu and Kashmir, have become critical issue in Indo-Nepalese relations. The hijacking of the Indian Airlines aircraft from Kathmandu in December 1999 was a manifest concretisation of Indian apprehensions about Pakistani intelligence activities originating in Nepal. That Pakistani intelligence agencies in collaboration with anti-Indian elements in Nepal are active in fomenting anti-Indian feeling in that country was proved late last December or early in January when large-scale anti-Indian agitations occured in Nepal against alleged anti-Nepal remarks made by Indian film star Hrithik Roshan in a television interview with Simi Grewal. This was a successful exercise in psychological and propaganda warfare against India which mercifully did not prolong. The fact of the matter was that Hrithik Roshan never made any anti-Nepalese remarks in any interview anywhere. Even the Nepalese media and Government have come to acknowledge this fact. The phenomenon, however, proved how fertile Nepal has become for entities aiming to fracture Indo-Nepalese relations.

Indo-Nepalese Foreign-Secretaries level talks in the last week of January, 2001 were held in this background. The Agenda of the discussions was rooted to these critical developments. The main items were: Discussion on the revision of the Indo-Nepal Treaty, the issue of *Kalapani*, further steps to be taken for the implementation of the *Mahakali* agreement, which are specific to Indo-Nepalese relations. The broader issues discussed were developments related to SAARC, feasibility of sub-regional cooperation, regional security and political developments and assessment regarding improvement of economic and trade relations. India's security concern in terms of externally-sponsored subversive activities was an item of special attention. Full details and the trends of discussions and resulting decisions are not made public. Naturally so, because requirements of transparency have to be tempered with the sensitivity of the issues discussed in the context of Nepalese and Indian concerns. However, there are indications that the discussions were characterised by a constructive and practical approach. India is not averse to revising or replacing the 1950 Treaty by an agreement of a normal type which governs inter-state relations. But then Nepal should accept that the special relationship and facilities which characterise Indo-Nepalese relations will become irrelevant if the relationship is to be formal, replacing the special relationship which has lasted for nearly 50 years. On *Kalapani*, India has emphasised the legitimacy of its presence in the area and the logic of it in historical, legal and strategic terms. On other issues, both sides seem to have agreed to evolve practical solutions keeping in mind the substantive concerns of each other.

This round of talks, therefore, in some ways was significant to the critical context in which they were held. It is clear that close relationship between the two countries needs stabilisation in the context of the asymmetry between Nepal and India, of differing concerns and attitudes on certain issues. Indian policy-makers are conscious of their special responsibility for fulfilling this objective but progress towards it also depends on Nepal's capacity for responsiveness, particularly to India's security concerns. This cannot be a one-sided unrequited exercise.

15

DEVELOPMENTS IN NEPAL— TRAGEDY COMPOUNDED BY POLITICAL UNCERTAINTIES

Two weeks have gone by since the bloody assassination of the Royal family of Nepal by Prince Dipendra. A two-member Enquiry Committee comprising of Chief Justice Keshav Prasad Upadhyaya and the Speaker of the Nepalese Parliament Taranath Ranabhatt has submitted its report confirming the fact that Dipendra murdered his family members and then turned the gun on himself, ending his own life. People of Nepal are still living under the shock. Their collective recovery in psychological and emotional terms would be slow because the Monarchy in Nepal has been and is more than a political institution. It is underpinned by emotional, religious, cultural and social impulses as a cementing factor of Nepal's national identity. The details of the events in the Narayanhity Palace on the first of June have been reported in detail in sub-continental as well as foreign media. The reasons leading to the assassination, attendent events and later developments are now a matter of public knowledge. Though the conspiracy theorists still insist on questions which they say have remained unanswered even in the Enquiry Report of Justice Keshav Prasad Upadhyaya. More important is to assess the implications of the traumatic event in deeper and long-term political prospects.

The first point to be made is that some of the political confusion and resulting uncertainties could have been avoided. The official statements after the assassination that the deaths were due to an accidental firing off of an automatic gun and then Dipendra being declared the King while he was in deep coma with certainty of impending death was motivated by Palace establishment desire to protect the image and credibility of the Royal family and to cover up the physical, psychological and emotional aberrations and controversies which affected the royal family. This assessment is further confirmed by the fact that Prime Minister G.P. Koirala was informed of the accident nearly an hour or an hour and half of the assassination. Even then he was given wrong initial information by the Palace that King Birendra had suffered from a stroke. This exercise at preserving the image of the royal family was patently inept and obfuscatory. The moment Dipendra died and the Royal Advisory Council decided to nominate Prince Gyanendra as the King, this effort at cover up had to be abandoned and the new King himself ordered the inquiry with the stipulation that a report to be submitted within three days. He also took the radical step of giving free access to the Members of the Inquiry Committee to the venue of the assassination and the Members of the Royal family. But the damage had already been done. The basic facts became public knowledge, and available to the media within hours, despite the first official statements of the government of Nepal. The issue became politicised rooted in the political orientations of the various Nepalese political parties. The public in general was not willing to believe governmental information. The Communist Party (Maoist) took full advantage of the situation and immediately propagated the theory of conspiracy, accusing Indian and American intelligence agencies of organising the assassination, of making Prince Dipendra the scapegoat with the ultimate aim of destroying Nepal's sovereignty and independent identity, and merging it with India. They also asserted that King Birendra was generally aware of this conspiracy and was therefore in touch with top leadership of their party (Communist Party-Maoist), ironically through Prince Gyanandra, the new King. The alleged objective of King Birendra to persuade the Maoists to join the National Coalition. It is necessary to recall the political developments during the last decade to understand Nepal's current predicament and future prospects to some extent. The restoration of democracy in Nepal has been a difficult experiment. There have been nine or ten Governments in Nepal with the Communist Party and the Nepalese Congress alternating in power. Each of the political parties is faction-ridden. Each of them when in power has been accused of corruption and mal-administration. The most remarkable achievement of King Birendra was that of his nurturing this faltering democratic experiment within the framework of the role of the constitutional monarchy which he voluntarily assumed when he gave up his over-arching executive authority in 1990. The processes of governance in Nepal, particularly over the last three years, has been afflicted by its lack of control over administration, particularly at the district level.

There are reports that Communist Party (Maoists) is running parallel administrations atleast in six to ten districts of Nepal. It is in this context that King Birendra authorised the deployment of the Royal Nepalese Army in 5 districts to control the situation reversing his earlier decision of refusing to allow the army to get involved when Prime Minister Koirala asked for it last year. While the Maoists questioned, and would like to continue questioning the legitimacy of King Gyanandra, the other political parties notably the Nepalese Congress and Rashtriya Prajatantric Dal would aim at sustaining the succession and nurturing the monarchical institutions, so that the Nepalese Maoists' objective of abolishing the Monarchy and establishing a communist Nepalese Republic does not succeed. That is why Prime Minister Koirala was quick in recognising the succession and supporting the transition to new Monarch. The new Monarch himself will be subject to imperatives of the status that he has acquired. King Gyanandra is reported to have been opposed to revival of democracy in 1990. He is reported to be politically more ambitious and functionally more assertive. An additional strength which he has is, the economic resources at his personal command. His main challenge would be that of adjusting to the role of a constitutional Monarch on the basis of the example set by his brother, late King Birendra. He will also have to shed his somewhat distant and elitist persona and work at reaching out to the people, to gain their goodwill and confidence. His overall task would be to restore stability and nurture democracy. The success or failure of his efforts in this regard would depend on the interaction between him, the Nepalese army and the political parties. The Army High Command has been deliberate in not getting involved in the feud of the royal family, leading to the assassination and its aftermath and at the same time not taking any overt stand in the interaction between the political parties and the King. The attitude of the Royal Nepalese army would be a decisive factor influencing the post-assassination structuring of the politics of Nepal.

At a deeper level, the socioeconomic predicament of Nepal needs to be taken note of. Nepal is a landlocked and amongst the least developed in the world. Within Nepal itself there are internal socioeconomic disparities of a critical nature. The Kathmandu valley and portions of eastern Nepal are comparatively well to do, when one looks at western Nepal. Nearly half of the country, therefore is in need of purposive governance and developmental inputs.

This can be achieved only if there are minimum levels of political stability and continuity. This would take some time given the turmoils generated by the assassination.

The disturbed and unstable Nepal can create serious political and security concerns for India. The floating Nepalese population between Bhutan, India and Nepal, with indeterminate national identity will provide fertile ground for violence and other categories of crimes. An instable Nepal would provide greater opportunities for the ISI of Pakistan and terrorist and separatist elements from the North-Eastern states of India, a phenomenon which already exist in Nepal. Nepal is an important buffer state between India and China. Nepal in turmoil due to instability and fractious politics can get enmeshed in foreign policy and security decisions, which can have a detrimental effect not only on Indo-Nepal but Sino-Indian relations. It is in this context that India was prompt in sending a message of support to Prime Minister Koirala and in recognising King Gyanandra the moment he was installed as King. The Indian response to the crisis was measured, practical, sympathetic and respectful to the sense of national identity of the Nepalese people. Once the situation gets stabilised and some political normalcy returns to Nepal, India should be promote in enhancing economic and commercial cooperation with Nepal.

The most productive potentialities of bilateral cooperation lie in the sphere of coming to agreements on water resource sharing between India and Nepal. All of Nepal's important rivers flow to into India. Nepal's hydro-electric power potential has been assessed at between 43,000 to 45,000 Megawatts. The geographical predicament of Nepal is such that its hydel resources can be developed only with India as a partner, subject to Nepal's voluntary desire and willingness. India should indicate its inclination to cooperate with Nepal on the Chisepani, on the Karnàli and the Pancheshwar Project on the Mahakali which would be particularly beneficial to the economically deprived regions of western Nepal. Parellely both governments could initiate action to implement Barakshetra Project on the Saptakosi River in eastern Nepal. This along with the Burhi Gandak Project, if made operational will be mutually beneficial. There is also considerable scope for Indo-Nepal cooperation in the sphere of environment management, flood control and agricultural cooperation.

On territorial dispute like Kalapani, India should adopt an imaginative and accommodating approach to the extent feasible. While these potentialities exist, the over-riding complexity which impacts on them as a limitation is the profound sense of national identity and pride of the people of Nepal, and we should be sensitive and responsive to this factor. The very commonalities between India and Nepal generates complexes and apprehensions among the Nepalese which we should understand and assuage. Indo-Nepalese relations are at a critical juncture due to the departure of king Birendra from the scene. The capacity of Nepal to return to normalcy and stability in a democratic framework and India's ability to be supportive without being prescriptive would be the factors which would determine the future of Indo-Nepal relations.

16

INDIA AND MYANMAR— A CRUCIAL RELATIONSHIP

The recent visit of General Maung Aye, the Deputy Chief of the military Government of Myanmar revived the debate about the advisability of India nurturing and expanding relations with Myanmar when it is under military rule. General Maung led a 16-member delegation to Delhi and had extensive discussions with our Prime Minister and Minister for External Affairs and with officials of our Ministries of Defence, Home Affairs and External Affairs. This high-level visit is a continuation of the process which had commenced in March 1972, when the then Prime Minister Mr. Narasimha Rao took a decision to activate relations with Myanmar which were in a drift particularly after the Armed Forces High Command of Myanmar refused to hand over power to Ms. Aung San Suu Kyi.

Recalling the background in which the current phase of Indo-Myanmar relations have evolved and the factors influencing them would be pertinent. It is to be remembered that in the initial period after India and Myanmar (then Burma) became independent, Indo-Myanmar relations were very close. Pandit Jawaharlal Nehru had visited Rangoon during 1945-46 and was a strong advocate of Burma's independence. His relations with Col. Aung San Founding President of Burma, the father of Aung San Suu Kyi and with the 2nd Prime Minister U Nu were based on their historical experience against colonial rule and a conviction about convergence of mutual interests.

Indo-Burmese relations were negatively affected for long years when General Ne Win held power in Rangoon. There was no break in relations but they were maintained at only the formal level and there was not too much economic, political or technological cooperation in bilateral relations during this period. The only exception is the strong and vibrant linkage of Buddhism remaining unaffected after the disappearance of democracy from Myanmar. Another factor which created distances between the two countries was an amount of discriminatory treatment which persons of Indian origin in Myanmar were subjected to. Myanmar's refusing to become a member of the British Commonwealth and of the non-aligned movement in its initial stages also contributed to a lack of depth in Indo-Myanmar relations. This situation characterised a profound contradiction in India's relations with one of its most important neighbours, because in terms of geo-strategic location, security considerations, the availability of markets and complementarity of mutual economic needs, India's relations with Myanmar, should have been multi-faceted and substantial. The initial insularship of the Myanmar Government and India's ideological reservations about military regimes were the root cause of this contradiction. Rajiv Gandhi tried to resolve this contradiction towards the middle of his tenure as Prime Minister in the late 1980s. Some expansion took place in bilateral trade relations and a beginning was made in providing some defence supplies to Myanmar. Things went into a spin again when the military authorities of Myanmar refused to accept the electoral verdict of their people in 1990. In any case, the V.P. Singh and Chandra Sekhar Governments were so enmeshed in domestic political uncertainties that they were not able to concentrate on forming a cohesive foreign policy with a clear sense of priorities. It must be underlined that the Government of Myanmar dealt with India's critical reaction to their assuming power with sobriety and without any polemical reactions. Nor did they react to Indian public and media criticism, and our Government's attitude by doing anything negative against India during the period 1989 and the beginning of 1991. It would be relevant to mention here that important western powers like the USA, the United Kingdom, Germany, and Japan from Asia, tried to generate political pressure on the military regime of Myanmar at the political level to give up power, to Aung San Suu Kyi, the leader of the National League for Democracy. These powers also formally requested India, to join their embassies in Rangoon to present a formal protest to the military regime for its not respecting the results of the elections. The industrially advanced powers were hypocritical in this exercise because while indulging in general political opposition to the military regime, they continued their investments in Myanmar and their export trade to Myanmar. While India did not join them, it did convey its disappointment at the negation of democracy in Myanmar through bilateral diplomatic channels.

There were some considerations which influenced India to revive relations with Myanmar. First, Myanmar is geo-strategically important for India. Myanmar abutts on our sensitive North-Eastern States and portions of Bangladesh. Myanmar shares an equally significant border with China. Thus the northern frontiers of Myanmar constitute a tri-junction with Bangladesh, China and the eastern Frontiers of India. Myanmar is also important country on the rim of the Bay of Bengal, lying astride India's South Eastern trade routes. The South Eastern Coast of Myanmar is close enough to the Nicobar and Andaman islands of India, so developments in that area could affect our security interests in the Bay of Bengal.

Secondly, India-Myanmar cooperation to counter drugs smuggling, narcotic crimes, insurgency and security threats to our north-eastern states were acknowledged as imperatives for our foreign policy. It was equally important to ensure that Myanmar does not become part of an exclusive area of influence of other powers in the region with whom India has uneasy relations, China for instance. This is an objective which would be shared by the people and governments of Myanmar also with a view to maintaining their independence and freedom of options in dealing with their foreign policy and security concerns. It was, therefore, considered necessary to normalise relations with Myanmar regardless of the kind of government in power there. The third factor was clinically rational. While India remains committed to democracy and related values, there was no reasons for India to unilaterally assume responsibility of creating democracies in other countries. This had to be the choice and responsibility of the people of the country concerned, in this case the people of Myanmar.

Preliminary discussions were held between the Government of India and the Myanmar foreign office between February and August, 1992. I was a participant in these discussions, which ultimately led to the visit of the Vice Foreign Minister of Myanmar U Baswe, to India between 11th and 13th August, 1992. Myanmar's delegation outlined three points during this visit. Myanmar respects India's commitment to democracy and hopes India would be patient about the revival of democracy in Myanmar. Secondly, Myanmar acknowledged that there exist security and political concerns which are shared by both countries. Myanmar was therefore willing to cooperate with India in taking joint action to meet the security and strategic interests of both countries. The third point which U Baswe made was that Myanmar was eager and willing to increase economic and technological cooperation with

India. Another important anxiety of India was the increasing strategic linkages between Myanmar and China. The Chinese had already built an all-weather road from Kunming in China to Mandalay in Myanmar, which they were planning to extend to Yangon. There were also reports of the Myanmar Government providing some visiting and berthing facilities to the Chinese Navy. When these points were raised with the Myanmar authorities, they responded by saying that they would be ready to accept India's assistance in building up the transportation network in their country. They indicated that they would like India making the road from Imphal and Mandalay and then on to Yangon as a parallel to the Chinese road building activities. They denied any military facilities being given to China and added that they would be willing to give general facilities to the Indian Navy also in their ports and on their coast. There have been visits of the Home Secretaries, the Controller of Drugs, Ministers of Commerce, between the two countries between 1993 and now. Myanmar becoming a part of ASEAN and ARF over the last five years adds to the legitimacy of the Myanmar Government in the eyes of other governments in the region, which by extension lends validity to our having relations with that country.

The visit of General Maung Aye, is, therefore, timely and contributive to strengthening our bilateral relations. The visit will increase Indo-Myanmar cooperation to prevent insurgency along the 1600 kilometre sensitive Indo-Myanmar border. Myanmar has problems with *Kachins,* and we have problems with *Naga* separatists. There is extensive complementarity of needs in the economic, commercial and technological spheres between Myanmar and India. Activating economic and technological cooperation was an important objective of this visit. If India speeds up the building up of Imphal-Tamu-Kalemayo Road, a true beginning would be made to consolidate Myanmar as a land bridge between India and South East Asian countries.

Dealing with a government in effective control in Myanmar which is recognised by all the important powers in the region does not imply any dilution of India's commitment to democracy. It is sufficient if India focusses on strengthening its own democracy instead of moralising about it to the other countries and other people. The overridding consideration in our relations with our neighbours should be safeguarding our interests and contributing to the stability and well-being of the other country concerned.

Strategic Importance of Myanmar for India

The pre-occupations with the presentation of Railway and General Budget, the continuing concerns about initiating a dialogue on Kashmir, preceded by a further extension of ceasefire, and such other domestic pre-occupations led to only marginal notice being taken of Foreign Minister Jaswant Singh's important visit to Myanmar in February, 2001. The visit was an important step towards structuring Indo-Myanmar relations in a practical framework. Jaswant Singh's visit was a follow up of the visit of the Vice President of Myanmar, Mr. Maung Aue to Delhi from 12th to 21st November, 2000. The most important event during the visit was the inauguration of the *Tamu Kalewa* Road being built in collaboration with the Government of Myanmer by the Border Roads Organisation of the Government of India. Geo-strategically Myanmar straddles an area which dominates our security perceptions in more than one dimension. Myanmar borders the north-eastern states of Nagaland and Manipur which have been the scene of separatist movements having links across the border with Myanmar's militant groups, sharing both ethnic and linguistic connections. Myanmar's north- eastern borders constitute a trijunction of India's borders with Myanmar and China. The south-western coast of Myanmar straddles India's shipping lanes through the Bay of Bengal to South East Asia. This coastline is close enough to the Anadaman and Nicobar Islands, the importance of which in India's security planning has increased over the years. A cooperative and friendly relationship with Myanmar is of utmost importance to India in terms of India's political and security interests. The issue of idealistic and moral dilemmas of dealing with a military regime which did not allow a power to a democratically elected political party, the National League for Democracy, led by Ms. Aung San Suu Kyi had inhibited India's reviving normal relations with Myanmar in the late 1980s and early 1990s. These inhibitions have receded gradually since 1992 on the basis of the following rationale.

The first and foremost, India's vital security and political interests require that we had a working relationship with whichever government is in effective power in Myanmar. Secondly, while India's commitment to democracy is incontrovertible, India need not take on the responsibility of sustaining democracies in other countries in a situation where the people of the country concerned themselves were re-conciled to their regime. Third, there is an increasing trend in Myanmar's politics where the military regime is engaged in negotiations with Aung San Suu Kyi and the political parties in Myanmar. Fourth, the countries of the ASEAN, who have a closer relationship with Myanmar were inclined to deal with the military regime considering it effective and stable enough to make Myanmar a member of the ASEAN and its Security Forum. And fifth, there are potentialities of long-term mutually beneficial economic relations between India and Myanmar. The sociological dimension of internal politics in Myanmar is that though the military regime, the State Peace and Development Council, may not have the full acceptance and support of the people of Myanmar, but popular attitude of the people believes in the credibility of *Tatmadaw* (the armed forces of the country) as a stable instrumentality of governance. The militarisation of Burmese society since the days of General Ne Win has resulted in almost every family having some personal connection with the Burmese armed forces, according to Dr. Mary P. Callahan. There is also the curious but interesting phenomenon of the armed forces being the main avenue of upward social mobility and economic well being. In may ways the military regime is considered a beneficial institution. Another specialist on Myanmar's political situation David I. Steinberg, in a recently published book; *Burma Myanmar-Strong Regime Weak State*states that the Burmese people perceive power as finite. This means that the sharing of power implies giving up power which is not easily undertaken either on an individual or institutional basis. In such circumstances power and *loyalty* become personalised. And therefore there is an inclination to accept authoritarian regimes if they give stability and minium economic security to civil society, it would be pretencious to claim that India's policy of reviving sustaining contacts with the military regime was rooted in such a deep intellectual analysis but a general perception on these lines reflected in the political situation in Myanmar, was also a factor in India's establishing communications with the military regime of Myanmar.

Jaswant Singh's visit was the culmination of a process on these lines which commenced under Narasimha Rao's regime in March 1992. The initial contacts were between senior officials of the foreign ministries of the two countries, the home ministries and then between officials of our Ministry of Commerce and Department of Drugs Control. The specific objectives of reviving relations with Myanmar were first to create cooperative arrangements between Myanmar and India to counter secessionist and terrorist activities on both sides of the Indo-Myanmar border. Secondly, to ensure that Myanmar's security and foreign policies remain balanced in terms of Myanmar's relations with China on the one hand and India on the other. A third objective was to enhance mutual cooperation in controlling the illegal trafficking of drugs from the "Golden Triangle" across sub-continental India, to other parts of the world. The fourth objective was to create equations with Myanmar to safeguard our security interests in the Bay of Bengal and the shipping lanes which are of considerable importance to Indian trade. There was series of hiccoups in Indo-Myanmar relations in the mid-1990s when India awarded Jawaharlal Memorial Prize for International understanding to Aung San Suu Kyi, overruling reservations of Myanmar's military regime. Then there was our Defence Minister's accusation that Myanmar's relationship with China implied a security threat to India and that Myanmar was becoming a partner in the Chinese objective of strategic encirclement of India. However, by the end of the year 1999, Jaswant Singh's interaction with his Myanmar counterparts at various meetings at the ASEAN removed the misunderstandings and distances created by these events.

It would be relevant to mention that China's South East Asian policies have become a major factor influencing India's policies towards the ASEAN region and specially towards Myanmar. China since the middle of year 2000 has launched a special programme of developing its South western Province of Yunam. China is developing the capital of the Province of Kunming as a regional energy and transportation. China is also developing airports, river ports and land corridors from Kunming towards South East Asia through Myanmar. There is a discernable Chinese objective of reaching out to the Bay of Bengal through Myanmar. Paralleley China is creating communication networks in the South East Asian region, participating in the construction of several trans-Asian roads and railway projects in collaboration with Myanmar, Thailand, Cambodia, Laos and Vietnam under the umbrella of the six-nation Greater Mekong Sub-Regional cooperation arrangement.

India's regional foreign policy orientations therefore necessarily involves sustaining a normal relationship with China and at the same time structuring substantial economic relations with the countries mentioned above. Myanmar being geographically the most proximate South East Asian country, has a high priority in India's regional policies. China has substantive defence cooperation arrangements with Myanmar. This relationship viewed in the background of China seeking to link up with ports in Myanmar through *Mekong* and *Irrawady* rivers and China having logistical facilities for its navy on the south western coast of Myanmar have obvious strategic and security implications for India. It is in this context that parallel to Kunming-Lashio-Mandalay road, India negotiated the construction of *Tamu-Kalewa* road which was inaugurated by Jaswant Singh during his February visit to Myanmar. The extension of this road further south is under discussion. Two subjects of equal significance discussed by Jaswant Singh with his Myanmar counter-parts were a move forward on the six-nation *Ganga-Mekong* project linking up the two river basins for communication and developmental purposes. The countries involved are India, Myanmar, Vietnam, Thailand, Laos and Cambodia. If this grouping succeeds in developing an integrated programme of regional transport, it would contribute to the larger Asian Highway project which has been under discussion now for nearly three decades. The second subject discussed was the possibility of importing natural gas from Myanmar into India. There are possibilites of constructing a gas pipeline from the *Kaladan* basin, Assam and Meghalaya. Another or alternative gas pipeline could be built from Akyab (Shitwe) to West Bengal. Jaswant Singh's visit and discussions was first affirmation of the fact that Myanmar with its location between South Asia and South East Asia, its western coastline dominating India's coastline to the eastern reaches of the Indian Ocean has the potential to be a major South East Asian power. Secondly, his visit and other high level exchanges over the last two years are the acknowledgement that recognising this potentiality India wishes to build a substantive and long-term relationship with Myanmar. Myanmar, in many ways is the pivot for security arrangements of special interest to India. The beginnings made in recent years in establishing durable equations with Myanmar are timely and relevant.

17

REGIONAL FORA : ASEAN AND SAARC

In current situation, three elements constituting the additional positive dimensions in our relations with ASEAN are :

(i) We have moved from our status as a partial dialogue partner to become a full dialogue partner of the ASEAN.

(ii) We have been admitted to the quasi-institutional security arrangements being put in place for the ASEAN region, namely, the Asian Regional Forum (ARF).

(iii) The ASEAN has stopped linking their interaction with India with their relations with Pakistan in the regional multilateral context.

India getting full dialogue partnership, in my assessment, was the result of the following factors:—

First, the tangible results of partial dialogue status cooperation which included interaction between the private sectors of India and the ASEAN countries were sufficiently satisfactory to convince the ASEAN countries of the desirability of expanded full dialogue status cooperation for mutual benefit. Secondly, the pace and orientation of India's economic reforms, and market and joint venture potentialities of such cooperation were assessed as complementary and responsive to the interests of the ASEAN countries. Thirdly, the Western democracies led by the United States which have considerable influence in the

ASEAN region, might have advised the Governments of ASEAN countries to expand their relations with India, arguing that it would support India's economic liberalisation policies and ensure India's becoming an increasingly useful partner in new global economic equations being structured under the leadership of the United States. Fourthly, a large economy like that of India's getting involved with the ASEAN could have been considered a factor balancing the presence of other powerful economies in the ASEAN market.

The transformation in attitude of ASEAN reflects the ASEAN countries having undertaken a long-term strategic introspection about regional security beyond the short-term limitations on which they had based their initial objections about an Indian role in regional security arrangement. India's geo-strategic location, its military-technological capacities, and its over-arching position in the South Asian region have been acknowledged as a factor affecting the stability not only of the South Asian but the extended South East Asian region also. Secondly, all the major Asian-Pacific powers were being included in the ARF, namely, USA, Russia, China and Japan. To exclude India, straddling the southern extremities of the Asian land mass and the Western and Northwestern flank of the ASEAN region would have led to an anomalous situation. Bringing India into the ARF would ensure for the ASEAN a security environment in which all the important powers which could impinge on the safety and stability of ASEAN countries undertake the responsibilities and obligations envisaged in the terms of reference of the ARF. Having China and India both in the ARF by which both these countries would accept the obligations of the security arrangements would reduce the prospects of negative competition between them in dealing with the ASEAN countries. Added to this was the assurance which India has been conveying since 1991 that in conformity with its policy regarding participation in multilateral arrangements, India would not bring up bilateral issues or controversies in such a forum. There is also the speculative expectation that India becoming a part of the ARF would temper its nuclear weapons ambitions.

In the new equations that India has to establish with different power centres of the world, a positive and substative equation with ASEAN is and should be a matter of high priority.

II

Some time towards the end of 1961, Pandit Nehru presided over a meeting of Indian Ambassadors in South East Asian countries in New Delhi. Needless to recall that the system of military alliances led by the United States and engineered by the Western powers were in full operation. Apart from the NATO, the CENTO, the SEATO, and ANZUS were bastions of the "cordon sanitaire" against the Soviet Union, China and the Communist bloc. There were a number of Indian Heads of Mission in the meeting who expressed their unhappiness at India's not having good relations with countries of South East Asia. They were of the view that geographical, historical and cultural factors should have made India more attentive to the area stretching from "Indo-China" and "Myanmar" to the Philippines. They were also of the view that India isolating itself from the South East Asian region was not in India's strategic interests. Panditji's reported response was brief and ascerbic. He said that India should not be expected to run around "coca cola governments"!

The considerations, the mindset, and the compulsions of Indian foreign policy at that time manifested a schizopherenic approach towards South East Asia. On the one hand we chanted the patronising mantra of having deep rooted historical and cultural ties with the peoples of

South East Asia; on the other we lectured them on the unwisdom of becoming part of military alliances organised by the United States primarily for its own interests.

The result was our creating distances between ourselves and the South East Asian countries and generally perturbing or offending them on both counts. Our emphasising the origin of their social and cultural systems based on Indian contributions offended their sense of self and individuality. Our critical evaluation of their foreign and defence policies at that point of time, in their opinion showed a lack of understanding on our part about their worries and concerns at that time regarding the threat of Soviet or Chinese expansion in South East Asia. The consequence was a politically tenuous and formalistic relationship between India and this region and economic interaction only at marginal levels.

Both India and the ASEAN countries have come a long way since then. ASEAN is emerging as a primary area of attention in India's foreign and external economic policies. This voyage of transformation and the evolving closer relationship with South East Asian countries has not been without its ups and downs. Any prognosis of future relations between India and the ASEAN should take into account the different factors and developments which have contributed to this change.

The post-Vietnam period witnessed the fading away and the reduction of the operational relevance of the system of military alliances. Economic policies of ASEAN countries ultimately leading to the creation of the ASEAN, followed by the continuing success of this regional arrangement gave South East Asia clout and importance in the Asian region. The second half of the 1970s and the decade of the 1980s saw South East Asian countries overcoming their major internal differences and disputes and achieving greater cohesion in economic and political policies. Disintegration of the Soviet Union, and developments in China which qualitatively changed China's internal politics and external postures, resulted in foreign policies of the ASEAN countries becoming more Asia-centric and exploratory for developing new equations with countries of the region.

It is relevant to recall that India was invited to become a member of the ASEAN in its beginning years and we demurred for political reasons and specially because of our economic policies and methods of economic management being at variance from those of the ASEAN countries. While this basis for having reservations about joining the ASEAN might have been valid till the late 1980s, the situation changed for India also with the disintegration of the Soviet Union, the beginnings of our own economic reforms, our own search for markets, investment sources and opportunities for economic cooperation.

Mrs. Gandhi initiated the process of giving more political and economic content to relations between India and South East Asian countries, her visits to countries of this region after she came back to power in 1980 laid the foundations of our current approach to this region. Mr. Rajiv Gandhi furthered the process not only giving an impetus to India's bilateral relations with individual countries in this area but also conveying a signal that India is desirous of a close multi-dimensional relationship with ASEAN collectively. There was a hiatus in this ongoing process during 1989-91, because of the political uncertainties which affected us during this period. Since the middle of 1991, the process has picked up again. The consolidation and expansion of our relationship with ASEAN is of vital importance. ASEAN has a big market and is a source of investment of several million dollars if one takes into account the ASEAN's external investment activities. The region is endowed with raw materials like petrol, rubber, palm oil, tin, petroleum, natural gas, coal and iron ore. It has the necessary human resources as well as requirements for joint ventures in different industries and manufacturing sectors. The economic involvement of important industrialised countries of the West and Japan with ASEAN countries makes it a catalyst through which India can have access to investments and technologies. Our initial experience with ASEAN countries so far shows that it is an important and growing area for Indian investments, joint ventures and trade promotion. There are a number of Indian companies operating in the ASEAN region at present active from the textile to the steel sectors. The total volume of bilateral trade between India and ASEAN runs into billions of dollars.

The strategic and political importance of ASEAN for India needs no over emphasis. The political and security situation in these countries on our South Eastern flank necessarily affects our security environment. These countries like astride our trade routes to the Asia Pacific region as defined now.

These factors have led to a conscious decision to give more content to our relations with countries of South East Asia and also to diversify them. Though delayed, purposeful negotiations led to ASEAN accepting India as a sectoral dialogue partner in 1992.

SAARC

India has always been committed to regional cooperation in the economic, political, social, technological and cultural spheres. Pandit Jawaharlal Nehru in his foreign policy statements during the first decade of our independence repeatedly stressed that nurturing peace is not merely an abstention from war but that it involved encouragement of continuously expanding cooperation between nations, particularly of the Asian region.

This commitment of India, however, at the macro-level, has psychological and political constraints. Regardless of India's professions and advocacies of cooperation, all of India's neighbours had apprehensive perceptions about India. This could not be wished away. Therefore, while advocating regional cooperation, India did not make any proposal for institutional arrangements for this purpose because it anticipated suspicion, even resistance from its neighbours, if India were to take the initiative in the matter.

The disparity in size, demography, resources, and levels of development between India on the one hand, and all its immediate neighbours on the other, led to this approach. The additional factor of a number of political issues on which there were (and are) controversies between India and its neighbours underpinned India's reticence in this matter. Hence, it was with caution that India viewed the proposal for South Asian regional cooperation put forward by the late Zia Ur Rahman of Bangladesh in January, 1980. There was the perception that in view of the perennial tensions between India and Pakistan and the distance which characterised India's relations with Bangladesh and Sri Lanka, Zia-ur-Rahman's proposal would be a purely cosmetic exercise. There was also the apprehension that the forum, if created, would be a regional platform for 'India bashing'— for putting collective pressure on India on matters of individual concern to each of the other participant countries. Non-participation would have laid India open to the accusation of scuttling an innovative proposal for regional cooperation, despite being the most socio-economically endowed country in the region. Taking all these factors into consideration India ultimately joined the negotiations for the creation of SAARC. It came into existence after four years of sustained negotiations in December, 1985.

SAARC has had a chequerred existence ever since due to political controversies, impinging negatively on areas where there could have been meaningful cooperation. Second, SAARC countries have to evolve a practical framework and realistic terms of reference for cooperation in substantive matters for mutual benefit, based on mutual complementarity. Future prospects depend on whether South Asian countries can make this beginning and then move on to concrete interaction. We must examine in the light of the experiences of other regional groupings as to what are the factors which lead to and stabilise regional cooperation in an effective manner.

First, of course, is the elemental phenomenon of geography. Physical proximity inevitably results in interaction. This, however, need not necessarily be positive in content; interaction can be negative and adversarial, as our experience has shown. In the course of time, the futility and wastage of an adversarial relationship are realized, as revealed by experience and developments in different parts of the world specially since the early 1970s, when there was a thaw in the Cold War culminating in a total transformation of the global scenario in 1989.

The new equations, and the new regional groupings which have and which are emerging since then, confirm that the logic of geography, whether in terms of continental closeness or in terms of the ocean rims, impels countries towards cooperative arrangements. The geographical factor argues in favour of South Asian Cooperation. It also raises question on defining regions; where should South Asia begin? Should it begin at the Durand Line or should it begin at the axis to include Afghanistan in the SAARC? Where should the SAARC region end? Should it end at India's north-eastern extremities bordering Myanmar? Or should it end at the southernmost point of the borders of Myanmar to include Myanmar in the SAARC Arrangements? The point to be noted is that the geographical parameters of regional or sub-regional cooperation are not determined by the logic or public perception of national or regional boundaries, but by political inclinations and economic requirements. In this context, there is ambiguity about defining the South Asian region. The enthusiasm or willingness of various countries to be part of a South Asian arrangement, therefore, depends more on economic and political considerations.

The second most important factor contributing to regional cooperation is the mutually beneficial complementarity of the economies of the countries of the region. It is seen that the characteristics of the economies of South Asian countries (those which are members of the SAARC are not mutually complementary. They have more or less similar endowments and have the same limitations. Despite all the developmental activities and steps taken for industrialising and modernising the economies of these countries, countries of the SAARC region have predominantly agricultural economies with more or less similar crop and agricultual product patterns. In terms of man-land ratio the situation is highly complicated by the fact that the density of population is coupled with extensive use of cultivable land, unlike in countries like Japan, where population density is matched by intensive and optimal use of land.

In addition, there is a dichotomy between the size of the national economies of the region and their resource and technological bases. In this respect, India is in a category of its own. Pakistan and Bangladesh have large economies in terms of geography resources and population. In contrast Nepal, Bhutan and Maldives have unidimensional smaller economies. Sri Lanka because of its timely concentration on the goods and services sector and liberal trading policies has developed a more diversified economy. The nature and orientation of the economies of the region have been different. They did not mesh with each other till the last decade. Only since the last three years have free market economic arrangements become a common phenomenon in all the countries of the region. This should lead to a greater willingness and capacity on the part of SAARC countries to explore possibilities of devising mutually beneficial, complementary economic arrangements. A shared approach based on transparent and technical interaction between member countries can lead to substantive economic and technological cooperation. Optimum utilisation of resources, productivity, a cost benefit oriented restructuring of the industrial and manufacturing sectors of member states and an integrated regional common market arrangement, should be accepted as objectives by SAARC countries collectively. Another area of possible substantive cooperation, provided the political apprehensions and suspicions are overcome, is in the core developmental sectors of the South Asian economies. Such cooperation is possible in sectors of transportation, telecommunications, hydro-carbons, energy, machine tools and engineering. Cooperation in these vital areas would give a boost to individual national economies, and to regional development as a whole. It would change the context and scope of cooperation qualitatively which, at present, is limited to marginal spheres and data and information exchanges.

Ethno-cultural affinity or similarity provides an intellectual emotional and social impetus to regional cooperation. There are both positive and negative elements affecting this factor in South Asia. Linguistic, ethnic, religious and cultural traits of the people of South Asia transcend the national frontiers of the seven member countries. The people of these conuntries also follow the same religions. All this should be a potent impulse for cooperation. Paradoxically, it is this very commonality of ethno-cultural and religious heritage which has created problems of national political identity amongst India's neighbours, especially in Pakistan and, more recently, in Bangladesh. Despite the shared socio-cultual and religious inheritance, the assertion of a separate political identity necessitates and results in countries of the region pulling back from processes of economic and socio-cultural cooperation. Their apprehension of being merged or marginalized by India remains an obstacle in the process of consolidating regional cooperation.

Cohesiveness in terms of the institutional framework of the power structures of the states in the region, shared ideas about the organisation of government, shared values shaping the political system of countries in the region, add to the prospects of cooperation. South Asia have to strive towards such cohesion; there is some distance still to be covered before this objective can be realised. At the time of the SAARC's inception the member states were a disparage group in these respects. There were two monarchies (Nepal and Bhutan), two military dictatorships pretending to be democracies (Pakistan and Bangladesh) and three democracies (Maldives, Sri Lanka and India). At that time one of the democracies was, in essence, a one party state (Sri Lanka). Since 1989, however, the scenario has changed. Leaving aside tensions and uncertainties, all SAARC countries have democratic governments with elected legislatures and ministries conducting affairs of state. This is a positive trend which should encourage regional cooperation. Having said this, one would expect elected governments to be subjected to increasing domestic political pressures and prejudices if the choice is between issuing the survival in power and contributing to regional cooperation. However, noble the latter objective may be, it is the former which will often find favour, therefore, only the stabilization of democratic institutions which will overcome this interim hinderance.

Last, but also the most important consideration impinging on regional or sub-regional cooperation, in any part of the world, are commonality of perceptions concerning the manner in which regional stability can be ensured, and a shared approach to strategic and security issues affecting the region. Objectivity requires that India clinically analyses the attitude of its neighbours towards it, while deciding on the manner and extent to which it wishes to participate in the regional cooperation effort. While Bhutan, Nepal and Maldives have no palpable reservations about India in matters relating to strategic and security concerns, Pakistan, Bangladesh and Sri Lanka do harbour such doubts and reservations. Whether these are valid or justified is beside the point. It followed therefore that until a number of complex bilateral political issues between India and its neighbours are resolved, these countries will : (a) continue to look for balancing equations with other countries outside the region; and (b) to that extent their willingness to participate in regional cooperation effort will be both limited and inhibited. In the foreseeable future, therefore the processes of cooperation will gradual.

India's approach till 1991 was to steer SAARC towards projects and programmes which were practical, feasible and devoid of political controversies. It was also opposed to SAARC expanding its activities to areas which would create political problems or which would encourage extraneous non-regional interference and presence in regional affairs. It introduced a nuance in its policies towards SAARC in November, 1991. Later, however, India decided and conveyed to other member countries that it would join cooperative effort at the level, extent and tempo acceptable to other members. It also reiterated that it would not oppose the SAARC Secretariat's efforts to initiate contact with other regional groupings and countries so as to explore potentialities for additional resources and information inputs for SAARC's activities, provided these activities conformed to the stipulations of the SAARC charter and provided the external inputs, so sought and obtained, did not contradict the terms of reference of cooperation within the SAARC region. The poverty alleviation programmes and the establishment of SAPTA follow from this policy stance of India.

Here the political approach should transcend technical and material, excessively Indo-centric advocacies. India should not compromise on issues which are of genuine national interest, i.e. its security and economic well-being but subject to this consideration, a willingness for accommodation rather than insistence on reciprocity should govern its negotiations. Even on Kashmir while no solution based on unilateral claims by either side is feasible, a military adventurer or conflict to solve the problem is not acceptable to public opinion in India and Pakistan. This is more so in the case of regional and international public opinion. This trend should contribute to the political will of the power structures in both countries to move towards a purposeful dialogue to resolve the problem, however slow and tortuous the process may be. There is also the problem of identity crisis facing India's neighbours, because the more significant components of their socio-religious, ethnic and lingual collective persona are derived from the Indian connections. Geography underlines this predicament as India's land and sea borders about on all the other six countries of SAARC while none of them is a direct neighbour of any of the other. The solution lies in a conscious, continuous, even repetitious assertion and emphasis by India on the separate political identity of all its neighbours along with the communication of firm assurances as often as necessary that India does not have any aspiration to reintegrate them into any contrived or centralized 'Indian sub-continental political system.'

As far as the strategic and security aspects of regional cooperation in South Asia are concerned, the cardinal factor is the Indo-Pakistan adversarial relationship. There can be no overnight solutions to this. The situation is compounded by the nuclear weaponization factor, which Pakistan has progressively used as an incremental pressure on India. This approach will not work. Nor would both the countries getting enmeshed in an arms acquisition race will solve any problem. Regardless of Pakistan's obduracies, we must persist in lowering tensions through adoption of confidence building measures (CBMs), including the nuclear sphere. We must generate regional as well as international pressure on Pakistan to adopt the CBM tract to eliminate possibilities of conflict and to stabilize the regional security environment. We must explore possibilities of a multilateral agreement for peace and stability in South Asia amongst SAARC, countries embodying mutual CBMs, commitment to the non-use of military force to resolve issues between countries of the region, and to the non-first use of any weapons of mass destruction.

Having said this in my view the time has come for the SAARC not to shy away from becoming a forum for discussions on political issues which afflict the countries in the region. I therefore see no reason why the Heads of State and Government of the region should not exchange views on political issues putting their heads together to evolve practical and viable solutions. This would not imply any mandatory jurisdiction of the SAARC on such issues or interference into sovereignties of the States in South Asia. The agreement just suggested should signal a willingness to reduce defence expenditure as well as the size of the armed forces on the basis of negotiated norms of mutual security and reciprocity. There will be resistance even outright rejection of such initiatives in the beginning, but such political initiatives backed by increasing economic cooperation should create a practical and durable framework for stable regional equations.

There is a trans-reginal dimension to structuring regional cooperation. If the effort is successful, it will draw other regional groupings to the potentialities of economic and political returns from the region concerned. The European Community and ASEAN interacting with each other, and the way they have attracted attention of other emerging regional groups proves the point.

Trained human resources, the competitive labour force, the availability of raw materials, natural resources and the large market of the South Asian region should attract other countries of the world to this region. An environment of political stability, and a proven capacity for coordinated economic performance within the region are prerequisites to achieve this. The emergence of democratic political systems, the restructuring of national economies in conformity with global trends, and the shared attitude of the peoples of South Asia to move beyond conflict and mutual antagonisms provide the necessary basis for a concerted effort by South Asian countries to meet the above objective. The positive ramifications of interaction with the EEC, the APEC, and ASEAN or NAFTA need no emphasis.

India has a more complex and difficult role to play in this process, compared to the other countries in the region. It has to re-assure its neighbours while being firm about, and safeguarding its substantial political, security and economic interests, India's predicament is difficult because of its neighbours judge its bonafides towards them on the sole criterion of whether it accepts their suggestions in totality for resolving problems affecting its relations with them. The chemistry of emotions and inherited attitudes and the compulsions of realpolitik combine to create a volatile atmosphere in which all nations are seeking to fashion reasonable institutional mechanisms for meeting their more fundamental aspirations. India being the largest polity in the region necessarily has to take a lead in forging stable regional equations.

The avoidance of 'big brother' attitude, a willingness for reasonable accommodation of the concerns of its neighbours, adopting policies which will further their stability, sense of security and development are norms which India should follow. This approach should be adhered to even if it goes unrequited.

INDEX

N

O

P

R

S